MW01442935

Don't fall for it!

CONTENT RATING
A Courtesy of DHK Creations & Publications, LLC

<u>Violence & Drugs:</u>

↑ ↑ ↑ ⇧ ⇧

Violence (Including Both Acts & Mentions) Is Rated as a 3/5

Mentions: Mild – But Clear – Mentions of Domestic Violence Throughout Book, Abortion

Actions: Scene of Briefly Described Violence (Pgs. 86-88)

Graphic Scenes: None. While The Violence Is Shown & Described, It is Never Graphic.

Drugs/Alcohol (Including Both Acts & Mentions) Is Rated as a 2/5

Mentions: Brief Mentions of Drug/Alcohol Use

Actions: Drinking, Implications Drug Use,

<u>Language:</u>

↑ ↑ ⇧ ⇧ ⇧

Language Is Rated As A 2/5

For Brief Use of Mild Cursing During Recounts of Real-Life Experiences

Pgs: 53-55; 87; 89

<u>Explicit Scenes:</u>

↑ ↑ ↑ ⇧ ⇧

Sexual Scenes (Including Both Acts & Mentions) Is Rated as a 3/5

Mentions: Mild Implications Throughout Book

Actions:

Graphic Scenes: None.

We Recommend "Don't Fall For It" for Readers +18

This book talks about the true struggles of the author's life, including mentions of abuse, abortion, adultery, & addiction. While these subjects are talked about & addressed, they are never graphic or made light of.

Create in me a clean heart, O God and renew a right spirit within me.

Psalm 51:10, ESV

Copyright © 2023 | Lisa Dee Dunnam

All rights reserved.

No part of this work may be reproduced, stored in a retrieval system, or transmitted in any form by any means, electronic, mechanical, photocopying, recording, or otherwise, without written permission of the publisher. In order to maintain anonymity in certain instances, some names and characteristics have been changed. This book remains a truthful account of actual events in the author's life.

Paperback ISBN: 979-8-218-96822-9

E-Book: Available on Amazon.com

Publisher: Lisa Dee Dunnam

Foreword: Cody Carnes

For Rights & Permission: lisadeedunnam.author@gmail.com

Editor: Ashley Newman

Cover Design: Cody Williams

Powered By: DHK Creations & Publications, LLC

Website: www.dhkcreations.com

Contact: dhkcreations@outlook.com

DEDICATION

First and foremost, I dedicate this book to Jesus Christ, my Savior. He made me write it. It's been Yours from start to finish, Lord. Do whatever You want to with it. *"... and all Mine are Yours, and Yours are Mine, and I am glorified in them."*

~ (John 17:10).

Secondly, to my precious sons, Cody and Will, who couldn't pick their family. They had a front row seat to this saga growing up. Truly, they are my earth angels God entrusted me with, who gave my life meaning and purpose. Now I get a front-row seat watching them both fight the good fight and finish their race. I love you both more than what my heart can hold. Thank you for loving Jesus the way you do and making me look better than I deserve as your mama.

To my close friends/cheerleaders who have covered me in your prayers through this process. You know who you are. I'm forever grateful for your love and constant support.

Last but not least, to my amazing husband, Craig. He has endured four years of sacrificing many hours of our time together to allow me to put my story on paper. He walked with me through the tears and pain of reliving some of my darkest days. He was a big part of my healing process with attentive ears, strong shoulders, and a huge heart. I've never met a more loving, supportive, and non-judgmental person in my life. He's my safe place God led me to so that I could find my true self again. I am so grateful to God I get to do life with him forever. I'll always love you, Honey, in this life and throughout eternity.

FOREWORD BY
Cody Carnes

This is the first foreword for me to write and it couldn't be for a more special person. Lisa Dee Dunnam is my mom. Mama, as I like to call her. She's a great woman. A strong woman. She has lived through many storms – storms that would wear many people down next to nothing. This book describes many of them. But my mama stands today more refined, beautiful, strong, and faith-filled than ever. She's in one of the best seasons of her life. God has carried her through and brought the kind of healing and freedom only He can.

God has done the same for me. Most of my childhood was spent living with my mom and my little brother in little apartments or houses. Usually, a different one every two years, but always with our mama. We'd call ourselves the Three Musketeers. My brother and I had separate dads that we'd see fairly often. Thankfully, both of our dads loved us very much and we had a good relationship with them. I remember my mom working multiple jobs and going to college for her bachelor's degree while I was growing up. She worked hard and prayed hard because most of the time, she didn't fully know what the next day would hold. *Would we be ok? Would we have enough?* It was hard. It was stressful. Now, being an adult and leading a family, I often think about the situations my mom was in and I really don't know how she did it. I don't know how I could have done it. God undoubtedly brought us through. He proved his faithfulness time and time again. We saw miracle after miracle, including the fact that the Three

Musketeers love Jesus and each other today. We're all in healthy places in our lives thanks to the love of God. Things should have and *would have* been very different without Jesus.

My mom took us to church and prayed with us often. She likes to joke that the reason she took us to church so much was because it was full of free activities for me and my brother. To this day, I laugh every time she says that. True. The Holy Spirit uses everything to draw us into His family. Because of what my mom did, I developed a love for church and the presence of God from a young age. Many of my best friends growing up were at church. My first experiences singing in church were with my mom. We would sing "special songs" on Sundays a few times a year, singing along to a cassette tape. They were songs we'd practice for weeks on our little karaoke machine at home. When that Sunday would come, I'd walk up the stairs to the church stage in my church clothes and my mom would walk down from the choir loft in her choir robe to meet me, and we'd sing a duet together. That's where it started for me. Side by side with her. I went on to lead worship in my youth group in that same church throughout high school. That's where I fell in love with what I'm doing now - leading worship, and creating music that leads people into the presence of God.

This book is very vulnerable. She lets you in on the darkest parts of her journey. In that darkness, you'll see the beautiful ways Jesus rescues, redeems, and heals. Growing up, I got to see a mom who held onto her faith through it all. In fact, she knew it was the only way she'd make it. As I witnessed that, it established an important foundation for my faith. I saw that Jesus is real. His peace that passes understanding is real. His provision and protection are real! Many things about my childhood should have been better, but I'm thankful for the ways I got to see Jesus for who He really is in it all. We don't have to clean ourselves up to come to Him. He is in the mess. He does incredible work in the mess. He's simply that good. I know you're going to see that as you read this book.

↑ *Lisa Dee Dunnam* ↓

I pray that the Holy Spirit would reveal Jesus to you, show you the incredible love He has for you, and the ways He wants to work in your life as you read it.

- *Cody Carnes*
4-Time Grammy Award Nominee
Christian Recording Artist/Songwriter

INTRODUCTION

As a mother of two, I have wondered about this many times; even before I had my sons. Why do most women yearn to be a mom? I discovered after having my boys, that I was created for the relationship that I have with my children. I experienced such joy in having little humans with my very own traits. My heart was ignited with untapped emotions as I first gazed upon their newborn faces. I will always love them unconditionally. This is true companionship to the very core. We are created to yearn for true and lasting companionship.

By becoming a mom, I discovered that's how God sees us. He created us in His likeness as He yearns for that same relationship with us – His children.

Genesis 1:27 says, *"Then God said, "Let us make man in our image, after our likeness, and let them have dominion. So, God created mankind in His own image, in the image of God He created them; male and female He created them."*

As He loves us unconditionally, He yearns for us to love Him in the same manner.

"We love because He first loved us." **(1 John 4:19)** In His great love for us, He desires that we trust and obey, doing what He tells us to do, because He loves us. *"For this is the love of God, that we keep His commandments. And His commandments are not burdensome."* **(1 John 5:3)** This is exactly what we desire for our children. We want them to obey us because we love them and we know what is best for them.

As my children grew into adulthood with rights to make their own decisions, I no longer had parental rights as "ruler" over their lives. My position as a parent with *control* changed to a parent who only could encourage them to make good decisions. I offer advice, ONLY IF ASKED. Ultimately their choices are theirs to make as adults. This includes having a relationship with me and to be a part of their lives – or not. If their choice was to not love me back, it would hurt deeply. I cannot force them to love me. I can only hope that years of raising them and loving them through their youth were enough to make them want a relationship with me as adults. It's not authentic love if my children stay in a relationship with me out of a sense of obligation. I only see it as a joy when they love me and want me in their lives simply by their own choice.

That is the same as God's love for us. He loves us unconditionally and He is jealous for our love for Him alone **(Deuteronomy 4:24).** Jealousy in this scripture means He loves us so much that He wants to be first in our lives. He is jealous FOR us, not *of* us. He also gives us free will when He created us. It is our decision to choose Him or not. He gave us the Bible – His unchangeable, LIVING Word - in hopes we would read it and understand who He is, what His nature is, and that He loves us unconditionally. He knows what is best for us. He cares about us so much that He wrote a playbook for us to live by. The Holy Bible is God speaking to us in black and white so we can know Him; and most importantly how we can live with Him in paradise throughout eternity! He foretells the future and lets us understand history since the very beginning of mankind's existence.

God won't force us to love Him back. He is a Gentleman. He did not create us to be robots that are under His command. He wants an authentic love relationship with all of us. This is only possible with those who choose to love Him back. He is blessed when we *invite* Him to be a part of our everyday lives. *We* are ABUNDANTLY blessed when we choose to make Him LORD of our lives. That means we surrender to His will

– learning about Him, talking to Him, and asking Him to guide our decisions that will please Him. *The God of the Universe is sovereign over everything, yet He wants a personal relationship with us – His creation! Knowing Him and understanding just how much He loves us makes all the difference.* His PERFECT WILL is to provide what is BEST for us in all areas of our lives.

I sure wish I had known this truth as an adolescent. As a child, I was taught to see church as a building of tradition and going through the motions under the yolk of religion. My view of God was anything *but* a personal relationship with a Savior Who knew everything about me. I thought He was just this "Big God in the sky" who only saw believers as a whole group. I did not believe He really saw me individually.

To illustrate my wrongful view of Jesus, think of it like going to a rock concert. Jesus is the star. I have my ticket, so I am allowed to enter and find my seat to watch Him perform. He cannot see *my* face. I am lost in the crowd of faces. As a young girl, I thought accepting Jesus as my Savior was just my ticket to get into Heaven. *"God has so many believers, He can't possibly see each person. He just loves us all as a collection of believers."* That was my limited view of God. We all tend to put God in a small box for our limited understanding to be able to comprehend Him.

I had what I call a "Celebrity Jesus" viewpoint. I knew about who He was. I knew what He was famous for, and I was a fan. I did not know Him personally. I had no knowledge of His nature; I didn't know of His personality, and I certainly didn't know He wanted to be my Best Friend beyond being my Savior.

Due to my blind, misguided understanding of who Jesus is, I had a misguided understanding of who I was. *I did not know, understand, or trust Gods' love for me personally.* I was bound in a web of lies as far back as I can recall. This took me down a long winding road of bad decisions that caused me to live in darkness for almost 4 decades. That's right . . . FOUR DECADES!

I pray as you read this book, you can begin to recognize some possible beliefs you have developed about yourself that are NOT true. I pray you discover that the lies you are believing about yourself could be affecting the choices you are making. No matter what age you are now, you are still on this planet for God's purpose.

CHAPTER ONE
We Were Created For Greatness

"Oh yes, You shaped me first inside, then out; You formed me in my mother's womb. I thank you, High God – You're breathtaking! Body and soul, I am marvelously made! I worship in adoration – what a creation! You know me inside and out, You know every bone in my body; You know exactly how I was made, bit by bit, how I was sculpted from nothing into something. Like an open book, You watched me grow from conception to birth; all the stages of my life were spread out before You. The days of my life all prepared before I'd even lived one day."

~ Psalms 139:13-16; (The Message).

One of my favorite fictional movies is titled, *I Feel Pretty.* It is a fantasy film about an "average" insecure woman, named Renee'. She suffers from low self-esteem. Renee is a full-figured girl with a limited sense of style. She constantly compares herself to every thin, beautiful woman she sees and is overtaken with obsessive admiration. One night, in desperation, she tosses a coin in a wishing well and yells, "I wish I was pretty!" Superstition was all she knew to cling to.

The next day, she takes an awkward, accidental fall in a spinning class where she suffers from a head injury. This blow to the head results in something "magical" that happens when she regains consciousness. She now sees herself as a super model when she looks in the mirror. To everyone else, she appears unchanged, and still "average" Renee'. In her own eyes however, she is a "new and improved model-material Renee" with six-pack abs. She gives the Wishing Well all the credit.

Her improved self-image completely changed her mindset. Her "fantasy figure" heightened her self-confidence and changed her behavior, revealing her TRUE inner self. She carried and operated in her unique gifts, talents, and strengths. She received appreciation from the types of women she always aspired to be. Instead of being snubbed or overlooked as in the past, people now drew near to her!

She became brave enough to apply for her "dream job as a receptionist" at a major cosmetics company. This position was typically an entry-level job for women seeking a career in the modeling industry. For Renee' it was her ULTIMATE dream career; answering a phone, greeting clients, and serving coffee to the executives. Her life goals matched her poor self-image with sub-par goals, limiting her full potential.

Most of the staff belittled her at first. However, because of the "new and improved" way that she saw herself, she was oblivious to their sarcasm. She took their remarks as compliments instead. She soon became known as the best receptionist in the history of the company. She always went the extra mile with a cheerful smile and an eager attitude. She was constantly praised for her professionalism. Every day, she looked forward to going to work with the public – instead of her previous job – alone, hidden in a basement on a computer. ALL this came about because she finally loved herself.

She also found true love in THE man she had been waiting for. They met in line at a dry-cleaning business while she was dropping off. She initiated the introduction; all because she felt confident to boldly approach him. Her quick humor and high self-esteem intrigued him. The love affair took off from that one encounter.

She later discovered she was meant for greater things than a receptionist. Without the limitations of insecurity, she began offering her input on what the everyday woman is looking for in cosmetics. She quickly gained respect and recognition from the company executives and became a nationwide spokesperson for the cosmetic industry. She went from a girl who used to hide from crowds to a girl who embraced large crowds, just because of the drastic change in her self-image.

It's my favorite movie because of the way it ends. She takes another blow to the head in an accident that reverses the "wishing well magic". Tragically she sees her reflection in a mirror. She discovers she looks the same as she always did, on the outside. Reality TRIES to knock her down. Instead, she has an epiphany. It wasn't a magical physical transformation after all! Instead, her TRUE INNER SELF gained her popularity and success. This self-discovery happens while she is speaking in front of thousands of beautiful women.

Her closing remarks went something like this---

"When we were young girls, we were so confident. We would let our bellies hang out, dance when there was no music, pick our noses, say whatever was on our minds, while laughing and playing with no regard to how we looked. Then something happened along the way. Someone says something mean to us on the playground and our sense of self-confidence is shattered. We grow up learning to compare ourselves to others and start hearing inner voices that tell us we aren't smart enough or pretty enough."

She continues with an incredible message of self-realization. She is received with loud cheers and acclamation, as she concludes her speech with, "*We should all realize we are unique individuals. We are not supposed to be like anyone else. We should be confident in who we are!*" Her powerful message had me tearfully cheering in my living room too!

It's important for us to ponder the dark side of that lesson. We start out being carefree, confident children but many of us grow to develop a damaged self-image with crippling insecurities. I believe the root cause goes deeper than just a mean kid on the playground. There is a more sinister plot against us. The Bible says we are created in God's image. Because of this, *we all* are caught up in a spiritual battle of good versus evil.

Let's go back a little further to investigate. This "elementary"

Sunday school lesson will highlight the foundation of my own personal story. That's why I tell this Biblical truth in my own words.

In Genesis, God's Word teaches us that in the beginning, He created Adam first, then Eve – the first humans – created in His own image. This meant they were created to be God's children – with His DNA – to love and obey Him as their adoring Father. He instructed them to populate the earth where we all would become His children created in His own image and live in Paradise forever. This was God's "Plan A". To be in close communion with His children, guiding them under His loving authority to keep them safe. He basically had one rule for them - to just obey what He tells them to do – and not to do. This plan failed when Adam and Eve disobeyed God and ate from the Tree of Knowledge of good and evil, when God clearly told them not to. Only one rule -- and they blew it. Due to their disobedience, God had to take paradise away from them, just as He had warned them that would happen if they disobeyed.

As Christians we are taught Adam and Eve are to blame for "The Fall" - the big C - "The Curse." They caused paradise to disappear in a fleeting moment because they disobeyed God's one command, *"Don't eat from the tree of knowledge of good and evil, lest you die."* **(Gen 2:17)** That temptation was too enticing. Someone more sinister was really to blame. Satan twisted the truth just enough to get them to believe the lie, "That won't happen; you will not surely die – you are being cheated out of a good thing". (my own translation). Immediately, the paradise we were meant to live in forever became the broken world we now know. God meant they would die spiritually, not an immediate natural death. Satan took what God meant and turned it around to cause them to see with their natural eyes instead of their spiritual inclination. So, we have all been taught we live in a fallen world because Adam and Eve ate the forbidden fruit.

I think Adam and Eve get the blame more than they deserve. This is not the real beginning. There is another beginning that happened long before this event that needs a closer look. Yes, they were guilty of sin, and it did cause the Fall of mankind. But what was the root cause?

Something else transpired before "Plan A" on earth. The event occurred in the third Heaven – in Glory. The Heaven where God, The Creator, sits on His throne. The book of Ezekiel, chapter 28 describes an "anointed guardian cherub" **(Ezekiel 28:14)** – a *created being* that lived in Glory with God. He was an angel by the name of Lucifer, which means "light."

Life was good for Lucifer, the "angel of light." Lucifer was the main worship leader in Heaven. Musical instruments were part of his makeup as he made beautiful sounds of worship to God. "He was blameless in his ways . . . until wickedness was found in him." (V. 15)

Lucifer became puffed up with pride, declaring that he was equal to God, refusing to bow to God any longer. He thought he should be worshipped. So, God changed his name to Satan, which means "slanderer/accuser." God hurled Satan down from Heaven and cursed him to roam the earth. **(Isaiah 14:12-14)** God made a special eternal home, a pit of fire and torment, designed only for Satan and 1/3 of the "fallen angels" who chose to follow him. **(Revelation 20:10)** This new home for Satan is a place called Hell. Hell was meant to be an eternal place for him and the fallen angels **alone**. Hell is still the ultimate destination for this enemy of God. Have you heard the saying, "a criminal who has been given a life sentence in prison always wants to take friends with him"? It's the same with Satan. He is determined to take as many humans with him as he can. His daily, unending agenda is to spread his curses [and his lies] and seek whom he may devour. **(1 Peter 5:8)** Let's review Adam and Eve's story again going a little deeper.

Genesis teaches us that when Adam and Eve disobeyed, it was because the serpent (Satan) tempted them with a doubt and then a LIE! "Did God really say you'll die? You will not die, but instead be like God; to have His same knowledge of good and evil." **(Genesis 3:1,4-5)** They fell for it and "bit off more than they could chew" by eating the forbidden fruit. They fell out of a relationship with God and caused the rest of mankind to be born with a sinful nature, starting with their seed. From that time, God allows "the serpent" to roam around Earth, until his time (according to God's timeline) to be cast down in the "lake of fire" – his eternal destination. Adam and Eve were created to have authority over the earth. **(Genesis 1:26)** They surrendered that right over to Satan, when they disobeyed God. **Satan tricked them into giving up their authority with a lie.**

Plan A failed, but God still had another and GREATER - "Plan J." Thousands of years later, Jesus left His throne to come to Earth as a newborn baby. **(Luke 2)** He grew up as a human just like us but being both God and man. He chose to give up His royal crown in Heaven to come put skin on and show us by example how to inherit the Kingdom of God. At age 30, He began his ministry on Earth (Luke 4) to teach us who God REALLY is. Jesus came to dispel the lies Satan was spreading through the judgmental attitudes of the Pharisees. These religious leaders kept the Jewish and Gentile people bound in guilt/shame, or self-righteousness.

At age 33, Jesus WILLINGLY went to the Cross and died a tortuous death to take our place. **(1 John 3:16)** He became the sacrificial lamb to atone for OUR sins (not His – He never sinned). He died for my sins and FOR YOURS. **(1 John 2:2)** In the Old Testament, Jewish law called for a spotless lamb to be sacrificed annually to cleanse the Jewish people of their sins. **(Numbers 6:14)** In the New Testament, Jesus came as the ultimate Spotless Lamb to be sacrificed for ALL of our sins – past, present, and future. This is why Jesus is referred to as The Lamb of God – He took our place. His death, burial and resurrection reconciled us back to God, where we are given back the authority over the enemy that Adam and Eve forfeited. **(2 Corinthians 5:18)** Those who believe this Gospel can have victory in Christ over the enemy!

Until Jesus comes again **(Matthew 24:30),** the enemy of God is still free to roam the earth. "Be alert and of sober mind. Your enemy, the devil, prowls around like a roaring lion looking for someone to devour." **(1 Peter 5:8)** Those "someone's" on his radar are us. The children of God. We are the devil's worst enemies. He hates us because WE are made in God's image. He thought he was like God, so he despises us with a jealous hate. He also knows Jesus gave US back our authority over him when He defeated death on the Cross. Satan tries hard to prevent us from knowing our God-given authority over him. Satan knows if we grow in our relationship with Christ from an *early* age, we can grow up knowing how we can defeat him. That's when he is powerless over us. Early childhood is when our mind, emotions and will are molded into what we believe when we get older. This is why Satan starts lying to us when we are still children in our developmental stages. We are vulnerable to misunderstanding the world around us. His constant game is to steal, kill and destroy our destiny as a believer in Christ.

As I said earlier, Satan knows his eternal destination is the lake of fire and he does NOT want to go alone! He wants to take as many people as possible with him. Unfortunately, he succeeds in his plot many times with lies. The Bible describes him as the author of lies. He is good at it. He succeeds in deceiving a lot of people into rejecting the Truth and believing the Big Lie – God doesn't exist.

Typically, unbelievers have a pretty calm life on planet Earth. Many atheists contend that Heaven is what we make of it on Earth and there is no such thing as an after-life. Unfortunately, they are deceived in this notion of "their own heaven on Earth" because the enemy does not target them. He leaves them alone to live out their carefree lives before he takes them to Hell. They think everything in life is smooth because THEY are in control of their destiny. So, these people are no threat to him. The horrendous lies Satan tells people are: **1)** *he* (Satan) doesn't even exist (many intelligent people with good intentions would never follow a devil if they thought he was real); **2)** all "good people" (ones who don't commit the big sins) go to Heaven automatically; or **3)** we evolved - we were not created; we live here and then we die without any eternal judgment.

On the flip side, WE . . . believers in Christ, who know the TRUTH, are commissioned to expel Satan's lies and tell others the truth about Heaven and Hell. We must tell people how to escape Hell and get to Heaven (only through Jesus). We ARE a threat to

Satan, and he is constantly looking for ways to shut us up. This is why Jesus warns His followers, *"... In this world you will have trouble but take heart – I have overcome the world."* **(John 16:33).** Look around today and it is easy to see that Christianity is the #1 criticized and attacked belief system on the planet. We are constantly being criticized, attacked, and persecuted, while other religions (Muslim, Hindu, Buddhism, etc.) are never subjects of any protests. This is because protests against Christians are more of a spiritual war than a political one. Any belief apart from Christianity are false religions that will not allow followers to live in Heaven. These are religions Satan inspired to deceive many people. This is why Satan leaves these individuals alone to live peaceful lives on earth – because they will live with him in eternity where he gets to torment them forever. The trick is on them!

Look at all the upheaval we have seen in our country and around the world over the recent war in Israel. So many people are against Israel and see that as a political war over territory. It is not. It is a spiritual war, where Satan is influencing people who don't know Jesus and convincing them that Israel is the enemy. The Jewish people just want to live in peace with their neighbors in the Midde East. Instead, they are constantly having to defend their rights to live in the land God gave them. Israel is Satan's enemy because they are God's chosen people, and their bloodline is where Jesus came from. Satan only attacks Christians because we are his true enemy – we are his biggest threat in telling people the Truth. The Truth will set people free from his demonic grip and he hates us for that.

We, as believers in Jesus live by faith and store up our treasures in Heaven for our eternity, a forever paradise. Until then, believers and potential believers are constant subjects of harassment from Satan. He wakes up EVERY DAY with only two goals in mind: 1) lie to as many people as possible about God, to *prevent* their salvation; OR 2) to target believers (who *have* been saved) and *destroy our effectiveness* in spreading the truth of the Gospel of Jesus Christ.

Are you depressed by now? Don't be! This is a gloomy subject, but please BE ENCOURAGED! Jesus defeated Satan at the Cross and He equips us to defeat him every day! Never forget! We, as believers in Christ, have authority over Satan. We live under the protection and provision of Almighty God! Satan has no real power over us – when we choose to believe what God says in His word - and live by it! WE are the overcomers because Jesus defeated Satan at the Cross!

Therefore, Satan is infuriated by our existence! He STILL TRIES the same tricks he pulled on Adam and Eve. I'll say it again, the only agenda on his mind is to try to steal, kill and destroy this love relationship with our Creator and to ruin God's purpose for our lives. **(John 10:10)** Many times, he is successful by destroying our understanding that we are children of the Most-High God! We often times don't realize we are fearfully and wonderfully made by our Creator – who loves us unconditionally!

Every believer has the commission (our ultimate purpose) to spread the Good News of the Gospel and lead others to Christ. However, that looks different in the delivery for every believer. God is not a "cookie-cutter" Creator. He made each of us with UNIQUE gifts and talents to accomplish that purpose in our own way. We have our own unique stories to tell about our PERSONAL RELATIONSHIP with Christ.

Our uniqueness is exactly what Satan is after.

He tries to get us to play the "comparison game" so that he can deceive us into believing: **1)** we don't fit in; **2)** we don't measure up; and **3)** we don't have a purpose. If he can enslave us, he can slow down the spread of the Gospel. Again, he still thinks he is as powerful as God. NOT TRUE. Nothing can stop what God can do.

Satan knows he cannot steal our salvation, nor our position as children of the Most High, nor God's purpose for our lives. He CAN however steal our KNOWLEDGE of these things. We are all born with a "spiritual target" for Satan to shoot his arrows of deceit. He targets our most vulnerable areas. He whispers suggestions into our sub-conscience at an early age with the only language he knows – LYING! He can influence people in our lives to do his bidding. This can be accomplished without them even realizing it. My story will explain this concept in greater detail in a later chapter.

Back to Renee's speech, I propose (based on my life experience) that THIS is how we go from being care-free confident children to becoming insecure adults with a warped self-image. We lose sight of how God sees us, as unique and beautiful. As I said, there is something more sinister going on than just a mean kid on a playground. We believe the lies we are told by His enemy – the devil – in early childhood. His lies are so cunning and subtle, we don't even recognize them.

Somewhere in Renee's life, she may have been teased about being chubby, or less-than in some way. This teasing could have even come from people who love her with pure intentions – oblivious to the power of their tongue to speak life or death. **(Proverbs 18:21).** She began to believe the lie that she didn't measure up to greatness. She was only average and undeserving of an abundant life. She relented to the belief she could only fulfill her dreams by living vicariously through others -- watching beautiful women live out their dreams she had for herself. The enemy saw she was a threat to the kingdom of darkness because she carried a UNIQUE source of light. A personality that drew people to her. So, he started lying to her while she was young and vulnerable. Although "Renee'" is a fictional character, her story is a true example of what many of us experience. The Bible teaches the ultimate TRUTH about us, His beloved.

God loves us individually with a love that is as personal as the way He uniquely created us. When we truly grasp this truth, then we discover who we are and what we were created to be. ALL of God's children were created for greatness in fulfilling His purpose for our lives. Jesus came to show us in the flesh who God our Father really is. Jesus is more than just our Savior; He is also our True Best Friend who never turns His back on us. He is "with us always." **(Matthew 28:20)** He guides us daily with His truth and unfailing love, through the person of the Holy Spirit. THIS is God's true desire; that we know this from the moment we invite Jesus in our hearts. When we know Jesus is with us always, we are more inclined to surrender our lives to Him as our PERSONAL Lord and Savior.

Based on my own experiences, my personal definition of living a life with Christ is this. We can never out-sin God's grace, *no matter how bad we act*! I'm NOT SAYING, by accepting Jesus we have a "license to sin" and don't need a relationship with Jesus. What I AM saying is He constantly judges the condition of our hearts, not necessarily our outward behaviors. Once we confess our sins and invite Jesus in, He will relentlessly go after us, *pursuing* that close relationship of *mutual love*, even when we are still bound in the sin(s) that snare us. He never loses HIS desire to be in fellowship with us. In other words, He gets us – more than we understand ourselves. He is always working to get us to a place where we can finally repent of our sins . . . . TURN from our sinful living and enter into a beautiful relationship with our perfect Savior. Repentance is ABSOLUTELY necessary to have a relationship with Jesus. We don't have to figure that out on our own though! *He* helps us to repent when we really want to. He helps us make good decisions to live an abundant life of JOY, peace and protection on earth. My favorite catch phrase I have learned over the years sums this up perfectly. "We don't have to clean up before coming to Jesus – we can come to Jesus first – with all of our filthy rags - and He cleans us up – from the inside out – no matter how long it takes."

My story also illustrates how He is slow to anger, quick to forgive and never gives up on us. **(Psalm 103:8)** The following chapters explain my journey of ups and downs; good decisions and a whole lot of bad ones that lasted for half of a typical lifetime. It's a story where Satan tried to take me out, but my God never took His eyes off me. Even when I was making poor decisions, the Holy Spirit never left my side. He stayed silent in those times I grieved Him with my bad decisions, but He was *always present*, beyond my comprehension. He was constantly working out the escape plan from my own self-destruction. The "Ancient of Days" spent all *my dark* days waiting for the moment my heart would be ready to cry out to Him. He guided me on a LONG road trip to self-discovery of who I am in Him, what I was created to be and how much He loves me.

He is always working on our behalf for our good – whether we realize it or not.

I know I have been very repetitive in this chapter in teaching these principles in God's word. It's because I REALLY want it to sink in the very depths of your soul. My prayer is that my story highlights the most important truth. God loves YOU, with a deep/abiding love; a long-suffering (patient) love, willing to wait as long as it takes. His reckless love will kick down walls to get to you, no matter where you are in life. The sooner you discover His amazing way of life in obedience to His will, the sooner you will have everlasting JOY, no matter what circumstance you find yourself in. GUARANTEED! Read my story and hopefully you'll know why I am completely convinced of this.

Let's get started.

CHAPTER TWO
My Beginning

"They have known me for a long time and can testify, if they are willing, that I conformed to the strictest sect of our religion, living as a Pharisee."

~ Acts 26:5

My definition of a Pharisee is a person who shows outward signs of a follower of Jesus, without possessing a true heart for Jesus. In other words, someone who goes through the motions of religion without a true burning desire to follow Jesus and know Him personally.

That was me.

I was raised in a Christian home and heard about Jesus as far back as I remember in my childhood. Our family went to a "very pretty" formal Protestant church. We always dressed like it was Easter Sunday. We put on our finest outfits to match our painted smiles and best behaviors. Church was also social hour. We usually only met once a week, so pretenses were easily accomplished in a short time, all while wearing our "church masks." We never shared the troubles we faced as a family at home. Church seemed like a place to go to check off a box, to say we did our "Christian duty". Church is supposed to be a community of believers for our family to do life with. We lacked the spirit of community as followers of Christ. Church should be an extension of family, as children of God – where we can be real with one another and share each other's burdens.

In **Luke 5:31-32,** the Pharisees chastise Jesus by asking, *"Why do you eat and drink with tax collectors and sinners?"*

Jesus said, *"It is not the healthy who need a doctor, but the sick. I have not come to call the righteous, but sinners to repentance."*

Looking back, I believe my family missed the whole purpose of gathering with the "assembly" of other believers. I have since learned the church is supposed to be for broken people who need a touch from Jesus. This is why the Bible tells us, *"let us not neglect meeting together, as some people do, but encourage one another, especially now that the day of His return is drawing near."* **(Hebrews 10:25 NLT)**. We are to stay connected to teach, encourage and pray for one another. It's the only way to stay strong in our faith. Instead of a place where you wear a mask and pretend you are perfect, church is supposed to be a place you can safely take off your mask, let down your walls and be able to say, "I need prayer! I am not ok!" Then, we can leave feeling lighter from our burdens when we refuse to keep our sin a secret. That's where freedom is found.

Despite the access we have to the Holy Spirit, the Pharisee spirit still sneaks into many congregations today. Church can often be a house we gather in to socialize while hiding our struggles. We can ask "How are you?" and hear "I'm fine!" without stopping long enough to hear and address how we are *really* doing. Unfortunately, it is because many churches today do not make people feel safe to share their darkest secrets. Gossip and judgmental attitudes are prevalent because as my pastor says, "Satan comes to church too." The spirit of religion IS a demonic spirit inspired by Satan himself. It creates barriers and division among the Body of Christ. When we attend a church bound by this spirit, we often leave the "hospital" in the same broken condition as we entered in. It is VERY important to find a church home where you feel safe to be yourself and feel accepted in spite of your struggles. They are out there – but unfortunately my family didn't raise me in one. My parents were not raised in one either, so the cycle continued.

My Sunday school class consisted of kids from the opposite side of town. I considered them to be the "rich kids." My family of five lived in a three-bedroom house where everyone had ten minutes each sharing one bathroom. At a young age, I remember feeling like I was competing with my Sunday school classmates in wearing the latest fashion. The girls showed more interest in what I was wearing than learning about Jesus. My J.C. Penney dresses never won me any favor with the elites of my classroom. I felt the sting of "not fitting in" the very place I should have learned "God loves me just the way I am."

There was no "Children's Church" during my era. We were required to sit with our parents in "big church" and were given strict instructions, "Don't make a move and don't make a sound." The only time this rule did not apply was when the formal ceremony cued us to "Stand and follow along in the responsive reading." I learned to recite those words by memory. Also etched in my brain were songs we sang at the close of the responsive readings. Same ritual, every Sunday. We sang the same songs so often; I could sing them in my sleep, while not having a clue what the words really meant. Sleep was the escape plan I took many times to help me obey the command of being quiet and still. You get the picture. My religious upbringing was just that; religious – in the sense that it was guided by traditions apart from knowing why we did them. I was going through the motions of all the rituals without much thought and very little revelation of who Jesus was.

My so-called "conversion" was also decided *for* me at man's appointed time. Guided by tradition, I was required at age eleven to take "Confirmation Classes." At the conclusion of the course, I would be presented with my "Certificate of Confirmation" in a Sunday morning church service. By this time in my life, we had moved to a smaller church in the same denomination. I felt more at home, with families from my own neighborhood being fellow members.

I enjoyed the confirmation preparation classes with other kids my age. We would play around and socialize the way kids do, by passing notes and kicking each other under the table. I did not have a CLUE what we were there to learn. Then came the Sunday morning when "Confirmation Graduation" was to be part of the morning service. All I knew was that I was going to have to respond to three questions.

Getting ready for church that morning, I was so nervous! I felt like I was about to take a quiz I had not studied for and was soon to be subjected to great embarrassment. I remember saying to my older sister, "I am scared I am going to give the wrong answers to those questions! What are the questions?"

She replied, "Don't worry, just say "Yes." That's the correct answer to all 3 questions." Whew, what a relief! Thank goodness she had gone before me to prepare me!

My automatic "Yes" to each of those questions awarded me a piece of paper with my full name, written in bold calligraphy. It looked so pretty and official! I felt like I had *actually* achieved something. If only I knew what. I went home and hung it on the wall in my room. I was now confirmed. My only understanding was knowing it was my framed ticket to Heaven. I had completed the task I was taught to do; say, "Yes, I believe in Jesus." I truly did believe in Jesus. I had heard about Him for as long as I could remember. I didn't know much about Him. I believed He was real, and He was important - especially if I wanted to go to Heaven. That was the extent of my theology at age eleven.

At age twelve, I was invited by some friends to attend a crusade that was coming to town. The speaker was Nicky Cruise. He was one of the main characters portrayed in a motion-picture film that was based on a true story and released in the '70's. The story line was about an evangelist, David Wilkerson, who was called by God to live in the streets of the Bronx and minister to gang members. One of the meanest gang members was Nicky Cruise. *The Cross and the Switchblade* was a very emotional film that stirred something in my heart. I cried and cheered at the end. It was an encounter with the Holy Spirit, even when I did not understand what I was experiencing.

Months later, my friends and I were excited about the news that the actual man, Nicky Cruise, would be coming to our hometown for a crusade. Nicky, the most violent gang leader in the movie, was radically saved and converted overnight. His life mission from that time on is to travel the world talking about his experience and leading others to Christ.

Through his message that night, I heard something for the very first time. I couldn't get to Heaven based on my church attendance. Heaven was not a guarantee just because I'm basically a good person, who completed a class and received a certificate. I learned I had to acknowledge that I am a sinner in need of a Savior. It required me to intentionally invite Jesus to come into my heart. Though I wasn't fully aware of the entirety of what that meant, I did know my heart was stirred. I could not fight back the tears and I could not stay in my seat. My friends and I eagerly responded to the altar call to "give our hearts to Jesus." It was an emotional night, but not a *complete* revelation. I did feel different when I left from when I went in. Now that I intentionally received Jesus in my heart, what next? I do remember the incredible feeling of peace after that event. That was the extent of my 12-year-old understanding of what had just happened.

John 3:16 says, *"For God so loved the world that he gave His one and only Son, that whoever believes in Him shall not perish but have eternal life."*

I know that I wholeheartedly accepted Jesus that night at the crusade. The Bible also says in **Revelation 3:5,** *"He who overcomes shall be clothed in white garments. I will not blot his name out of the Book of Life, but I will confess his name before My Father and before His angels."*

I believe God's Word and know my name was forever safe from being blotted out of the Lambs' Book of Life from that night on. The only way that could be reversed is if I explicitly deny Christ and outwardly declare I reject Him and keep that stance until I die. Thankfully I always knew to never do that.

Unfortunately, I *still* had very little understanding of what to do with this life-changing decision. I knew all ABOUT Jesus but I did not know how to walk with Him personally. No one taught me that Jesus was not *just* my Savior, but that He was also my Heavenly Daddy and my Best Friend. I didn't understand, nor was I taught, that He wanted to be involved in my everyday life. I thought the rituals of religion (like attending church and behaving to the best of my ability) were the requirements for Jesus to love me. I thought His love for me was based on my actions. I didn't yet understand the TRUTH. My behavior, good or bad, could never change what HE did. Jesus loves us FIRST, so much so, that He took OUR place, by dying on the Cross for OUR sins, so that we could be reconciled to God, PERIOD. That's the simple Gospel. If we truly believe the Gospel, HE will change us from sinful rebels to faithful followers

Notice I said faithful followers, but I didn't say *perfect* followers. Not possible. FAITHFUL followers are those who *trust* Him to guide us daily. It has taken me a LONG TIME to understand the simple Gospel. We cannot do anything good enough - on our own - to receive salvation and we cannot do anything bad enough to lose our salvation – apart from outright denying Him. To deny Him is to deny the salvation that He freely gave through His death for our sins. We put our trust in *Jesus* and HIS finished work on the Cross that we might be saved. After that step, it's a lifetime journey of knowing Him and how much He loves us. He wants a deep abiding relationship with us! This is why He gives us the Holy Spirit the minute we say yes to Him. The Holy Spirit is the one who will constantly guide and convict us when we sin. Many people call it their "conscience" – believers know it's Holy Spirit leading us to repentance. He can be a loving nuisance. When we truly belong to Jesus, He never gives up on helping us understand when we fall short.

I always had an innate yearning for Jesus. I didn't know it *wasn't* about my *perfect performance* (which is impossible for any human). Performance doesn't impress Jesus. Humble devotion moves His heart. It's about HIM. We can never be enough apart from Him. He loves us unconditionally and He just wants a relationship with those He *already* loves. There is nothing we can do to make Him love us more. There is also nothing we can do that will make Him love us less – even if we reject Him. It grieves His heart when His children reject Him, but He never stops loving us. It's our choice – not His - to receive His love and salvation and go to Heaven or reject it and go to Hell. He leaves that decision totally up to us.

That's why Jesus suffered a torturous death on the Cross for me and for you. He took the punishment WE deserve, so that we don't have to be punished in eternity. I thought I had to earn that kind of love. When I felt good about my behavior, I ran straight to Him. Every time I knew I messed up; I ran as far away as possible to try to hide from Him. Sound familiar? Just like Adam and Eve. We all have their same nature. The Gospel teaches we should do the exact opposite. Our sinful mistakes are the times when we should run straight **into** His arms and let Him fix our brokenness.

The Bible illustrates this fact with the parable about the prodigal son. If you're not familiar with this story, I recommend you read it. Especially if you're in a place where you think you've messed up too bad to receive God's forgiveness. You'll find it in **Luke 15:11-24.**

Although I sincerely gave Jesus my heart at age 12, I didn't come to KNOW Jesus personally until I was 38 years old. So, if you do the math, that was 26 years of "in-between" time. I basically drifted spiritually through life, being a "good Christian girl" who went to church and checked off my Sunday ritual box.

I also made a whole lot of bad decisions that took me on a dark journey, trying to figure out life *all on my own*. My "relationship" with Jesus only meant going through the religious motion but never asking Jesus to guide me in my decisions. Never knew that was an option. This lack of knowledge made me a perfect target for the enemy. He shot his arrows of deceit to get me way off course of the destiny that God had planned for my life.

I always thought that my problems started at age 15. After becoming baptized in the *Holy Spirit* (different than water baptism) at age 53, I came to understand that the root of my problems was planted way *before* age 15. It began early in my childhood. Holy Spirit lifted the veil at age 53 and took me down memory lane into my childhood. He showed me how Satan started telling his perverted lies to me around age 6 and convinced me to believe that I was someone I was NOT.

CHAPTER THREE

The Formative Years

"Now the serpent was more crafty than any of the wild animals the Lord God had made... "

~Genesis 3:1

Webster's Dictionary defines the word "formative" as "serving to form something, *especially having a profound and lasting influence on a person's development.*" It's easy to see why psychologists refer to our childhood as the formative years. Depending on the environment we are raised in, our upbringing during formative years can shape our self-image and our view of the world. Psychological studies seem to overlook a deeper truth.

There is a spiritual battle influencing our environment as well.

I have many fond memories of my childhood. It was a happy and carefree period of my life. I was raised in a loving home with a great family. We were, by no means, a perfect family. We were the "typical" American home with two parents and three children. My siblings and I were neatly stacked in age, about two years apart from one another. I was the youngest. The oldest was my sister, Lori and my brother Mark was sandwiched between the two of us. Lori was the opposite of Mark and me. She was the type of child that never disobeyed and always made right choices with little guidance. As a natural rule follower, Lori never received one spanking growing up, that I can recall.

Mark and I took her share of spankings! We were both a handful. I admit I was probably the most challenging. As the baby of the family, I seemed to get away with more than my older siblings. By the time I came along, my parents were busy and too tired to be consistent in their discipline. They began to let the little things slide. It took too much effort to try and bridle my hyper-activity and rebellious nature, so "Brat" became my nickname.

Lori and I were also *complete* opposites in our physical appearance. To this day, we look nothing alike. I used to say she got *all* the best features from my parents. She has Dad's thick hair and my mother's beautiful smile, complete with perfectly straight teeth and high cheek bones. She also inherited Mom's smooth, olive-tone skin that tans easily in the sun without ever developing one freckle.

I always joke that I was born with the "leftovers." I got Mom's straight, fine hair. My Dad had thick hair, but it also had unruly waves in weird places. Instead of thickness, I got those unruly waves. Dad had fair skin with freckles and a small mouth with no cheekbones. Same here. Thanks Dad!

My parents' personalities were also complete opposites. Dad was loud and boisterous and loved being the center of attention. Mom was quieter and more reserved. She hated being the center of attention in any situation. She was a very patient and nurturing mom. She absolutely LOVED having all the neighborhood kids at our house. The sound of children's laughter always lifted her spirits. Dad on the other hand was a bit impatient with young children. He liked his house to be orderly and quiet when he was home. It was God's plan to give him a career as an airline pilot where he traveled a lot. This kept our home balanced with opportunities to be rowdy and play while he was away and then to quietly keep the peace when he was home.

Dad had a quick temper, and his overbearing personality could either speak life or death. When he was happy, everyone was happy, and our home was full of fun and laughter. When Dad was mad or in one of his "moods", fear and silence would rule the atmosphere. Like an overgrown kid, he would throw tantrums when he didn't get his way. I learned to walk on eggshells as a child, trying to escape Dad's wrath when his "fuse" was short. I learned to love my dad with cautious adoration, always trying to keep him happy and content, in order to avoid an explosion.

My parents argued a lot and every fight was about money. Dad liked to spend it and mom did her best to save it. When money was tight and bills were due, the screaming would start. As children, we would run and hide in the shelter of our bedrooms, until the storm passed.

Dad did have a fun side. He was the entertainment at adult parties. My dad loved to make people laugh. It was his constant practice to take any conversation and find a joke in there somewhere. It's quite possible he was the one who started the trend of cheesy "dad jokes." He was known for making them up on the spot.

I looked and acted a lot like my dad. That's probably why he seemed to have a soft spot for me. He showed me lots of affection, as long as I behaved. My relationship with Dad grew closer and more enriching as I got older. Dad seemed to relate better with older kids. We easily got on his nerves when we were toddlers. I get it now. I turned out to be the same type of parent. My patience wore thin when my boys were in the "wrestling on the furniture" stages. I was much more patient with them as teenagers, when I could hold their attention for meaningful conversations. My dad and I became close friends in my young adult years. He was my cheerleader and my constant source of support, even when my life was a mess.

Dad went to Heaven almost instantly from a sudden heart attack at age 72. He and Mom were on a trip with their Sunday school class. His passing is one of those amazing stories of God's mercy. Although Dad was a real "stinker" during my upbringing, he had rededicated his life to Christ in late adulthood. He spent the final seven years of his life on earth dedicated to sharing the Gospel. He was passionately involved in prison ministry and spent much of his time serving the inmates, teaching them about hope in Christ through Bible study. God was so gracious to take him in the "prime" of his spiritual life, while he was making a difference for the Kingdom.

I am thankful Dad finally experienced joy in life by following Christ instead of the world. My parents' marriage transformed from arguments over financial struggles to a life shared in the joy of the Lord. I was in my 30's when Dad made a 360-degree turn in his faith walk. After his rededication to Christ, he became a gentle, patient and joyful man who was the one who kept the peace in his home. It wasn't up to the rest of the family to tiptoe around him to keep things peaceful. Best of all, Dad loved sharing Jesus with others with child-like boldness.

Many times, I think about the different possibilities for my own life, had Dad made that life-altering decision while I was still young. In my early years during my parents' marriage struggles, I grew up loving my dad but was also fearful of him. His affectionate name for me was "baby daughter" and yet I often felt distance from him and uneasiness in his presence. The conflict I experienced as a child in relationship with my earthly father formed my view of God as my Heavenly Father.

I knew God loved me because "the Bible tells me so." However, my experience and understanding of "unconditional love" from my earthly father skewed my perception of God's "unconditional love" as my heavenly Father. My spiritual life as a child was somewhat rigid with religious rituals. So I grew to believe Gods' love was conditional according to how I acted, not according to who I was as His child. My understanding swung on a pendulum between the wrath of God and the unconditional love of Christ. This pendulum found no healthy balance that the truth of God's Word teaches. I couldn't truly see myself as the apple of God's eye where I could hide under the shadow of His wings. **(Psalms 17:8 NKJV)**. I kept my comfortable distance to avoid His wrath when I misbehaved.

However, I looked up to my older sister and truly believed God has His favorites and she was one of them.

CHAPTER FOUR
Sibling Comparison

"Favor ain't fair" ~ Christine Caine

" . . . but I am a little child; I do not know how to go out or come in."

~ 1 Kings 3:7

One of my favorite pastors of all time is Alex Seeley from The Belonging Co. Church in Nashville, TN. As a successful published author she says this in her book *The Opposite Life*: "When you are a favorite within a family, it is definitely not a good thing. You automatically have a target on your back the moment you are singled out and favored among others. Jealousy is a horrible curse that comes straight from the Enemy who is himself consumed with jealousy for God." I read this book only a few years ago.

Alex's statement helped me to eventually understand my fate with the enemy. It also explained Lori's fate in a struggle with her health in later years. I'll explain in a minute, but first here is some background. Although my mom was equally loving to all three of her children, Lori was mom's favorite, if she would have had to choose. Lori was definitely our "Mamaw's" favorite when we were growing up. Mamaw was Dad's mother, and she too was impatient with rowdy and unruly children like me and Mark. She could easily relate to Lori because they shared the same interests, like sewing and cooking. Lori has always loved Jesus. She was the one in our family who taught me the meaning of the Gospel. Lori is a rule keeper and has always lived a life of obedience and self-control. Mom loved watching her first-born experience all the "firsts" in the stages of her life. I recall so many times Mom would anxiously wait for Lori to get home from school, so they could sit at the kitchen table and talk about her day. I also remember getting scolded if I interrupted the conversation. So, I would just sit quietly and listen as I aspired to be more like her.

Lori's beauty, leadership qualities and obedient nature won her popularity among her peers, teachers, and other adults. As a teen, Lori's favorite past-time was to spend time with our Mamaw and learn how to make crafts, sew, bake and all other facets of excellent homemaking. Most teens would rather be with friends than their grandmother! Those days have paid off for Lori because she is what I call a "domestic diva". She's a talented decorator, a great cook and she can sew anything. She's very artistic and exhibits all the domestic talents that Mamaw had. She also taught junior high school biology until she retired. I, on the other hand, found my joy as a child building forts with rocks and hunting horned-toed frogs. As a teenager, I definitely chose friends over grandparents any day! This is why I'm NOT a good cook, nor a decorator and can barely sew on a button.

Lori's obedient life continues into adulthood, and she is continually surrounded by God's hedge of protection. The enemy tried to trick her into marrying the wrong man, her high school sweetheart, who was clearly not good for her. Thankfully, God spared her from a lifetime of sorrow. The blessing was disguised as heartache when her sweetheart broke up with her a few months before the wedding date. It was a difficult time in her life, but God's mercy and grace eventually led her to her perfect life mate. She has enjoyed a stable and fulfilling life in a Christ-centered marriage of 45 years, with two successful adult children and five "perfect" grandchildren.

Since Satan couldn't break through Lori's devotion to Christ, he went after her health instead. She was the last person in our family who deserved breast cancer. She takes very good care of her body. She has ALWAYS lived a healthy lifestyle, following all the rules of moderation. I remember when we were children, my brother and I would have a contest to see how many pancakes we could eat when we stayed with Mamaw and Papaw. I would be nauseous after over-indulging those empty carbs drenched in syrup and butter. Lori, as a child, would ask for only 2 pancakes with a little dab of butter and NO SYRUP. She was definitely an anomaly.

Satan was threatened by the Christlikeness created in her. At age 40, Lori was suddenly diagnosed with Stage 2 cancer, when she found a walnut-size tumor in her breast.

I remember pacing back and forth in the waiting room during her surgery. At that time, the family was uncertain about the seriousness of her condition, and afraid her life would be cut short. Lori had lived her entire life devoted to Biblical principles. I was the total opposite. By this time, I had 36 years of rebellion under my belt. I wept with guilt and shame thinking I should be the one on that operating table. Lori had been faithful to lead a clean life of self-control. I, on the other hand, had abused my body in more ways than I cared to admit.

But, God! In His miraculous power, He still had Lori in the palm of His protective hand. The doctors were astounded by the results of the biopsy. It showed that the cancer had not spread to her lymph nodes. With only a lumpectomy, five rounds of chemo and several rounds of radiation, Lori was able to defeat cancer. She has been cancer-free for almost 30 years now.

Alex's statement also makes me ponder the thought of my brother's fate being an act of God's mercy. Unfortunately, Mark was caught in the middle of two daughters who were the apple of each of our parents' eyes. As the typical middle child, Mark seemed to be overlooked and made to feel insignificant. Dad was harsher in his correction on Mark than he was on us girls. This made my brother believe Satan's lie that he was not enough and could never do enough to earn Dad's affections. Mark began to hang out with the "wrong crowd" as soon as he began his high school years. The "at-risk students" in school helped Mark feel important. They looked up to him because of his keen intelligence. However, Mark was unable to lead them to improve their choices and instead, they convinced Mark to follow their bad choices. Mark battled a 40-year struggle with addiction. His life was a rollercoaster ride of slow, steep climbs into recovery, followed by high-speed descents back into relapse. His "clean" periods would last a while. During one period, it lasted almost a decade. He kept a steady job and married a hometown girl from a good family. They tried to raise their own family. Instead, they suffered through tragic heartache and loss, having a stillborn baby boy in the 5th month of pregnancy.

Sadly, Mark didn't get to be my parents' favorite on earth. Throughout Mark's life he and Dad would quarrel and held animosity toward one another. So, Satan attacked his self-image early on. However, he was favored in God's eyes. Even though he walked through the shadow of the valley of death for many years, God was still with Mark. He spent the last five years of his life successfully walking in recovery and we knew this time it was for good. He successfully completed a 30-day recovery program, followed by a 12-month stay at a halfway house to insure there would never be another relapse. He made it his life mission to help other addicts stay clean too. He was a faithful follower of his 12-step program, and he served as a sponsor and keynote speaker in the AA community. Most importantly, he became a sold-out, faithful follower of Jesus Christ with no reservations. He found a church that made him feel at home and helped him grow in his relationship with Jesus. He had a bold, child-like faith, never holding back in sharing the Gospel. Mark had found joy and he constantly expressed it on the job and in his clean and sober social life.

I believe God's mercy allowed Mark to leave this fallen world at age 57. His great reward was to go home to Heaven and be with his only son, Mark, Jr. Little Mark would have been the same age as my oldest son. My big brother was in the prime of his life; drug-free and serving God, when he was suddenly killed on the job in a freak accident. He never knew what hit him. According to settings on his phone, we know he was listening to worship music when the accident happened. He suffered a head injury in "the blink of an eye" that left him in a 6-day coma before finally crossing over into Glory.

These stories of my siblings' journeys are examples of how we are all born with a target on our back. BUT GOD! We have a constant Shield Who stays with us in the battles and fights FOR US. Whether we make good choices like my sister, or not-so-good choices like me and my brother, we are all in a spiritual battle while we are living on Earth. But, be encouraged! *"If God is for us, then who can stand against us?"* **(Romans 8:31)**

My sister was the "good child." My brother would be deemed in society as "the black sheep." As the youngest sibling, I was the grey sheep, who swung on a pendulum between good and bad behavior. My good decisions were influenced by Jesus, and those in my life who followed Him – like Lori and my mom.

My bad decisions were influenced by Satan with the string of lies he began whispering to me in my childhood. As I grew older, those whispers escalated into a loud voice that drowned out God's voice. Satan twisted a tight cord of deception into a noose around my neck and led me into dark places. I was naïve in thinking it was "just life." It was actually total bondage.

Here's my story of many tragedies and eventually one great triumph.

LORI | MARK | ME

FAMILY PHOTO

DAD AS A TEEN	MOM AS A TEEN
DAD	MOM
DAD FISHING	MARK

CHAPTER FIVE
Lies Children Believe

"Many of them will stumble; they will fall and be broken, they will be snared and captured."

~Isaiah 8:15 (NKJV)

LIE #1 – I was an accident, and my name is "Damnit"

By this point in my life, my natural world was very stable and peaceful, I was 58 years old when Holy Spirit began the process of healing me emotionally and spiritually. I had already traveled a long road back to full dedication to Christ. I was baptized in Holy Spirit at age 53. I thought I had finally reached my destiny of freedom in Christ, living a life of fellowship with Him and in a God-centered marriage. I decided to read a book that Alex Seeley, the author I mentioned earlier, had just written. It was her very first book titled *Tailor Made – Discover the Secret to Who God Created You to Be*. The book is about finding our true identity in Christ. She is an amazing pastor, and I basically ordered it, just because I loved how she preached. So, I knew I would love how she would write. I was expecting to be entertained more than being enlightened. However, I discovered through Alex's teachings that I still had deep wounds in my soul that needed healing. These wounds were from years of toxic relationships and marriages that were NOT God-ordained. This God-centered marriage is my fourth and FINAL one. Anytime I meet someone new who is curious and asks about my family and my background, my go-to reply is always, "I've got a story. It's too long to explain, so that's the short version." This usually happens when they discover both of my sons, and myself, all have different last names. So, that reply is the least complicated.

At this appointed time, I realized there were still truths about my life I had never discovered before. As I began to dive into Alex's book, Holy Spirit revealed to me the lies the enemy had whispered to me as a young child. In one of her first chapters, Alex, directed me to pause and ask Holy Spirit, "Show me a lie I was told as a child." Upon taking her advice, I was ASTONISHED by Holy Spirit's revelation!

The very first lie He showed me was in a sudden vivid memory of a conversation I had with my parents when I was elementary school age. I asked them, "Where did my name come from?"

Mom replied, "From my best friend in high school. Her name was Maxi Dee and she was very special to me, so I named you Lisa Dee after her." I remember feeling so special from my mom's answer.

Then came Dad's answer. . . a perfect setup for one of his instinctive jokes. "Yeah . . . and Dee is also short for "Damnit", because that was my *first* thought when I found out we were pregnant again! Hahahahahaha!"

Dad was notorious for laughing the loudest at his own jokes. I knew my dad adored me, so I never consciously took offense to that joke at the time. I even laughed along with him because we had the very same sense of humor. But on this present day, as I asked Holy Spirit to reveal the lies I was told as a child, I began to see the sinister plot behind the joke "that happened to pop in" Dad's mind.

Today, I realize Satan began to whisper lies into my subconscience as a young child. This was his first, and it was an effective groundbreaker. He took that one little joke and turned it into a huge false belief about my life. *"So, you weren't planned, huh? Hmmmm. Well, that means you were an accident. You were not supposed to be born. You are not supposed to be here!"* This abrupt discovery turned on a bright light of revelation. "So THIS is why, as a child, I NEVER had 'the dream' of what I wanted to be when I grew up!" WOW.

Outwardly, I didn't THINK to dream about or plan for my future. Inwardly, I realize I didn't think much about it because I subconsciously believed *"I wasn't planned and didn't have a purpose. Why would God need me to do anything? That's for the children who were wanted."* This sudden realization opened the door of truth wide open and shined light on the OTHER lies I had heard and believed throughout my upbringing. This revelation caused me to see and understand why I traveled on such a long, dark path in life.

The Bible says the power to speak life or death is in our tongues. **(Proverbs 18:21)** As parents, we must consider the words we speak to our children, knowing that what we speak will affect our children's soul. God's word spoke the earth into existence, and we carry His power of the spoken word as believers. Our spoken word can create a blessing or a curse. My dad was oblivious to the fact he had spoken a curse over me by referring to my name as "Damnit."

As I said earlier, Mom was a very patient and nurturing parent. She loved children and had a high tolerance for the noisy, chaotic atmosphere that children bring to the surroundings. However, I recall on more than one occasion she would get very frustrated with me. I constantly tested her patience. I was a reckless handful. In a moment of frustration, Mom would say in her tired, gentle voice, "Lisa Dee, why can't you just be more like your sister and behave?"

The enemy was lurking around ready to pounce on me with another lie. *"Yeah – why can't you be more like your sister? You can never measure up to her. Look at her. She is beautiful and you look nothing like her. So, that means you are ugly AND an accident. You're not even supposed to be here."* Satan used the innocent frustration of my sweet mom to speak more death into my mind. He is a sneaky snake. My ears never heard those filthy lies, but my soul heard every single one as they began to form my self-image.

LIE #2 – "You don't measure up"

Despite our family's slight dysfunctions and occasional

spankings growing up, I still had a happy childhood with a lot of fond memories. My elementary school years are an era I'm still most fond of. I was blessed to grow up in a great neighborhood. There were many children on my block to play with. There were mostly boys, but also a few girls that became my very best friends. From first grade to the present, Alisa, Debra and Toni are still like sisters to me. We continue to meet together for "girl's weekend" once a year to catch up on life and are in constant communication on a group text. It was a happy time of walking to school with them in the mornings, having the same teacher, and playing outside with them after school and on weekends.

As a child I loved playing outdoors! In the summertime, all the neighborhood kids would stay outside all day playing games and exploring, until the streetlights came on at dusk. I knew that was the strict rule in our house – "when those streetlights turn on, you better be in the house!" Because of my love for the outdoors, recess was my favorite subject at school. I was a "straight-A student" on the playground in a game of kickball.

However, inside the classroom it was a whole different "ball game." If they had known about Attention Deficit Disorder back in the 60's, I could have been the poster child for their research. I had a tough time focusing, to put it lightly. Back then children like me were called "daydreamers." I was sent out in the hall numerous times for talking out of turn. Grade after grade, the teacher would sit me in the front row to keep me from being a distraction to other classmates. To have any chance of hearing the lesson, I needed to sit straight with eyes forward, focused on the teacher. I was successful at looking the part. As the teacher would give the instructions for the next assignment, I had my stance down. Sitting up straight, shoulders back and both eyes wide open and affixed on her. Unfortunately, my mind didn't follow suit. Within the second or third sentence of her instructions, my mind would wander off into a fantasy of riding my new bike or playing with my puppy. I was in a happy place. I would soon be snatched from that happy place. With a clap of her hands the teacher would say, "Ok everyone – get started." As I quickly woke up from my dream, I would frantically look to my left and my right whispering to Toni or Debra, "What are we doing?" Thankfully, they were loyal friends who had my back. They would quickly whisper a short recap with just enough information for me to complete the assignment and receive a "satisfactory" mark.

So, I did struggle somewhat in academics. I still managed to pass each grade with basically a "C" average. I never earned any of the "EXCELLENT" marks. I was always noted as a "Satisfactory Student". School was one of my favorite places to be for the social aspect, but not necessarily for the learning experience.

I now see that this was the time in my life when the enemy started whispering, *"You need to take the easiest path possible to get through school. You're just not as smart as the other kids, so take the path of least resistance. Besides, you don't need a formal education anyway – God doesn't have a purpose for you – you're not even supposed to be here, unplanned child."*

Satan planted the seed of self-doubt in my soul in Elementary school. He watered that seed until it grew into a full-bloom negative self-talk. By the time I was in high school, I declared often "I'm not cut out for college." So, I would tell my high school counselor at the beginning of each school year, "Put me on the easy track to earn my diploma. I'm not going to college. It's just not for me." So, my high school education consisted of the basic diploma track with entry-level courses, and no college-preparation courses.

LIE #3 – "You are only accepted by association"

Despite my attention problem, I still loved my elementary school years. Life was so fun and carefree. That happy time ended in the summer going into the 6th grade. My parents decided to buy a bigger house on the more affluent side of town. The new neighborhood looked much different than my old, familiar surroundings. Our new street consisted of large homes with manicured lawns. They were the homes of doctors, lawyers and other professionals who were successful and prosperous. Although our modest house was larger than our previous, and provided an additional bathroom, we still looked like the "poor folks" next to our neighbors.

When school started soon after our move, I was placed in a "foreign land" and felt the pressure of being the new kid in class. I had no idea how to MAKE new friends. From the early age of three, I always just HAD friends, naturally bonding as we grew up together. Here I was, plucked from my upbringing in the middle-class district and placed in the upper-class side of town. I felt like a small fish in the big, wrong pond.

I became a completely different person - much quieter, shy and insecure. This "foreign land" had "natives" staring at me as "the stranger from across the tracks." Academics became an even greater challenge! The teachers used bigger words. I didn't have the privilege of asking my buddies what the classroom assignment was. I was not about to embarrass myself by asking a stranger for help. I just sat in silence, hoping for a miracle to ward off the threat of being labeled weird AND stupid. I was still daydreaming during those instructions, but it wasn't about puppies. I was constantly thinking about my old life on the other side of town. I missed my friends. I felt so alone. My life was over! (We can be so dramatic at age 11).

Then, after school one day, I got acquainted with Katie at a Girl Scout meeting. She was one of the smart girls in my class. We soon discovered we had similar personalities. We made each other laugh and instantly bonded as new best friends. Katie wasn't just smart; she was also popular. All my classmates liked Katie and since I became her new best friend, I was finally accepted among my peers. Katie helped me be included *AND* she helped me with my homework. Just when I thought I was surely drowning in a pool of doom, Katie threw me a lifeline. I became Katie's shadow. Everywhere Katie went, I went. I was practically glued to her hip and let her do most of the talking in a group.

This friendship with Katie allowed the enemy to plant another seed. "*You do realize you are only accepted because of her. It's not about you* – **it's all about who you know**. *That's your ticket to popularity*

– just be seen with the popular kids and be recognized by association."

When we reached Junior High School, I was still stuck in unfamiliar territory on a grander scale. My hometown had two junior high schools during those years. My childhood friends attended junior high in my old school district. I was required to attend junior high in my new school district and still had to meet *more* new people from the "foreign land of the snooty".

As the crowd of "foreigners" increased, so did my insecurity and self-doubt. My body image really took a plunge too. My boyish, athletic physique began to take on a new shape, with curves I was not comfortable with. I was plagued with the "puberty pudge". So, I became even more insecure and shy.

Thankfully, Katie continued to pull me along as a lifeline. Her popularity grew at the same rate as my insecurity and self-doubt. In the halls between classes, Katie would get invited to the Friday night parties. I would always overhear, "Hey Katie! Party at my house Friday night - 6:00!" She would respond, "Well, is Lisa invited?" "Ummm, who's Lisa?" they asked. "She's my best friend and she's spending the night with me. So, if she's not invited then I can't come." I barely got my foot in the door of those parties by riding Katie's shirt tail. I never had a fun time either. I would sit quietly in the corner and watch Katie socialize. If there were any conversations around me, I would just observe, but never engage. I was just a fly on the wall that no one even noticed to swat. The "fish in the wrong pond" syndrome became increasingly more of a reality.

LIE #4 – "You need to settle"

Finally, in mid-term of my 7th grade year I got some social relief. My parents noticed my grades dropping drastically as my sadness and depression kept rising. So, they agreed to transfer me to the other junior high school where I would be back with my childhood friends. That was a happy time! I was back in my comfort zone and the "real" Lisa Dee started blooming again. Besides being with my old friends, I also made new friends who were a lot like me.

I felt right at home. We had all our classes together. They were "average" students taking the easier classes too! Hallelujah! I had arrived.

Junior high school is a time when I started noticing the opposite sex. I started having an attraction to boys for other reasons besides playing kickball with. Most of the boys in my classes leaned slightly on the rebellious side. They were "too cool to follow the rules." They had an edge to them that was mysterious and attractive. The best part was that they noticed me and would engage in conversation. They seemed to speak my language and were easier to talk to than the male class leaders and star athletes. I was attracted to these "at-risk" type of guys because I didn't feel the sting of not being enough. My poor self-image began to improve, even while I was still a little on the "pudgy" side.

The enemy whispered, *"You need to look for a boyfriend in this group. You don't really have what it takes to attract a popular boy. Besides, the rule-keepers are boring anyway. These cool boys are more exciting and romantic.* **You just need to settle** *for one of these guys. They weren't planned by their parents either."*

That's when the seed I call my "bad boy syndrome" was planted in my soul. For many years I "settled" into the belief that I was destined to be with a bad boy. The good guys were just "too boring" and "too good" for me. Although I still saw myself as a "good girl," it became my "calling" to date "bad boys" because they were the type I was attracted to. As I grew into adulthood, I believed the lie that I could "fix" them and lead them to Jesus.

It was also in junior high when Satan continued to use my sister in his comparison trap. By the time I was in 8th grade, Lori was a senior in high school. She was well known as a school leader and all-around successful student. She made the cheerleading squad all four years of high school, and voted a top-4 finalist in the school beauty contest. Lori was also chosen to play the leading role in the school musical, "Oklahoma", as "Miss Laurie", and was favored by all of her teachers for her grades and excellent work ethic. She was also very popular with all of her classmates. During her junior and senior years, she had the same steady boyfriend and they dated all through college and eventually became engaged. In high school, Lori constantly had other male admirers visit her frequently at our house. It was obvious they were attracted to her but settled with being her close friend. Lori was always a loyal girlfriend to her beau. I could keep going about Lori's accomplishments and attributes, but surely, you get the picture.

I started noticing that people, who typically ignored me, suddenly treated me differently when they discovered who I was kin to. I would often receive comments like, "Oh wow! You're Lori Fort's little sister?" Their puzzled looks gave way to an obvious thought, *"Hmmm. I wonder if she's adopted, I just don't see it."*

The enemy took the opportunity to drive his lie even deeper. *"Let me repeat, LOSER. It's not about you, it's about who you know. No, you can never be your sister or accomplish anything she has, but you CAN gain attention by using her name."* So, that's when I started introducing myself a lot as "Lori Fort's little sister." My own name just never made an impact.

During these formative years, the enemy had completely stolen my sense of identity. He convinced me I was nobody and I would be lucky to attract *anybody*. He had me right where he wanted me to lure me into his next trap of deception. It was the grand finale of his plot to throw me into a cage and lock me into a lifetime of bondage.

CHAPTER SIX

The Beginning Of My Downhill Slide

"So the serpent spewed water out of his mouth like a flood after the woman, that he might cause her to be carried away by the flood." ~ Revelation 12:15 (NKJV)

This is the longest chapter in the book for a very good reason. I'm determined to give a clear picture of a potential danger in your own life.

High School was new, exciting, and frightening, all in one. I did gain respect and popularity with my new "title" as Lori's sister and was elected cheerleader my freshman year of high school. As I advanced in grade, I was faced with new challenges academically. As I mentioned earlier, I still had the same plan Satan had planted in my elementary school years. I was to *get out the easiest way possible because I am not college material.*

In my day, school counselors were never charged with the duty of helping students choose their career paths, set goals, or guide them on paths of success to fulfilling their purpose. Unfortunately, counselors were often over-loaded. They could only assist students who were self-driven and had their life goals in mind on their own. Counselors didn't have time to guide a "satisfactory student" who had no idea what her goals were. I didn't have any dreams of a career. I had simply settled for taking life as it came. I thought my destiny was to meet my husband and stay at home, raising kids. That's all I ever wanted. The "man of my dreams" was my destiny.

Aside from academics, it was an honor to be counted among the class leaders as a cheerleader. I really stood out from the "typical cheerleader" model. I was the chubby one with the goofy personality. I used to make the other squad members laugh a lot, *especially* when I would show up at the games, on more than one occasion, with the *wrong* uniform on! I would be greeted with loud laughter and exclamations, "Lisa! Were you not listening at our meeting?" *["Well, no, actually!" I was daydreaming as usual. Not about puppies though - about one of those dreamy "bad boys" in my class.]"* It was another example of my "uniqueness".

Homecoming my freshman year is a vivid memory. We felt like we were BIG shots. As freshman cheerleaders, we got to cheer with the varsity squad, in front of the entire student body, at the Friday night football game. However, I was also the *only one* who *didn't* receive a mum. When it came time to take a group picture for the yearbook, I *borrowed* one of FIVE mums from our most popular squad member, Irene. "It will balance us out" was my rationale. My fellow squad members gave authentic smiles for the camera, as they laughed with me, laughing at myself.

I quickly realized that the ability to laugh at myself also got me invited to parties. I didn't need Katie's shirt tail anymore! I became known as the funny girl with the "great personality." This meant I was everyone's friend but was not seen as girlfriend material. I didn't have a steady boyfriend like my other classmates but was asked "as a friend" to the dances. I was a pretty good dancer with some impressive moves. My more important quality, however, was being a good "wing man" for my "dates" to introduce them to my cute, female friends. I had settled into the role of flying solo, while many of my girlfriends were going steady with the boy of their dreams. By day, I was class clown. By night, I cried myself to sleep many times, thinking about all my flaws and shortcomings. The mousy girl in the mirror was destined to be alone.

The spring semester of my freshman year was a game changer. Finally, I was asked to the Spring dance by one of those boring "rule-followers." When the band took their first break, I secretly

↑ Don't Fall For It ↓

slipped out and went with my exciting rebel-friends to another dance across town. This dance was off campus. The patrons were mostly Seniors who were of legal drinking age. The legal drinking age back then was 18. Rules pertaining to under-age drinking and driving were more lenient in the 70's; especially in my small town. Luck had it, we were admitted with a "minor" stamp on our hands and "our word" we would not partake in alcohol. My fear of the wrath from Dad and the thought of making Mom cry, helped me to keep my word. I declined invitations from friends to partake in the liquor they snuck in. I was more of a "pseudo rebel." I played a role that did not match my true inner compass. I had no interest in drinking. I enjoyed the rush sneaking out on my date at the school dance to be in a risky environment. I felt like a rebel *with* a cause, pretending like I was one of the high school seniors. I was among the adult world, and I liked it!

It wasn't too long after we had settled down at one end of a long table, when I looked up and saw him. This guy at the other end of the table looked straight at me with sparkles in his eyes. It instantly captured my attention and my heart. It was like love at first sight. He was sitting with his friends, and something strange came over me, as he kept making eye contact with me. I mustered up the courage to go say hello to him. To my surprise, he asked me to sit with him and his friends. I feared his attraction may have just been due to his beer consumption, but I still accepted his invitation when he asked me to dance. He took an attraction to me even before I told one of my corny jokes. So, he saw more in me than just a "great personality." I quickly learned this guy was a senior too. Some of his friends had graduated already. I really felt like a big shot for being accepted into this group of older people. I was no longer a fly on the wall, but instead was suddenly the center of attention as introductions were made. I sat with them the rest of the night to get acquainted with this mysterious "older man". By the time I left the dance with my friends, I was "head over heels in like" with this guy. I only knew his first name. That didn't stop me from giving him my phone number when he asked for it. For the sake of anonymity, we will call him Rob. I was hopping around the house when I got home, with elation of "puppy love".

The next morning was Sunday and as I went to the breakfast table, Dad had his head buried in the Sunday newspaper. He held the newspaper in an upright position, where I could read the backside. I almost choked on my pancake when I took my first glance at the sports section. There he was! My dream guy was staring right at me in a photo of himself, running on a track, with a full-page write up. Rob was not just "some random guy." He was the star mile-runner of the track team! This was no "average Joe!" He was the town sports celebrity! I suddenly faced reality. He's too important for me. Even though he asked for my number, I'm never going to get a phone call. I suddenly felt like Cinderella when the clock struck midnight. Back to reality. As suspected, I never got a phone call that long Sunday in the spring of 1975.

To my surprise, he did stop me in the hall at school the next week and invited me to come and watch him in the district track meet, held at our high school. Talk about not being able to focus on class assignments! A few days later, the beginning of my destiny launched like the gun shot start of his race. The district track meet was about to begin. I remember shaking like a leaf as I entered the field with my friends. My eye immediately caught him stretching in preparation for his event. My stomach churned butterflies as I approached him. I kept telling myself to "act cool and don't say anything stupid." I was unsure if our conversation would flow as easily as it did that night the beer was flowing. I had already braced myself for just a quick nod or even a short greeting as a kind gesture. Instead, a huge smile broke out on Rob's face when he saw me. I was an instant catch! He asked me to go with him to get a coke after he won his event without barely breaking a sweat. That's where it all started. A coke date and an invitation for a second date.

Rob went on to win the state championship in the mile run at the close of season. This was his final victory as a high school graduate. My association with a state champion won me more popularity and a pretty big spoonful of pride. I had found my purpose, and it felt amazing to be on the arm of a "town sports celebrity."

↑ *Don't Fall For It* ↓

That summer was a fun-filled adventure. My parents allowed me to date this older guy, under the condition that I was not to be with him alone. If at least one friend was invited to go along, then I could go. This was a great arrangement for my friends, as well as for his single friends. They too, were older and single, and in search of girl companions. Although the attempted matchmaking did not catch on for them, we all hung out as friends. There was lots of laughter and good times.

I was considered the "summer hero" to my close friends because I rescued them from boredom. The tables were turned and now, Katie was riding MY shirt-tale! We were not yet old enough to drive, so cruising the strip on summer nights was not an option without my connection. So, my older boyfriend with a car and his friends with a ski boat, made for a fun summer in the sun. I learned to water ski and also discovered I liked the taste of beer. I knew if I was going to fit in with an older crowd, I had to act older. My friends grew to admire Rob. They witnessed how crazy he was about me. He got along well with my friends and was always willing to let them tag along. My friends saw our relationship as a model for their own "happily ever after." I was treated with love, respect and dignity. The way Rob's eyes continued to sparkle when he looked at me, made my heart melt every time. Our mutual admiration quickly developed into a steady, autonomous relationship, vowing to stay together forever. I knew I wanted to spend the rest of my life with him, even though my life was just starting. I had found the man of my dreams! I suddenly knew what my future goals were; to be his wife someday and have his children.

He came from a great family. His parents were high school sweethearts too. They found love at a very young age as well. They quit high school and got their G.E.D. so they could get married at age 16! They were hard workers and had built a good home with three children. Family time was extremely important to them. I loved going to their house for supper. They made it a common practice to turn off the TV and sit around the table, having meaningful conversation while dining. Many times, the conversation would last long after our plates were empty. They were a perfect model of a functional family. They had been happily married for over 20 years when I came into the picture. I saw a generational baton being passed on as our love story followed in their footsteps. Rob's mom was a stay-at-home wife and mom too, just like my dream goal. Getting to know and being accepted by his family only deepened my love and adoration for Rob. My whole world became all about his world. I couldn't get enough of his time and attention. I wanted to be attached to his hip and never be apart from him. That's why life became extremely difficult when September of 1975 rolled around.

My romance was being forced to continue long-distance. He was awarded a four-year track scholarship at a major university, about ninety miles from my hometown. When he left for college, we had only been dating five months. Those five months seemed like a lifetime already. The summer went by so fast because we were having so much fun. I rode with his family to get him settled into his dorm on that dreaded day. When we had to say our goodbyes, I felt like I couldn't breathe. I could empathize with those wives who have to say goodbye to their husbands who join the military. It felt no less agonizing to me. Females can be so emotional and dramatic at age 15 and I was no exception. My immaturity and inexperience in dating made this heartache even more painful. I thought I was going to drown in my tears on the trip home. Although he cried too during our goodbye, my mind was still riddled with fear he would find someone else in his new surroundings. He admitted to me later that he had the same fear I would find someone else back home. We talked for hours on the phone on school nights. Many times, we would fall asleep before we would hang up. We were full-blown in love and I could hardly bare being apart from him.

Luckily, we had a lifeboat. Lori had chosen the same college after she graduated high school two years prior. So, her private dorm room with an extra bed provided a place to stay when I went to see him on the weekends. His obligation to the track team did not allow him many chances to come home. It was hard being apart, but we made it work the best we could. I was having to juggle pursuing my own high school diploma, while constantly missing him. Now, my classroom daydreams were all about him as I doodled "Rob + Lisa = 4-Ever" all over my schoolbooks. My involvement in extra-curricular activities helped take my mind off my sadness. With a heightened self-esteem as "girlfriend of a track star", my confidence awarded me more popularity. I was elected to student council and made the top advanced choir with my singing voice. I was starting to embrace the high school experience while still pining for my long-distance Romeo.

I thought I was living a dream. I believed that God had sent me my destiny with a boy who, I would've never thought, wanted ME. I now know this season of my life taught me that just because something looks good, it doesn't always mean its God. Satan, the counterfeit loves to "copy" God's blessings in order to lure His children into a trap. For the remainder of this chapter, you will see some statements written in ***bold italics***. This is because I want to make sure you see the ***bold flags of a potential abusive relationship***. If you are just beginning to date and may be as naïve as I was, I want you to see the signs written in bold italics so the enemy cannot lead you blindly into the trap of abuse.

By the middle of my sophomore year and eight months into our relationship, Rob seemed to become more concerned and agitated about the distance between us. He suggested ways I could do my part in making this separation easier. He pointed out that all those extra-curricular activities were interfering with our limited time together. *"Besides Lisa – high school is dumb anyway. You're with a college man now. You can be up here on the weekends watching a college football game instead of cheering at some lame high school game. What's the use of cheering for a losing team?"* My hometown football team had a decade-long reputation for losing every game. He helped me to see that all my other commitments were taking time away from him. Serious relationships require sacrifice and commitment. I marveled at the fact he loved me so much he could not stand to be apart. So, I ultimately sacrificed my entire high school experience to jump start my life with the man of my dreams. I devoted all of my time and attention to him alone. ***Abusive relationships almost always begin with isolation and control.*** He wanted me all to himself because, in reality, he was afraid of losing me.

I began to puff up with pride as I strutted down the halls of my high school. Internally, I began to belittle my school and the students my own age. I had a new routine that made me a "big girl." Each passing weekend, I would travel on the Greyhound bus to the university, all by myself, to be a "college student." I felt like an independent adult, making my own decisions. I developed an attitude of "I just don't fit in with these people my own age. They just don't get me." I loved the life of a weekend college girl. I didn't even pause after dropping out of all my extra-curricular activities. My love of singing and socializing were now put on the back burner. I had "bigger fish to fry." When I informed my choir instructor and my sponsor for the student council that "I'm out," they tried convincing me to rethink my decision. It was no use. My deep love affair with my new beau paved a "better road" I was to travel.

Proverbs 16:18 says, *"Pride goes before destruction, and a haughty spirit before a fall."* Pride is a dangerous trap set by our enemy. The devil loves to tempt us with pride, because we elevate ourselves so high that we fail to see the fall that is inevitable. Pride can disguise itself in so many subtle ways, even in a young girl who is incredibly insecure. *I became very prideful and unteachable when others tried to warn me.* Pride turned me into a rebellious teenager, refusing to listen to my parents, who constantly warned me to be careful with this older boy. They could clearly see the red flags but were the type of parents to allow me to learn my lesson the hard way. They relied on the belief I would grow tired of him eventually. However, the fairy tale was just too enticing for me to see the real picture.

Utopia had its first storm one night, not long after I made my decision to dedicate my life to this man of my dreams. The memory of our very first fight is forever etched in my mind. It was a weekend when he traveled with the track team, so there was no reason for me to go see him. At home, I was invited to go riding around with my girlfriends. That sounded like more fun than sitting at home on a Saturday night, missing him. After all, I was still a 16-year-old teenager. It was a fun night of "dragging the strip", talking about boys and laughing with my girlfriends. It had been a while since I had done that – just hang with my peeps on a girl's night.

Later that night, I was pleasantly surprised when we passed a familiar car. It was Rob, riding around with his buddies. He was in town! He had decided to travel home after his track meet. Those were the days before cell phones, and since I wasn't home to answer his call, he had no way of letting me know he was coming. I waved frantically when we passed him and his friends. They followed us as we all pulled into a nearby parking lot to hang out. I could not contain my excitement as I bailed out of the car and ran as fast as I could to give him a big hug. Suddenly, my sprint of enthusiasm was stifled by an angry look on his face. He chastised me for being associated with these girls who "were obviously looking for 'love' (sugar-coating his words)." I was dumbfounded. These were my very same girlfriends he knew from last summer who went with us on group dates. He had come to know them as his friends too, so I was completely confused. Now, he was accusing them of unspeakable intentions and prosecuting me by association. *An abuser will use outlandish accusations, guilt and shame in order to keep the victim isolated from a free world.*

Where was my Prince Charming? It was the very first time I saw anger on his face, much less to hear the terrible comments he yelled at me as he peeled out of the parking lot. I was suddenly in a nightmare. It felt like someone just punched me in the gut. I couldn't breathe. I couldn't believe what had just happened. I went home and cried myself to sleep. I quickly discovered that fighting with him was not an option. *It sent me into a whirlwind of panic and depression. Life without him was impossible. This is the definition of co-dependency when a person can control your emotions by their actions.* If I only knew then that the only Person life was impossible without, was Jesus. If I had known He is my Best Friend and was talking with Him daily, He would've told me that no other human being on this earth gives me life, but Him. Instead, the enemy kept whispering his lies that this broken, insecure human being was my god. I believed Rob was my only reason for living.

Thankfully, Rob calmed down and called the next day. When I heard his calm and apologetic voice explain what angered him, I started exhaling again. He was actually "angry at my friends for putting me in that position." He was "more concerned about my innocent reputation being tarnished by riding around town. That would give others the perception that I was in search of other guys." He helped me to see from a guy's perspective, what "girls appear to want" if they are riding around town. So, we came to the agreement that I would stay home on the weekends when I wasn't with him. There was no other man I wanted. If giving up my friends was required to stay pure, so be it. Besides, my purity was reserved for him.

Once we give our hearts to Jesus, our spirit man is made perfect. The enemy can no longer attack our spirit, so he goes after our mind, our emotions, and our will through the desires of our flesh. He will send people into our lives who are influenced by darkness but disguised as angels of light. It's his favorite way to lure us into a trap. My upcoming days are a perfect illustration.

Springtime came around and it was the eve of the second summer of our romance. College semesters always ended earlier than high school and he was back home before my sophomore year ended. I could not contain my excitement that he would be home for four months. I remember the first time he and his friends picked me up from school. I thought I was the envy of my classmates as they watched a sporty truck pulling a shiny new ski boat, full of older guys, pick me up in front of the main doors. The loud music coming from the truck made every head turn to look. Perfect set-up. Rob stuck his head out the window to start shouting my name, "Come on Lisa! We are burning daylight!" I waved good-bye to the "poor peasants waiting for their mommas." I was headed to the lake with my OLDER boyfriend and his OLDER friends for some after-school water-skiing. I had never felt "cooler" than in that moment. No more "Miss Wallflower." I was now the center of attention instead of the girl in the corner that no one noticed at parties.

I felt like I had won the lottery when this man came into my life.

How was I so lucky to be the one he chose? He was so much more important than I was. He was still winning track meets in college and receiving regional notoriety. He was so good at running; he began to teach me the correct form and technique on how to jog a long distance with endurance. I was so grateful because I quickly watched those puberty pounds melt away into a slimmer, more fit figure. He was my fitness coach, along with being the man of my dreams.

Rob and I were inseparable as the summer break came into full swing. By this time, my parents settled into the realization that this older boy was not going away. They had already trusted me on the weekends I had traveled to see him. So, they abolished the group-date rule and let me date him alone. Rob began trying to persuade me that it was time to take the next step in our relationship. I clearly knew I was not ready to take that step. The idea absolutely terrified me. It became the subject of our next and even bigger, fight.

On our usual date, hanging out with his friends at the local hangout, this night ended differently. He convinced me to go "parking" on a nearby secluded country road about 5 miles from my house, just outside the city limits. The kissing advanced into heavy petting and his wandering hands. As I stopped the party with a firm hand on his and a "No!" his frustration instantly turned into anger with an ultimatum. "You either [derogatory word] or walk!" My shock and anger prompted me to jump out of the car, slam the door and proceed to walk. I was determined to make a statement! My body, my choice! I felt confident he would pull up and say, "I'm sorry. Get in the car. I'll take you home." Instead, to my sobering error, he skidded right past me shouting "Have a nice walk, you tease!" He left me behind to walk alone, in the dark, all the way home. As I walked in a "zombie-like" state of shock down that country road, the only light guiding my way was the brightness of a full moon. I remember crying uncontrollably, riddled with shock and fear, as I was left for any predator to come along and grab me. *An abuser never cares about the safety of the victim. They are only interested in their own needs and desires.*

Today as I recall this memory, I wish I could go back and allow the 64-year-old me to speak truth and wisdom to the 16-year-old me. I would tell her that the full-moonlight illuminating my path was no coincidence. It was the love of Christ, the Keeper of the moon and stars. I was oblivious to the fact that Holy Spirit was right there with me, in me, protecting me and guiding me, lighting my pathway, literally. If only I had known then who I was and Whose I was, I could've seen the red flags of an abusive relationship right at my threshold. That lonely, scary walk could have been a time to talk to Jesus about all my hurt, anger and disappointment, allowing Him to speak to me. I imagine He would've said, *"Daughter, this is not the plan I have for you. My plans for your future are to prosper you and not to harm you."* **(Jeremiah 29:11)** Instead, because I had no idea who I was in Christ or that Jesus was my Best Friend, I only did what I knew to do. I was not equipped to hear Him guide me into better decisions. My mind was completely fixed on Rob and thoughts of how we were going to get past this. I continued down the same path of more hurt, anger and disappointment, disguised as "my destiny with my soulmate." This older, wiser boy had become my god and I put all my trust in him.

In my fantasy, Rob would show up at my house the next day with a humble, mournful look on his face, showering me with apologies and promises of never repeating that night. Unfortunately, that did not happen. I didn't hear from him for a while. The silent treatment led to many long days of depression and anxiety attacks, as I waited desperately for the phone to ring.

Instead, I soon learned he had found another girl to date. This girl was a year older than him, making her five years older and five years more experienced than me. The worst part of all - I had to work with her at the local country club pool. I had been hired as the pool waitress that summer. She was the lifeguard. She was an innocent victim in the whole scenario of our issue. She started dating him, oblivious to the fact that I was the "ex-girlfriend" he spoke frequently to her about. Her talkative nature at work brought much insight as she shared their conversations. I chose to keep his secret too, in order to get the inside scoop. These revelations were informative and excruciating. She always came to work with stories about their date the night before and what they planned to do that evening. I was devastated as I watched this nightmare unfold right before my eyes. She did not seem like his type at all. She wasn't considered one of the prettiest girls in town, but her "well-endowed" physique kept wandering eyes off her face anyway. It was obvious to me that it was no coincidence he had asked out a girl closer to his own age, who "just happened" to be my co-worker. He was deliberately punishing me by proving a point. Her "girl confessions" about their intimacy confirmed that he was getting from her, what he could not get from me.

This charade was short-term, however. Their breakup was quick and final, when he was tired of playing his "I can shop elsewhere" game. He came back around with a reconciliation proposal. I can't even recall his words that won me back. I'm sure they weren't anything too convincing. I can only remember being so grateful and relieved that I was going to get my life back. I decided to forget about that night he left me stranded. An apology was no longer necessary. Him, being back in my life was the greatest apology of all. He had me eating out of the palm of his hands and I agreed to go that next step with him. I was ready to devote ALL of myself to him. My emotions were standing at attention and willing, but my mind, body and heart were still saying, "Wait." *Manipulation in a relationship is a huge red flag of abuse.*

The entire experience of losing my virginity was embarrassing, disgusting and FAR from romantic. The act of the ultimate commitment to a man – the vow that God intends to happen on the first night of marriage – became a perverted, awkward and despairing life event that could never be undone. It felt like sheer duty with absolutely no pleasure. It planted the false belief in my soul from that day on that sex is dirty and only intended for the pleasure of the man. I felt filthy when it was over. Every time after the first time never felt any different, even throughout the entire period I dedicated my life to him. *I had signed my emotional covenant with this man through sexual intimacy. An abuser will not only go after your body, but also your soul.* I will explain the stronghold of "soul ties" in the next chapter. It is a real and serious trap that is tied to sexual sin, but it can be broken off through prayer and declaration.

Six months later, we slipped up and got pregnant, despite using caution with our limited knowledge of safe sex. I didn't know what to do. All I could think about was the look of sorrow and disappointment on my parents' faces with the news. I was doomed. I would now be known as an unwed mother. Then, I found out Planned Parenthood had a "way out." I knew other girls my age who had already experienced pregnancy and had gone to Planned Parenthood for "help." The lady we spoke to was so kind and non-judgmental and gave me the reassurance, "Having an abortion in this stage is not killing a baby. The embryo has not formed into a fetus yet, so it's just a seed with no heartbeat." She never talked to us about options other than abortion. There was no ultrasound offered. She even agreed to forge my mother's name on the release form.

That's how Satan tricks us today. He will disguise himself as our friend who has come to rescue us from the very trap he set in the first place. In the world of sin, facing our mistakes and taking responsibility for our actions is never suggested. Satan had now tricked me into taking the secret, easy way out. *"No one else will know and this little slip-up will be forgotten forever."* SO NOT TRUE. Although the PP consultant had a convincing argument, I wasn't fully convinced when it was over. I knew someone died in me that day. It's another memory forever etched in my brain, though I know God has forgiven me. I could not "just forget about it," but only add it to the list of issues I continued to face in this demonized relationship.

Hasty poor decisions will cause emotional wounds and leave permanent scars.

To make matters worse that day, I remember the difference in Rob's countenance from mine. Even before the abortion took place, I was scared, depressed and guilt-ridden. He was joyful and relieved, even excited, to escape the responsibility. I'm almost certain if I had been given other options, he would have still coerced me into this one. He even made up an "abortion song" on the way to the clinic.

I remained silent, trying my hardest to muster up a smile at his sick, light-hearted humor. I was dying inside. When we got back to his house after it was over, I only wanted to lay in bed with a severe case of cramps and a guilt-ridden heart. Thankfully, his parents were not home to inquire what was wrong. My innocence was stripped away even more. My heart was breaking. I was grieving the loss of someone that was a part of me, without thoroughly understanding that. Rob, on the other hand, wanted to go country/western dancing that night with friends. I declined the invitation due to a severe case of stomach cramps. He left the room and came back with the prescription bottle of pills I was given at the clinic. As I laid in fetal position on the bed, he threw them at me calling me "party pooper" and he left the room. *He was angry because I put a damper on his plans. This is another example of how abusers only care that their needs are met and have no consideration for the other person.* I cannot stress this point enough!

How could I not see the cruelty and harshness of this boy who had vowed he would never treat me this way again? Why was that not the deal-breaker that would give me the strength to leave this relationship? Why could I not see, it was just a precursor for worse times to come? I had no idea that I had a Savior who saw me as His beloved daughter and had a better plan for my life. I didn't see that I deserved so much better. Instead, I thought my only self-worth was found in being this college boy's girlfriend. I was blind to the fact that I was trapped. I was like a caged bird with the door open. It never dawned on me to fly away.

Domestic violence can become a self-fulfilling prophecy of submissive defeat when the victim becomes addicted to her assailant. *Low self-esteem is one of Satan's strongest weapons. He convinced me I was a nobody unless I remained in bondage to my abuser.* At this time, I didn't even recognize I was in an abusive relationship. It was just life – couples fight all the time.

After that day, I made an inner vow that I could never be with anyone else. I had given him my one treasure that was meant to be reserved for a wedding night. Therefore, I thought I could only excuse my sexual immorality by making an inner vow to stay with him until one day he would in fact be my husband - for a lifetime. I believed, if I stayed with him forever, God would excuse my sin. I relinquished my freedom to think for myself and to decide, for myself, what was best for me. Rob made all my decisions for me. I was bound for life. I belonged to him and him alone, no matter what happened. **I *knew if I submitted to whatever he asked of me, we were destined for a long and happy life together.*** Submission was the price I needed to pay in order to be in a happy relationship.

The next three years went smoothly as I settled into my proverbial prison of being this man's possession. If he was happy, I was happy. Life was good and we had some good times. I had a new normal of having one goal and only one goal - to shape my thoughts, actions and beliefs around whatever he needed them to be. This included making sure my physical appearance met his standards as well. Ironically, I had lost the identity of my own name a second time. Now I was known as "Rob's girl." That's how I was recognized. Again, my own name made no impact, so I thought.

Rob convinced me that I needed to graduate high school as soon as possible, so that I could enroll in the university and be with him full-time. He pushed me to take dual-credit correspondence courses from the same university during the summers going into my junior and senior years. While my classmates were making lasting memories at the local pool, movie theatre and skating rink – I spent my entire summers with my head buried in books, taking hard college-level courses that earned me credits toward graduation. It was NOT a fun summer for me, but I pulled off a "C" in each course. By the end of the fall semester of my senior year, I was a high school graduate. That landmark time in my life was not recognized by a ceremony with a family celebration afterward. Instead, it just consisted of walking to the Registrar's office, collecting my transcript with a graduation date to go with the application for admission to college. By the spring semester of what would have been my senior year, I was now an official full-time college student with a "secretarial science major". Luckily, my vocational classes that taught me how to work in an office came in handy. I was not college material. I was not there to earn a college degree. My goal was just to take classes, play the part and be at my man's beckoning call. I missed making all those "Senior Class memories" my classmates now talk about at class reunions. I now have to just listen and live vicariously through them about those years that were supposed to be my memories too. When they gather to look at old pictures, I'm not in any of them. The only proof I was even in high school are my individual class pictures of my chubby face with a funny hairstyle.

However, my first semester proved to be an exciting one as a college girl. Despite moving in mid-semester, the girls on my floor in the dorm were quick to welcome me and make me feel at home. My "acceptance by association" was related this time to my roommate, Jill. She was a popular girl from my hometown who had graduated a year earlier. Jill was now a sorority girl and had already established friendships with girls in the dorm. Perfect timing allowed me to fill the bed her previous roommate had vacated. So, I was able to get my foot in the door of this social group, on Jill's shirt tail. We would have late night "pow-wow's" and pizza parties. I had to study much harder than Jill, so classes were a little stressful. The dorm life however, proved to be a fun time to get some much-needed girl time, with "sisters on the 5th floor of Gates Hall."

Visitation hours put a real hardship on my time with Rob. He would get frustrated that the strict visitation rules were reinforced on my floor. Our Resident Assistant took her job very seriously. By the end of my first semester, he convinced me that I needed to move out of the dorm. Finding my own apartment would not limit the time he could spend with me. I had to obey my master. Thankfully, my grandparents supported the financial obligation, enabling me to rent a one-bedroom apartment within walking distance of campus. The deposit was made, and I would move in when we returned for the fall semester. I worked all summer, saving up for things I needed to be an independent adult at age 18, in my very own apartment. The future looked very exciting and adventurous.

The fall semester came, and this new living arrangement was quite different than my life in the dorm. I was no longer living around fun neighbors but instead, had to keep company with myself. I never got to know any neighbors in my apartment complex because I never saw anyone. Most of the residents were graduate students, who devoted all of their time to studying, not socializing. It was a quiet and lonely place. I had also reduced my full-time enrollment to part-time student. This allowed time for me to work and earn money to finance my new freedom. The days became even more lonely and mundane. I found a part-time job on campus at the student health clinic. It was a quiet and serious working environment. No one really socialized but instead, kept to themselves, with all focus on their work. My duty was to assist students with the admissions process when they came in for healthcare. I had no other duties so on slow days, I sat quietly at a desk, left alone with my thoughts.

Most of my thoughts were dreading going to class. That semester, for some insane reason, I took accounting. My academic advisor convinced me it would be as simple as the basic bookkeeping class I took in high school. That had to be Satan's idea to torment me! This "beginner" class was one of the hardest courses I had ever encountered. My professor talked about 100 words per minute, with a speech impediment, to add to my torture. I left every lecture riddled with discouragement and confusion. The condition only worsened as I would open my books to do my homework. It felt like I was taking a foreign language by immersion, with words that were way out of my grasp. The enemy's lie planted long ago that I was "not college material," was hitting home, deeper and harder. He was grooming me, knowing that I would believe Rob, when he began to tell me the very same thing.

So, I didn't bother preregistering for spring classes that year and instead sought out a full-time office job. My loneliness and depression grew stronger with each passing day. My only social life was attending sports events or frequenting nightclubs with Rob and his teammates. My own group of friends were no longer a commodity.

Christmas break that year was one I welcomed with open arms!

↑ Don't Fall For It ↓

I was never more ready to go home than that December. It was a festive time in my house. Lori was planning her wedding to her Prince Charming, to be held on December 29th. My family was extremely busy attending engagement parties, couple showers and bridal luncheons all while also preparing for Christmas family gatherings. It was a time of festivities: dressing up, reuniting with old friends, and celebrating Lori's new life with her forever boyfriend. My attention was engulfed in family matters. Rob was put on the back burner a lot, even though he was included in the festivities. The fact that he was having to share my attention did not sit well with him. We argued more than ever. I felt torn between my family and my slave master.

After the wedding, I was overwhelmed by the emotional crash, feeling "the party is over." I knew I had to start thinking about going back to my lonely dungeon to look for a job and be bored without friends. I dreaded it with each passing day. Finally, during another argument that had become our holiday routine, I told him I didn't want to go back. I couldn't stand living secluded with no social life. I suggested I stay home and enroll in the local community college, continuing our relationship long distance. He was not having that. He suggested we move in together. I was not having THAT! My parents and grandparents would disapprove, and the financial backing would stop. So, he gave me two options: **1)** I marry him NOW; or **2)** He would break up with me forever. FOREVER? That never crossed my mind. Forever meant to me that we would be together. I could not imagine my life without him. He was all I knew!

Yet, I wasn't ready to get married either. I wanted to wait until we could do it the right way. I had always dreamed of him getting on one knee and proposing, instead of an ultimatum. I wanted a big church wedding like my sister just had. He convinced me he was serious. An elopement was the only way to have my forever with him.

It was a cold, icy Saturday in January 1979. I was five days away from turning 19 years old. We were watching our college basketball team play a huge rival on TV, in my small apartment, that was soon to be ours. The score was close, and the game was a nail-biter. We had already made an appointment with a Justice of the Peace to officiate our nuptials at his home. Conveniently, our appointment with the JP was the same time as the half-time break of the game. We went to our private "wedding" dressed in our finest Sunday outfits, only to impress each other. It took only ten minutes to vow to "love one another until death do us part." There were no friends or family to stand by our side. The JP didn't even think it was important enough to put on a shirt. He married us in his trousers, held up by suspenders, over an undershirt. He also had the game playing on his TV in the background, which sped up the process. The quick ceremony and signing of the license enabled us to catch the second half of the basketball game. It was no more special than that.

As we left the JP's house, I slipped and fell flat on my butt, on the ice. That was the "icebreaker," pun intended. I could only control my emotions for a few short moments. As we sat down in the car, I looked down at my $20 wedding band we had picked out at Best Buy. I began to sob uncontrollably. It hit me like a ton of bricks. There was no turning back now. I was in communion with this person for the rest of my life. My lifelong dream of a big church wedding was no longer in my future. Satan had stolen that dream from me too. Although my head could not fully understand the scope of this mistake, my heart was fully comprehending the consequence. I began grieving with every teardrop in me. Rob began to get angry. No consoling words or concern for my tears. My future nightmare had officially begun with this man of my dreams.

Instead of whisking off to a romantic destination for a honeymoon, life went right back to normal as soon as we got home. I changed out of my best Sunday dress into jeans and a t-shirt and settled in with him to watch the rest of the game. It was as if we had left to run a quick errand. There was no celebration, not even a special, romantic dinner. My only positive emotion was a feeling of relief after telling my parents the news, over the phone. Even though their voices revealed shock and concern for my future, they accepted my decision and showed their support. It was a phone call I dreaded making, and I was glad when it was over. I think that is the only time I smiled that day, knowing my parents were not angry with me.

I became accustomed to my new life by putting my regrets behind me. I made a concerted effort to focus on the future and the things to look forward to. I told myself a fancy wedding is not the key to happiness. I settled for a post-wedding shower back home that our family and friends threw us, a few weeks after the "big day." That was the extent of our celebration to begin our new life together. I resolved that my life was supposed to look completely different from my sister anyway. It always had and it always will.

As an independent married couple, we needed more money to supplement our living expenses. I was hired full-time as an office secretary for a life-insurance company. This was my first real job where I could use the office skills I learned in high school. We settled into a routine. Rob was going to class and working out with the track team. I went to work every day from 8 a.m. to 5 p.m. His scholarship paid for his tuition, fees, books and one meal on campus. Luckily, the Volkswagen his parents refurbished for his high school graduation present was paid for. He didn't receive any other living expense compensation form his scholarship. So our rent, groceries and gas, had to be covered by my entry-level paycheck. We lived paycheck to paycheck and had little money left for entertainment or other luxuries. I always kept the hope of living on faith, encouraging myself that "life would get better once Rob graduated from college. For the time being, we were living on love and that was enough. Our future looked bright!" My self-talk stayed on repeat until I convinced myself.

Another aspect of our common routine began in our courtship and continued throughout our marriage. This was the daily battle to keep my figure. While dating long distance, he "encouraged me daily" to keep jogging those long distances and build my endurance (to keep me slim). He "coached me" with an inventory every night when he would call, "Did you get your 2 miles in today?" Again, he was always concerned about my weight. Jogging was the answer to rid me of those unwanted pounds. Those pounds *he* didn't want. A champion athlete could not have a chubby girlfriend or wife. This trap turned into an 8-year conversation centered around my physical appearance. After we married, he would not let me go to bed at night until I had jogged my two miles. But in his eyes, I was never quite there, no matter how much weight I lost. One day, I distinctly remember telling him with excitement "I've lost 15 pounds!" His response, "That's great - just lose 15 more and you'll be on your way." He never gave me compliments to keep me encouraged. Another vivid memory is during a heated argument (no idea what about) when he cut me deep with, "If you get fat like your mother, I WILL divorce you!"

Mom had a hysterectomy after she had me and her hormones and thyroid began to function abnormally. This resulted in massive weight gain that she struggled with almost her entire adult life. She fought obesity with every diet on the market, with no success. Ironically, she lost every bit of it in her 70's (without even trying) and she left this world in her late 80's as a size 6 petite. God's favor allowed her to enjoy her golden years in perfect physical health until He took her Home.

Although I had the "puberty pudge" when Rob and I met, I was nowhere near obese. I'm not sure why he was initially attracted to "pudgy me" considering his hangup in this area. Perhaps, he also had low self-esteem when we met, and he "settled" for me. My appearance became a frequent topic of discussion with ways in which I could improve. I became very self-conscious about my weight and did everything I could to keep a lean figure. No matter how thin I became, he seemed to see me as I was when we first met. I couldn't get thin enough to satisfy his fears of me getting fat. He could eat whatever he wanted and not gain a pound, yet he closely monitored what I ate. Later, I began to rationalize that his obsession with my weight was just because he was so lean. He needed me to be smaller than him to improve his own self-image. His fears caused me to grow an obsession with ALWAYS feeling fat. At one point, I got down to such a low weight, I quit having my monthly period.

This is when I knew I was in trouble. Luckily, I didn't develop a full-blown eating disorder, but I knew I was headed there if I didn't make a change.

After years of relationship with a man who was obsessed and critical of my physical appearance, I have had to continuously fight the false belief that says, *"If I get fat, I will be rejected by society."* I *still* struggle to overcome being obsessed and negative about my weight and appearance. Despite being an avid exerciser who eats healthy, I am ALWAYS concerned about gaining weight. If I gain a few pounds, I become depressed and angry. I am much better than I used to be, but I'm not completely free from this emotional stronghold. God is still working on me. Rob's critical words left deep emotional scars that have taunted me my entire adult life. *If you are with someone who is consistently criticizing your appearance, instead of lovingly telling you how pretty you look . . . RUN!*

My quest to please Rob's desire for physical perfection to prevent his verbal attacks is nothing compared to the next challenge I faced in this "tragic love story." Another lifelong dream was suddenly snatched away one memorable Saturday morning.

Most days, I fought my depression by trying to focus on the future. Most nights were spent locked in our tiny bathroom after Rob was asleep - silently sobbing until my tears ran out. A good cry always made me feel somewhat better. We were about 3 months into our marriage on this pivotal Saturday morning. We laid in bed talking a while, after waking up and before deciding to get up. It was a morning when we were being playful, with light conversation, like newlyweds are supposed to. I saw it as a perfect opportunity to talk about our future. I asked him . . .

"Have you thought about what you want to name our kids when we start our family?" That's when the bombshell hit.

"I thought I already told you that I don't want kids."

"Shut up," was my reply, "Stop messing with me! No really, what names do you like?"

His mood completely changed, "I'm serious Lisa. I do not want kids. I never have and I thought we had already talked about this."

[News Flash! I KNOW we had not talked about this because this could have very well been a game changer if I had known this BEFORE your "proposal" ultimatum!]

I wasn't going to give up so easily and tried to reason, "But honey, it is God's will for us to be fruitful and multiply."

"Well, that would be a great argument," he fired back, "if there was a God."

I felt like I had just been shot in the heart. I tried reasoning with him, but it was no use. I didn't dare argue further, knowing it would escalate into a fight. I didn't want to hear any more of these new revelations that would ruin the light-hearted moment. All I knew to do was to change the subject. This only deepened my depression. I survived on the hope that one day he would change his mind.

I continued my midnight crying sessions in our private bathroom every night trying to cope with yet another huge disappointment. I would also stew in my anger, agony and disarray. How could he not tell me this before? I began to realize that the fact he was an atheist clearly explained past events. No wonder he acted completely opposite of how I felt on the day we drove 30 miles to murder our unborn child. His demeanor was relief and happiness, while I was racked with sorrow and guilt. He had none of the conviction I was experiencing. I still had a hard time wrapping my brain around the fact that he was truly an atheist. His grandmother was a very devout Baptist. She told stories about taking him and his siblings to church when they were young, even though his parents never went. It had never occurred to me to have that very important conversation to find out where he stood spiritually. I just assumed he was like me, a believer that knew just enough about the Bible to know Jesus as Savior. As the days passed, those crying sessions turned to venting to myself in anger, as I felt my heart start to harden towards my husband. I felt tricked and deceived. Satan was laughing at the revelation that I had been duped. His best blow of all was still to come.

A NEW DAWN – WHEN DARKNESS APPEARED FROM THE HORIZON…

The memory is forever etched in my brain about as deep as the day I had my abortion. I woke up one weekday morning before the alarm went off. I didn't need the alarm clock because of the tremendous burning sensation in my throat. It felt like razor cuts in my throat and was more than I could bare. Chills and fever plagued my entire body. I had not felt that sick since my bout with measles at age 16. I tried taking an aspirin and hot shower to ease my symptoms, but they only grew worse. I knew there was no way I could make it to work, which was not good. I had not yet completed the probational period at my new job. So, I had not started receiving fringe benefits like sick leave pay nor health insurance. Going to the doctor was out of the question since we had no extra money for an office visit. Even worse, next months' paycheck would be less, due to missed work. I felt helpless but there was nothing to do except call my supervisor and tearfully explain my dilemma.

God will always shine His light in darkness to let His children know He is still with them. My employers were that shining light. I loved going to work every day. No matter how down and depressed I was before I got there, my spirits were lifted by the loving and supportive environment God led me to. Working with people who loved Jesus was a big contrast from living with a husband who didn't even believe in Him. That company had a staff of appreciative and encouraging mentors who constantly praised me for my efficiency and hard work. The more they showered me with compliments, the harder I worked. My job was a bright spot in my gloomy existence, helping me hold on to the little bit of self-esteem I had.

That morning of calling in sick for the very first time was no exception. My immediate supervisor, Debbie, and I had an immediate bond when we met. She treated me with such respect as she took me under her wing, becoming one of the most profound mentors of my life. She was patient and kind in every moment as she trained me in office procedures. She had a heart of gold and was so sympathetic to my condition that morning. As I hung up the phone, a wave of relief and warmth from her encouraging words and support helped me to feel a little better.

I didn't want to wake up Rob by going back to bed. I tried to just rest on our wooden-frame sofa that came with our furnished apartment. As I lay there with a thin throw blanket that didn't help my chills, I could feel the boards through the cheap, thin cushion press against my aching back. This, along with the agonizing burning pain in my throat, made any comfort impossible. I watched the sun come up through the small window as it began to light up the room. I had almost dozed off but was awakened by the sound of Rob stretching and going into the bathroom to take a shower. On a normal day, I would have already left for work. As he was getting dressed, I didn't bother trying to alert him that I was still home. My burning throat prevented any speech above a whisper. So, I just laid there, knowing he would see my condition when he came into the living room. I was expecting him to come to my aid and go to the store to buy something over the counter to ease my symptoms. My dreams of a loving and supportive husband were abruptly diminished.

My body jerked when I was startled with a loud, "What are you doing? Why aren't you at work?"

I mustered up enough voice to whisper, "I think I have strep throat. I've already called in sick."

"You did WHAT? We can't afford to miss a day's pay. You KNOW that!"

The anger I had been suppressing night after night was welling up like a tsunami, as he continued to gripe and complain, demanding that I go to work. Not one word of sympathy came out of his mouth. It was the "straw that broke the camel's back." I had all I could take of his selfish, controlling and unfeeling words.

I shot up from the couch with the loudest yell I could muster up, as I stormed toward the bedroom, "I AM SICK! I'M NOT GOING ANYWHERE, ASSHOLE!" The next thing I remember was an excruciating pain from behind that felt like I had been shot. He kicked me right in my tailbone with all his strength, with his steel-toe cowboy boots. The impact was so great, my legs almost came off the floor. I was stunned in shocking disbelief and even more angry. I slammed the bedroom door to lay down on the bed and immediately regretted it as I heard it fly open. He was on top of me before I could move and had his hands in a tight grip around my throat, pinning me in paralyzing fear.

"Don't you EVER talk to me that way again!" he whispered in a deep, demonic tone, through his gritted teeth. I was relieved when he stormed out of the apartment, slamming the front door, knowing he would be gone for the rest of the day.

I NOW realize that this was the day his control had turned up a notch. He was losing his emotional control over me. I was growing up and growing out of my naïve submission. Maturity and a supportive work environment helped me to realize I deserved better than how he treated me. I began to stand up for myself, so it was necessary for him to knock me back down to reality, physically. *Abuse always starts in a way that is unrecognizable until it turns into a world that's almost unescapable. Physical abuse is Satan's final act of slamming the door to your trap after years of grooming you to step into it. All other forms of abuse are the lure. Physical abuse is the final prison sentence that locks you into fearing for your life.*

After he stormed out, I remember lying in bed in total shock at what had just happened. Although so many signs pointed to the probability of this day, I hadn't seen that I was in an abusive relationship, until I was physically stricken. I never dreamed he would ever lay his hands on me. He wasn't raised in the typical environment of an abuser. His parents were loving and kind and in no way abusive to one another, nor their children. They practiced peaceful conflict resolution when they disagreed with one another. Where did this come from? It was still a little hard for me to wrap my brain around. "Surely, this is an isolated incident," I reasoned.

I grew up in an era of watching shows like "The Three Stooges" and "All In the Family." I know I'm really showing my age now! If you were born in the 80's or later, you're most likely clueless to these

TV shows. If you watch just one episode on Netflix, you will understand. I was conditioned to believe that hitting another person was comical and it was "normal and funny" to talk down to women. I believed that, unless I was physically beat up with black eyes and deep bruises regularly, I was not abused. I never was taught to look for *the warning signs of abuse: 1) isolation 2) control 3) manipulation and 4) belittlement.* [I'm being repetitive about these signs to make sure you can see them if they are in your relationship]. If I had been taught these truths, I would have seen at the beginning of our courtship, that he was an abuser alright! It took "a swift kick in the butt" to finally open my eyes. I never felt so afraid and alone in all my life. It was the day I finally realized I was married to a monster, who was not capable of sympathy, concern or support of another person – or at least, not toward me.

I laid in that bed sobbing, with a high fever and excruciating sore throat, along with my new degrading injury. Just like the long walk home on that dark road at age 16, it never dawned on me to cry out to Jesus for help and direction.

WHERE WAS JESUS?

If only someone in my formative years had told me that Jesus was more than just my Savior. He was also my Best Friend, who promises in His word that He watches over me; He never leaves me nor forsakes me. I realize today, He was right there, tears running down His cheeks, grieving over what had just happened to His precious daughter -- waiting for her to cry out to Him. He would have made Himself known in an instant, but He is a gentle God. He does not force Himself on any of His children. He gives us free will to *choose* Him. John 11:35 is the easiest verse to memorize in the Bible. It simply says, "Jesus wept." So, *we both* laid there in silence, grieving in the dark, as I held on to the little bit of strength I had *on my own*. Even when I had no knowledge of His presence, it didn't prevent Him from being there, by my side. He doesn't judge us. An earthly parent may say, "I told you not to marry him." Not our Heavenly Father. He never brings condemnation. He only offers correction for any of our mistakes. When we don't ask for help, He just weeps with us. He is with us, whether we know it or not. I realize that now because now I know who I am in Christ. I am a child of God. So are you. If I had known that back then, this day would have been the end of my nightmare. If I had cried out to Jesus for help and let Him guide me, He would have told me to pack my things and call my parents, asking them to make the 90-mile trip to come get me. I would have been gone, way before Rob even came home. Instead, my blind ignorance kept the doors tightly secured in my prison cell.

SIDE NOTE: Jesus doesn't just come to our side when we suffer from something that is not our fault - at the hands of someone else. He also comes to our aid as we suffer from the sinful acts of our own choosing. As soon as we confess and cry out for help, He is there.

There is a term I learned years later called Prevenient Grace. It is a nature of God the Bible teaches where He first loved us. **Romans 5:8** says, *"but God shows his love for us in that while we were still sinners Christ died for us."* Even before we accept Christ as our Savior, He still loves us and pursues us, desiring a relationship with us. Prevenient Grace means He woos us into a relationship with Him even when we don't realize it and even when we are living in sin. I had already accepted Jesus as my Savior when I was 12, and He never left my side, even when I knew nothing about Him - other than He died for my sins. I didn't really know the full weight of that love. **John 14:18** says, *"I will not leave you as orphans; I will come to you."* Throughout decades of wrong decisions, Jesus was ALWAYS THERE. All *I* needed to do was acknowledge His presence and cry out to Him for help. That's all He was waiting for. He was there with me through my abortion too. While I was a sinner, Jesus did not love me any less than when I was born. He didn't leave me. He didn't disown me. Even as I committed sexually immorality (out of wedlock), followed by one of the most horrific acts – killing an unborn child – it did not cause a blemish on His love for me. He simply waited PATIENTLY. He knew there would come a day when my eyes would be opened to the magnitude of my sin. He knew I would humbly confess in total repentance. He just waited with His unconditional love ready to forgive me. I am no exception to the rule, and neither are you.

God doesn't just love. God IS love. We can never out-sin God's grace, once we have surrendered our hearts to Jesus. Don't believe me yet? Let me confess to you something even more horrendous. I never thought this would happen during this time in my life, but later on in my 40's, I had 3 more abortions – even when I knew better but was a coward. You'll learn more about those dark days in later chapters. Right now, I just want to bring home the point of how patient, merciful and kind God is. I know now I am forgiven because I repented. He never gave up on me. I am an avid pro-life advocate because I still struggle with forgiving myself sometimes. But I know that I know that I know my God – in His infinite mercy – has forgiven me.

If you have repeated a sin or maybe still living in one – there is still HOPE for you. His name is Jesus. He died for your sins as well. Just confess and ask Him to help you turn from your situation and follow His lead. He will give you the strength to do it – one day at a time. This is called sanctification. Salvation happens immediately when we accept Jesus in our hearts. After that moment, sanctification happens gradually – throughout a lifetime – maturing us spiritually day by day, as we learn to walk, talk, and think like Jesus. He is patient and He is kind and there is no reason to hide from Him when we mess up. He already knows. Sanctification is a fancy word that means a very long process of getting to know and forming an intimate relationship with Jesus. The Bible describes this as "He takes us from glory to glory" – demolishing one sinful stronghold at a time. End of my sermon.

Back to my gloomy story . . .

As the days went by, I learned to protect my husband (and my dignity) by keeping his fit of rage a secret. I was still in denial that I was married to an abuser, and mostly embarrassed by it. For sanity's sake, I kept telling myself, "It will never happen again. After all, I started the fight with my yelling. I just need to honor him." I don't recall ever receiving an apology. Perhaps he did, but if so, it wasn't one I cherished in my memory bank. It was several months before the next physical attack occurred. However, the usual verbal jabs and

↑ *Don't Fall For It* ↓

emotional shackles continued. I was already accustomed to this lifestyle. I couldn't see that his hurtful words were abuse. An occasional kick or punch in the arm to get his point across became "normal human behavior." As my fear of his unpredictable outbursts grew stronger, so did the chokehold of his control over my mind and emotions. I knew better than to intentionally do or say anything that might provoke him. I certainly knew better than to share our secret struggles with another human being. I just couldn't take that chance. My self-esteem and self-worth diminished to just a glimmer of confidence, which I received daily, at my job. When he would make cruel jokes about my "inferior intelligence" or "chubby thighs," I silently took the jabs with a slight, tight-lipped smile. That silence kept fooling him into thinking, I was amused and unoffended. After all, I believed everything he said about me anyway.

Twelve months came and went. He graduated from college with a bachelor's degree in Geography. He was able to complete four years of college, debt-free, by running track on a full scholarship. It never dawned on him to visit the Career Center on campus and explore future career options that would be fulfilling. He was just there to compete in long-distance running, while getting a degree on the side. Geography was his favorite subject, so that was the extent of his decision-making in declaring a major, when he was forced to do so.

Unfortunately, there weren't many options for employment in this field of study. A driving force that would guide our future destination was the new state his parents moved to when his dad's employer transferred him. Their new home was in Mississippi, and we went to visit them during Spring Break of his senior year. It was on that trip that *Rob decided* we would be moving close to them when he finished school. I emphasize Rob decided; not *we* decided. He made it very clear that *he* would be making ALL our important decisions in the marriage because *he* was the one with the college degree. Although *he* was the one who talked me into quitting college. He could now use my "lack of education" anytime he needed, to make a point. The ole "lure and slap" routine - that is one of Satan's finest tricks. He looked more like the enemy every day.

After his graduation and spending the Christmas holiday with my parents in our hometown, we pulled out with a jam-packed Volkswagen, venturing off into our new life in another state, thousands of miles from home. I didn't stop crying until we got to the border of Louisiana, only because I ran out of tears. Not only was my future a mystery, but my sense of belonging was very frail. Any security from family and hometown friends, faded further away in the rearview mirror, as we traveled to the "land of the unknown."

Our original plans were to settle on the coastal beaches of Biloxi, close to his parents. That brought comfort since I was very close to his mom, and she was my safe haven. If I could've had my way, we would've even moved in with them and lived there long-term. These plans were soon shattered, as the job market did not provide hope for a college graduate with a degree in geography. Rob had to start hunting for any position above entry-level, that required a degree of *any* kind. He soon landed an assistant manager position at a lumber yard chain, in Jackson, MS, almost 3 hours away from safety. With my one-year clerical experience, I was hired at a large CPA firm in the clerical pool. Ironically, I made more money with no degree than Rob did with his formal education. This did not sit well with his ego. He hated feeling inferior. He began to hate his financial status, his job duties, and his supervisor. He was getting a small taste of the control and criticism he fed me. This did not create empathy in him – only more frustration and anger – and a stronger threat of danger for me.

He would relieve his frustrations on me, as his sounding board and punching bag. He was a novice at venting anger in a way that only left marks on the parts of my body that were clothed and protected from exposure of his bullying. The only exception was a night when he choked me so hard, his fingertips left bruises on my neck. His secret was guarded, as the girls at work teased me the next day about "my night of passion" thinking those bruises were "hickeys". What they considered to be marks of love and affection, were actually marks of hate and anger. This humiliation and embarrassment did not compare

↑ Don't Fall For It ↓

to the next horrifying incident. It is still a taunting memory as I remember every detail, even 45 years later.

Let me give you an idea first of our living situation to accurately describe my terror in my next round of abuse. The setting was downtown Jackson, MS in the early 80's, when racism was escalated with news stories of violence between black and white people. A popular TV series "Roots" was watched in most American homes, accurately depicting the horrors black Americans endured in the slavery days. The highly rated TV show, along with a concurrent gripping news story of a black man, killed by white cops in Florida, had created a race-war frenzy in the nation. It caused many riots to erupt in the Deep South. As racial tensions increased, I experienced discrimination based on the color of my skin, for the first time in my life. When riding the city bus downtown to work, I was forced to sit in the back of the bus receiving angry glares from people of color. It only increased my empathy for Rosa Parks in reverse discrimination. My incubated, small West Texas town, where we loved people of all colors, did not prepare me for this kind of life.

I'll never forget one night when I was alone in our apartment while Rob worked late. I was doing laundry that required me to walk a short distance to and from my apartment to the laundry room, between washing and drying cycles. With each trip, I kept noticing my neighbor, a young black male, looking out his window and staring at me with an angry look. I tried to ignore the suspected intimidation by blowing it off as my imagination. When I made my final trip to gather my last load out of the dryer, I saw him standing on his porch on my way back to our apartment. My heart raced when he didn't reply to my "Hi, how are you?" I quickly went inside and locked the door securely. The curtains to our living room were open and I became very alarmed when I looked out and saw him standing in front of the window banging one fist into his other palm, motioning that he wanted to hurt me. Racism was not something I had ever been faced with in my upbringing. My parents taught me to judge people according to their character, not the color of their skin. This was a whole new world in which I didn't know how to navigate, and I already felt unsafe IN my home. Now my world outside of my home was even more terrifying. Luckily, Rob got home soon after that and the situation fizzled. I tell you this story to emphasize the terror I felt in this next story. Unfortunately, the following incident of terror was caused by my *own* intimidator.

The CPA office I worked for was in the heart of the business district. By day, it was flooded with professionals in business attire. By night, gangs occupied the streets where drug deals were made. Homeless addicts found shelter in the dark corners of covered garages and alleys. It was not a safe place for anyone to walk the streets unarmed.

I worked in a typing pool, where four of us prepared typewritten tax returns for clients of major corporations. We were required to complete these tedious tasks with an electric typewriter, using "White Out" correction liquid if we made a mistake. No luxury of computers in those days. It was tax season, and, on many occasions, it was common for us to work after dark in order to meet deadlines for those clients. The stressful environment was not worth the "attractive compensation with good benefits" that lured me to this hell hole. On this day, I wasn't in the best of moods, due to the abuse I had endured the night before. It was hard to keep my "happy mask" on all day. Anger swelled up in my spirit, as the "movie" of him choking me the previous night, played on repeat in my mind.

Finally, I got some news that cheered me up. I had finished my pile of returns and my supervisor said I could go home at a decent time. I immediately called Rob at home to tell him to pick me up at 7:00. No answer. I figured he must've worked late, as he was usually home around 6:00. I called the lumber yard where he worked. His co-workers said he had left already. Without the luxury of cell phones in those days, I was forced to stay put at work, until I could find him on a landline. I ended up helping the other girls with their workload, while trying to call him at home about every 15 minutes. He was used to me working until ten o'clock most nights and sometimes even midnight. Around 11:00 p.m., he FINALLY answered the phone at the apartment. I could tell immediately he was tipsy from alcohol. At first, he tried to lie, saying he had worked late. I fired back that I knew he was lying because I had called the lumberyard. He then admitted he had gone to play pool with his co-workers, thinking I was going to still work late again. It never dawned on him to check with me first. Life was all about Rob. The girls in the office were finishing up and needed to lock up, so I ordered him to come and get me immediately. The distance between our apartment and downtown was NOT a short trip, however. I remember standing outside of our office building, with only a porch light, to keep me out of the dark. The last girl was leaving and offered me a ride home, since it was taking Rob so long to arrive. I declined, knowing he would be there any minute.

Looking back, I wish I had accepted her offer. When he finally showed up it was practically midnight. It was all I could do to keep my composure as I realized his level of intoxication. Instead of hearing excuses and apologies for his selfish behavior, the first words out of his mouth were, "Oh by the way, the guys are at the apartment, and we are hungry, so you need to cook us something when we get home." No thought or consideration that I had to get up early the next morning for another long day at work. That was it! The anger dam had burst! I blew up in a rage of anger from this preposterous display of selfishness! I yelled and screamed for about 10 minutes, until it happened. As we turned the corner onto one of the busiest streets in downtown Jackson, MS (which thankfully, was deserted at this hour) he slammed on the brakes, jumped out of the truck, walked around to my side, opened my door, grabbed me and hurled me out of the truck onto the street. It took me a few seconds to get my composure from the shock. When I looked up, he was back in the truck and peeled out at high-speed, leaving me stranded. This was the very same scenario I experienced with him, at age 16, on a deserted country road. This time though, home was nowhere close by. I went into panic mode trying to keep calm and figure out what to do next. All I knew to do was to find shelter under a covered garage, to stay hidden from any possible predator, hoping to stay safe until some kind of help came.

Although it was only several minutes, it felt like hours, when I saw Rob drive by looking for me. I ran out, hoping he would catch sight of me in his rearview mirror. The predator I married was a welcome sight in comparison to the fate I might have faced had I not eagerly jumped back in the truck with him. He laughed at my fright, "Did you think I was really going to leave you out here?" (Duh – you've done it before) "I just needed to get my point across and teach you a lesson. Maybe now you'll be a good little wife and not DARE mention this argument to the guys." I received nothing but a lecture and more instructions on that long ride home.

These friends weren't "guys" – they were more like boys! Rob found his tribe, as they were immature and just as selfish as he was. I quickly discovered after our move that these new friends and coworkers were predominantly chauvinistic. It was easy to see why they were still single. In previous seasons, all of Rob's friends back home had included me with great respect. In card games, lake trips, riding around on weekends, you name it. It was me and the boys and they always made me feel accepted. This was no longer the case. On the first night we invited his "buddies" over for a card game, to my shock and surprise, they rejected me from the game before it even started. So, on this night, it was no surprise to see them sitting in my living room with looks on their faces that said it all. "What took y'all so long? We are hungry!" I bit my tongue as I walked over to the freezer, grabbed a frozen pizza, slapped it on a cookie sheet, threw it in the oven and turned it to 400. I turned and said, "Your dinner will be ready in about 20-30 minutes – don't let it burn. I'm going to bed." As I walked into my bedroom to escape, I overheard, "What's up her ass?" followed by Rob's heartless reply, "She's just pissed because she had to work late, and I didn't. She'll get over it."

I could write a separate novel about the days of hell that followed, but I'm sure by now, you get the picture of my life with this "man of my dreams." Most of the time spent in this "holy matrimony" was a life in hell, with occasional good times. For the life of me, I cannot remember any good times after we married. We never went on romantic date nights. Only occasional nights out with friends. We never took vacations together. No picture albums of fun things we did together. Life just consisted of work, home, cooking, TV, bedtime. A dull life of following orders from my superior.

If you have never endured an abusive relationship, you surely must wonder by now, WHY? Why would I stay in a situation like this one? Abuse is like the analogy of the boiling frog. You can place a frog in a pan of water that is room temperature and GRADUALLY increase the temperature to boiling. The frog will not jump out as his body temperature gradually acclimates to the increasing water temperature. The adaptive creature doesn't realize he is being boiled alive.

Years of thinking and believing I was destined – by God – to be married to this man, kept me in that boiling pot. From an insecure girl at 15 to a heat-adjusted young woman at 20, I never considered other options. He took my virginity and that is where I sealed my covenant and my fate to be with him forever.

No apologies or changes in behavior took place after the abuse. Only affection, as though nothing had ever happened, followed those days. I learned to "just get over it and move on." His reign of terror over my emotions and my will kept me imprisoned. After a few more incidents of physical harm, he no longer needed to use physical abuse. I was completely chained in shackles of fearful submission under his authority. I knew better than to raise my voice at him in anger because I knew the consequences. I didn't even take chances by voicing my own opinions. When I did, I was shot down by insults or "jokes" about my lack of intelligence

The emotional and verbal abuse was a learned lifestyle. I became convinced that his verbal and emotional digs were actual truth about myself. I was constantly reminded, with insinuations and these sick jokes that I wasn't enough. My inner voice told me constantly I wasn't thin enough, I wasn't pretty enough, and I wasn't smart enough to ever attract another man. I was lucky I had him, and he was all I could ever have.

BUT, GOD.

I had no idea at that time but can now see so clearly; the God that I know now, was as close as my breath. He ordered our steps back to Texas, less than one year after leaving. Rob couldn't stand his job any longer and he quit with no notice, and we headed West. Soon, I was back home and near the safety of my mom and dad. Life became more manageable. Rob got a job at our local gas refinery with a promising career. He enjoyed his co-workers and the company provided great fringe benefits. I was able to find a job at a local CPA office, using the experience I gained at the CPA office in Jackson. Being close to my dad protected me greatly from any more physical harm. Rob dared not evoke anger in my dad, whom he was already leery of.

Our life settled into a calmer, content existence with one huge obstacle for me to overcome. I was no longer in love with my husband. I started to gain more self-confidence in a safe and familiar home environment. Being around supportive friends and an enriching work environment pumped life back into my veins. Unbeknownst to me at the time, Jesus started showing me that I was, in fact, intelligent and productive. He began to whisper, "Daughter – you ARE enough." Unfortunately, I didn't have enough affection for my spouse to be the type of wife I should. I cringed when he touched me. I was living a complete lie trying to pretend I felt like I did when I first met him. The more I failed in my attempt, the more frustrated he became.

Eventually God led me to a position at the local community college that would end up being my resting place for a future career. Campus was more than my workplace. It became my second home. It was not easy to get on the staff of this institution because they had a practice of promoting within. Usually, a new hire always had to start at entry-level. You had to know someone within the college to be hired into a higher-level position. I was one of those lucky ones. I knew a woman who was administrative secretary to one of the Vice-Presidents of the college. We had previously worked together at the CPA office before she left to work at the college. Due to her recommendation, I was hired as a department office manager. The "Rob chains" I wore in matrimony had prevented me from seeing the plans God had for me. I thought this was my destiny to just retire one day as a department secretary, but God had other plans. I would eventually finish my college education (years later) and build a professional career within this institution – my new life with my extended family.

I'm setting the stage to make another important point about what life is like with an abusive atheist. Even the daily struggles are magnified when you don't have a supportive partner.

Back then, as a brand-new hire, there was a HUGE hurdle to overcome, however. Little did I know about a situation I "inherited" that could make or break my employment.

If any of the red flags I've spoken of are sounding familiar to your own situation, please read the next story and ponder a possibility. This is the kind of life you could be stuck with if you marry a man who does not have Jesus in his heart. This is the sole reason I tell this story – to give you a real close look in the potential daily life of a covenant with an atheist. Know there are exceptions, but ponder the possibility of a similar situation you might face as you read this.

My supervisor, "Mary" was a true sweetheart. She supervised the operations of the department with a kind, gentle, upper-hand and had respect for her subordinates. She treated us more like friends and co-workers than employees. I always looked forward to going to work to be with my new best friends. It was a welcome contrast to my home life. I loved my boss, I loved my co-workers, and I loved my job duties. The job was interesting and challenging. One of my responsibilities was to manage the department's cash flow. About three months after starting this new job, it became very apparent that Mary was "borrowing" from the cash drawer. She had a compulsive spending problem and was on a desperate mission to cover up the spending addiction from her husband. Her intentions to pay it back were evident as she left little "IOU" notes to replace the missing cash. One day, I gathered enough courage to approach her about the missing cash. She assured me it was protocol. As time went on, the occurrences became more frequent. The amounts increased considerably. When I approached her again, she began denying the allegations or making up stories to cover her tracks. I knew I had reached a fork in the road. If I didn't say something, my job could be in jeopardy as the overseer of the department funds. The girls in the office were not surprised when I brought it to their attention. In fact, they admitted they already knew there was a problem, and this was the reason the previous girl had left this position. No one had the courage, nor the heart, to blow the whistle on Mary. She had become a close friend to everyone who worked near her.

I was between a rock and a hard place. It was THE hardest predicament I had ever encountered in the workplace, as a young adult of just 21 years of age. I had to build up the courage to take my co-workers' advice and meet with the Vice-President over our department about the situation. Vice-President Cheri Sparks was the only woman on the administrative staff. She was highly respected by her peers and her subordinates. To make matters more difficult, she had also been roommates with Mary in college and they were still very close friends. So, here I was, a new-hire and an outsider. I knew I was taking the risk of being labeled a troublemaker.

Cheri was reluctant to believe me at first. Being in denial that her close friend was capable of this, she kept saying, "There has to be another explanation." As I explained further, she still looked at me with slight suspicion. When I was finally able to show her solid evidence and Mary's secret could not be explained away, Cheri hung her head in shock and sadness. She instructed me to stay after hours so that she could conduct further investigation into Mary's records in her office. Cheri was once in Mary's position, and she knew what to look for in the record-keeping system. To our further shock and dismay, she discovered that Mary had embezzled over $20,000 in just a few years of her tenure. Her next words caused a huge lump to form in my throat. "We have to take this to the President." She thanked me for coming forward and dismissed me, telling me not to say anything to anyone but instead, to wait for further instructions the next day. That night, I received a phone call at home from Cheri. "You will need to meet with me and the President first thing in the morning to report our findings. Go ahead and report to your office and wait for my call." My heart sank and I began to shiver with anxiety that would not let up. How I dreaded the next day. How was

I going to be able to face sweet Mary? How was she going to take the news? What will be her consequences? Are they going to arrest her? Fire her? I couldn't touch my supper that night. I couldn't sleep. I couldn't concentrate. All I could do was sob with worry and dread. I felt so alone – because I was.

It was this night that finally broke my spirit in marriage and shattered any love I had left for my husband.

A loving husband, who promises to "have and to hold," should be there to hold his wife in times like these, to comfort and give assurance that everything will be ok. My husband, however, kept taking jabs at me, like jokingly saying I was hired to be the campus snitch. All his jokes did NOT make me laugh, but only increased my anxiety. Through him, Satan was taunting me with accusations and outright making fun of my dilemma. PLEASE READ THESE SIGNS AND KNOW. When you do not have a Christ-centered marriage – marrying someone who does not know Jesus – this is the type of covenant you are in danger of. This is why Jesus tells us in His Word to be evenly yoked. **(2 Corinthians 6:14)** Instead of marrying a man who loved Jesus and knew how to love *like* Jesus, I was with an empty soul who had no empathy to offer. I had no sensitive shoulder to lean on when I needed shelter. No comfort, no encouragement, and zero prayer coverage from my partner in marriage. That is NOT God's design for marriage.

SIDE NOTE: I realize this statement I make about unbelievers is a strong statement. I have members in my own family who would argue that not all atheists are this cruel to their spouse or significant other. Many have a good heart. Many are still kind without believing in God. I agree with this stance. To that, I would respond – are they a true atheist or a prodigal? Many people I encounter today who claim to be atheists have the same story. They were raised in church, accepted Jesus in their heart sometime in their life, but decided to walk away from the faith later in life. They still lead fulfilling lives as good people who still believe in treating everyone equally with love and respect. The following is my own philosophy about that, and others do not have to agree with me. Everyone has a right to his/her own opinion. I believe those who have this story are not atheists. They are prodigals. When you have sincerely invited Jesus into your heart at any point in your life and meant it, the Bible says in 1 **Thessalonians 1:4-5,** *"For we know, brothers and sisters loved by God, that he has chosen you, **because our gospel came to you not simply with words but also with power, with the Holy Spirit and deep conviction."*** When the power of the Holy Spirit has entered a person, they become a believer to their very core – apart from their soul and flesh. He resides in our spirit. He doesn't leave. He will be silent – maybe for many years – but I believe He will eventually lure the prodigal back home into his or her Father's arms. People who claim to have once believed but now deny their faith, but still operate in all the fruits of the Spirit are still God's children. He has a plan for their journey. He will bring them back into fellowship with Him by the conviction of the Holy Spirit that dwells deep within them. They will one day return to the belief they accepted as a child before the enemy attacked their minds and wrapped them in a web of deceit. God will still have His way in them before it is too late. **Proverbs 22:6** says, *"Train up a child in the way he should go, and when he is old, he will not depart from it."* Strong's definition of the word "depart" provides a deeper Hebrew meaning, "leave undone". They may think they are departing from it, but God will not leave that undone. God's Spirit is Mighty and Stronger than anything the devil tries to thwart. He will get through to his prodigals by the power of the Holy Spirit that still resides in them. Especially, when believers around them are praying fervently! That's my sound belief and I'm sticking to it!

This is totally different than someone who has never accepted Jesus in their heart. They've never accepted the gift of God's unconditional love and are absent from the power of the Holy Spirit. So, they are a pawn for Satan to use, without remorse or conviction. God has the power to change their hearts as well to be saved. There is POWER in prayers of the saints for the lost! God is able!

Sorry for the interruption . . . back to my story.

As soon as Cheri called me that morning and instructed me to report to the President's office, I felt faint. I excused myself with a vague reason that had Mary puzzled. I'll never forget that long walk across campus, praying for God to help me through this dreadful meeting. The picture of Mary's sweet face smiling at me as I left kept haunting me. I felt so intimidated walking into the President's office as Cheri sat across from his desk. This would be my first introduction and encounter with Dr. Hays, and it wasn't for a pleasant occasion. I was terrified he would drill me even more and I ran the risk that he would not believe my claims on the situation.

Thankfully, that did not happen. Cheri had already briefed him on what she had discovered and I was just there to be another witness to Mary's plight. It was excruciating for me to return to my office and act like nothing was wrong. My heart sank when Mary's phone rang, and she walked out announcing she had been called into a meeting and would be back soon. My coworkers and I waited anxiously with dreaded anticipation wondering what was happening with her. When she returned, I was SO relieved to learn the situation turned out better than we expected. Mary did get fired, but the college agreed to give her six months to repay the money, before they would prosecute.

To my surprise and relief, Mary took the confrontation with grace and dignity. I was shocked to hear her first words after returning from her meeting of fate. I braced myself for the worst, when I heard her say "Lisa . . . (as I lifted my head to look her in the eyes, I never expected her next remark) . . . thank you. This needed to happen. I have a terrible problem and I'm thankful you have forced me to face my demons and get this out in the open." It was a huge relief to all my co-workers because we had such an adoration for Mary. We all rushed to her side to hug her as we cried together with her. Holy Spirit was right in the center of the group hug as His divine healing process began for all of us. Even though I had no support from my husband at home, I had the loving support from the Lover of my soul, Jesus Christ. Looking back, He was so compassionate of my dilemma. He held me in His arms through the night and walked with me through that dreadful day. Holy Spirit took control of the office atmosphere, and it became a win-win for all. Mary was able to heal through therapy and pay back her debt, without prosecution. She continued her career working with children, in a position elsewhere she liked even better.

"Even though I walk through the darkest valley, I will fear no evil, for You are with me. Your rod and Your staff they comfort me... surely Your goodness and love will follow me all the days of my life..." **(Psalm 23:4, 6 NIV)**

Jesus planned my future and orchestrated this event to lead me beside "still waters." This situation helped me to grow emotionally, and love Jesus more deeply. Holy Spirit was building my tenacity to trust Him and choose life over death. I knew I was falling out of love with Rob but saw no way out. I had never shared about the abuse I endured at the hands of my husband. Though I wasn't taught much on this subject in my religious upbringing, I remember hearing that divorce, under any circumstance, is wrong in God's eyes. I knew God hated divorce, but I was beginning to understand that He hates abuse even more! I felt like I was suffocating in a loveless marriage where I had to pretend to love and hide my feelings of loathe. I began asking God, "Isn't it a worse sin to live a lie?" In one of His loving ways to answer prayer, Jesus determined my next steps in His divine plan to know His heart.

About a year later, I received my first promotion as an assistant manager to the campus bookstore. In my previous position, I became acquainted with one of the professors, who loved to hang out in our office to visit when business was slow. Professor King was an interesting man, and we had an instant bond. Although he was highly intelligent, he had an outrageous sense of humor. He loved to make people laugh, just like my dad. He reminded me a lot of Dad, and ironically, his wife, who was an English professor, reminded me of Mom - very reserved and lady-like. My new position in the bookstore offered more down time to be able to chat with campus visitors. We were busy only during the beginning and end of semesters with book purchases and book buy-backs. So, during our slow days, Professor King became a regular visitor to the bookstore in between his classes. The jokes my dad had told me came in handy to exchange with Professor King. We would belly laugh the entire time during our visits. It was so therapeutic! No matter how low my mood was, it immediately brightened my day when I saw him walk through the doors of the store.

Even more amazing was that Professor King was a deacon in the Catholic church. As we grew closer, I felt more comfortable sharing with him about my abusive homelife, while asking for spiritual guidance. I knew Catholics didn't believe in divorce and felt he could help me try to heal my broken marriage. On the contrary, he taught me what the Bible says about divorce and abuse is never a reason to stay in a marriage. **Colossians 3:19** commands, *"Husbands, love your wives and do not be harsh with them."* The Bible further instructs it is the duty of the husband to submit to God first, in order for the wife to submit to him. I had never heard that before. The apostle Paul instructed that Husbands are to love their wives, just as Christ loves the Church – His Bride. Wives are to do the same. Husbands are supposed to be the priest of the home and set the example. It was Rob's responsibility to love me as Jesus loves me. If he had followed that example, I would have reciprocated. Instead, I had a husband who didn't even know Jesus and didn't want to know Jesus. I learned a lot from this Catholic priest whom God had sent to be His messenger. Professor King helped me see that I didn't need bruises to recognize abuse. Verbal and emotional abuse are just as much of an abomination to God as the physical punches. The Bible does not excuse any kind of abuse. God's Word never says an abused person is to remain married to an abuser.

With each discussion, Professor King gave me more insight and strength to stand up for myself and choose a better life. So, as I became more confident in speaking up for myself, Rob became more combative. As I said earlier, when we moved back to Texas, he never lifted a hand to me because he was fearful of my dad, with good reason. However, his verbal and emotional punches never stopped in his attempt to control me and keep me inferior to him. I knew I had to leave my husband. He did nothing but speak death over me more than extending occasional compliments. I was done. I had nothing left to give him except all the material belongings that we had accumulated. I was willing to leave with nothing but my clothes.

My final night with him is still such a vivid memory. I had been contemplating for weeks how to gain the courage to tell him, face to face, that I was leaving him. I could have easily left without a proper goodbye because he worked longer hours than I did. The bookstore closed at 4:00 p.m., so I got home from work at least 2 hours before he did, every day. I could've easily packed my car and left with a note way before he got home. But "something" told me to take the narrow road, not the road of least resistance. I knew I had to bravely face my abuser for closure, yet I was still afraid of the unknown. I was unsure how he would react to the initial blow, but had a pretty good idea, it would not be pleasant. I was expecting hurtful words, but I also ran the risk of farewell bruises.

The interesting thing is how God brings people in our lives to do life with together, side by side. It had been 12 years since I had become best friends with Katie. Ironically, we walked through life together, in very similar circumstances. She, too, had married her high school sweetheart. He, too, was abusive. She had been married the same amount of time that I was. The only difference in our situation was that she had a baby with her abuser. She too was contemplating escaping her prison at the very same time I was.

That fateful day after work, I packed my car as tightly as I could, with only my personal belongings. All that was left to do was to have the hard conversation with him, before escaping from prison, in my 4-door compact car. As I watched the clock tick closer to his expected arrival time, my nerves increased into shaking hands. I was about to lose my courage and take my belongings out of my car, when the phone rang. It was my lifeline, Katie. Previously, in long phone conversations, we had made a premeditated plan on how to leave our abusers, on the same day.

"Are you ready?" were the first words from her mouth when I answered the phone.

"Ready as I am going to be. I'm scared though. How about you?"

↑ *Don't Fall For It* ↓

"I was able to get all my things in the car while he was sleeping this morning. I just have to wait for him to leave for work then I'll pack the baby's things."

Katie's dilemma was worse than mine. Her physical abuse had become more frequent, whereas my physical abuse had basically stopped. My loving dad with a slight temper was my safety net. Katie didn't have that luxury. She was still living in another city. Realizing her bravery in a dangerous situation, it helped me to be strong as well. If Katie can do it, I can surely do it. I only had to worry about my own safety, without the extra fear of a child being involved. I was spared that burden and realize now; it was a blessing that he never wanted children. His lack of desire had already killed the child we should have had together, but that act will never be considered a blessing – certainly not a better alternative. It was only a brief relief in this particular situation. I didn't have to subject a small child to the drama of a loveless marriage.

Katie and I sealed the plan with our goodbyes, "Ok, I will let you know when I've left, and you be careful. Don't tell him you're leaving him, until you have made it to safety," I encouraged her.

"Oh, don't you worry, girlfriend. I'm not about to take a chance with him hurting me and taking our baby away. Be strong. I'll talk to you when we are on the other side." I hung up the phone, took a deep breath and moved forward with my plan to leave.

Strange as it was, my plan included preparing Rob one last meal, before my departure. I admit, I sinfully considered slipping a few laxatives in his food, but feared he would taste it. I just wanted some kind of retribution. Then, I realized I was about to receive it.

Throughout our marriage, Rob was very insistent to have his dinner, on the table, at the same time each night, when he got home. That's how his mother took care of his family growing up, and he expected the same. So, that night, I prepared one of his favorite 5-course meals in hopes to put him in the best mood possible. "The way to a man's (cold) heart is through his stomach," so the saying goes. In four years of marriage, he drilled it into my head that, "a meal is not a meal without at least one main dish, three sides and a dessert." As I cooked that meal, I rehearsed over and over in my mind what I would say to him. I imagined our conversation would be at the dinner table over our last supper together. I memorized my speech as my nervousness grew more severe. I had timed the preparation so that the meal would be on the table when he walked in the door. Instead, I heard the front door open and close as I was about to take it off the stove. He was home early. Panic immediately set in as the plan was already being thwarted. Did he suspect something was about to happen (by seeing my packed car) and he had his counterattack ready? I was trying to swallow the big lump in my throat standing over the stove cooking. Before he came into view, I called out, "You're home early. Your supper will be ready in a minute." Those words barely left my lips when I saw him (from my peripheral view) walk right past the kitchen, headed toward the bedroom.

His very hoarse whisper responded, "I'm not hungry. I'm sick and going to bed." My heart jumped. *"He's sick? That means he is weak, so I am likely to get out without a physical fight."* My conscience started to bother me. *"Can I really leave him while he is sick?"* Then the vivid memory immediately came to mind. I remembered the abusive way he had treated me while I was sick, running a high fever with strep throat, in our first year of marriage. It was the first physical blow of many. It was all I needed to raise my head high, straighten my back, pull my shoulders back and go "face the music." I entered the dark room and saw him lying in bed with the covers pulled over his head.

"Can I get you an aspirin or something?" Admittedly, my tone was pretty sarcastic, lacking compassion.

"Get the thermometer and see if I'm running fever," was his stern reply. Such a cold order from a man who was at the mercy of a caregiver. It didn't win him any brownie points, for sure! It gave me the courage to get the thermometer, two aspirins and a glass of water before I went back in. This would be the LAST time I took orders from him. I took his temperature. It read 102. I could see he was riddled with chills. All I kept thinking about was that morning he had left me in my bed to suffer, after he had kicked me and strangled me, before leaving for class. A shrewd and unfeeling spirit came over me.

"Oh wow! You do have a temperature. 102! You probably should see a doctor. Here's some aspirin. If you get hungry later your supper will be on the stove." I then walked to the closet to grab the iron I realized I had forgotten to pack.

"Where are YOU going?" was the hateful inquiry.

Never a "thank you honey for all that you do." Just an interrogation of my whereabouts. I stood in the doorway of the bedroom with iron in hand and said, "I'm leaving you . . . hope you feel better soon! Bye-bye!"

I felt my heart beating so hard; it could've jumped out of my chest as I scurried down the hall. I made it to the front door and as I was about to shut it, I heard him from the bedroom, "Wait . . . WHAT?" I thought, *"Too slow, loser. You heard me. No explanation needed."* I shut the door and never ran faster to my car, starting the engine as if he was right on my tail. I was turning off our street when my heart palpitations finally calmed down. The plan was even more successful than I could've imagined. A case of the flu helped to make my escape quick and drama-free.

The next scene was me, walking into my parents' house. Mom was in her usual spot on the couch and Dad was in his recliner. They just looked at me with puzzled looks on their faces as I entered with an armful of belongings. "Well. I'm home. I finally left him." I was prepared to argue with them, if the "marriage-is work" speech was coming. They didn't know the whole story. I had spared them the agony of all the incidents of abuse, but I was ready to tell them the whole ugly truth if necessary. Instead, I was comforted by Dad's usual humor, "Well it's about time. What took you so long?" They never were fans of his. They saw ALL the red flags while we were dating, but couldn't get through to me, as a rebellious teenager. Instead, all they could do was hope and pray that one day, I would finally come to my senses and the day would come when I would leave. It did and they were more than supportive. The truth was more horrendous than their suspicions. If they only knew what took me so long and what I had experienced. I wasn't about to tell them. It would cause them great pain.

Rob finally accepted the fact I wasn't coming home. Before his surrender, he taunted me with endless phone calls that swung from pleading for me to come home, to threatening suicide, to cussing me out and threatening to harm me. Finally, he gave up and took his losses. I was able to convince him that his slave had found her freedom. He insisted on being the one to file for divorce to protect his pride and reputation in our small hometown. That was fine by me. I did not care. It saved me the expense of paying for it. The only thing I cared about was getting away from this loveless marriage, once and for all. I found out through mutual friends, his response when asked the reason for divorce, was; "I have no idea. I bought her a home, new appliances and then she left me." Wow. No admission to the years of torment. Narcissism (also known as "egoism") is a real thing.

The next blow was meant for my sweet dad. As part of the separation agreement, we agreed to put the house up for sale, to relieve both of us from a mortgage. The realtor advised us to keep the house staged to insure a quicker sale. So, we waited to split up the furniture and other belongings in the house, until after it sold. The only thing I wanted were my grandmother's prize-winning paintings she had entered in the county fair each year. They were no Rembrandt's, but they were equally valuable to me sentimentally and I had proudly displayed them on our walls. I could care LESS about the other items. I didn't want any reminders of this marriage in any way. I was ready to start fresh with all new things of my own!

One night during this phase, Rob's rage got the best of him, and he reared his ugly head. Sadly, my parents got to learn the truth about his abusive temper in a sobering way. I had encountered him at a local dance hall, while celebrating a birthday with a group from work. It was on a weeknight, and we practically had the place to ourselves. One of my friends saw Rob standing by the bar and warned me of his presence. I tried to ignore my nervousness and stay

↑ *Don't Fall For It* ↓

present in the conversation. Eventually, Rob came over to our table to ask me to dance. It was apparent he had been drinking quite a bit and I politely declined. He left and went to stew in a corner. A little while later, he returned to the table to tell me "I was acting like a whore". I guess "whores" are known for laughing with GIRL friends and colleagues, over drinks. I was sitting nowhere near a man. To Rob's demise, one of the people in our group was my supervisor's husband and he knew the owner of the club. It only took a short conversation between the two and Rob was escorted out by the bouncer. Little did I know, it sent Rob into a violent frenzy.

My former neighbor called me the next morning asking, "Are you ok?"

I answered, "I'm great, why do you ask?"

She and her husband were a couple we hung out with frequently. He worked at the same place Rob did and she worked at the college with me. Being neighbors made it convenient to get together and play cards on several weekends. The separation had happened so quickly and sooner than they realized, along with the town gossip. She thought I was still living two doors down from her. She explained, "We heard a lot of glass breaking last night coming from your house. Your motorcycle is laying in your yard, and it looks like someone ran over it." It was also stated in the separation of assets agreement that I would be awarded the motorcycle. I planned to sell it for the extra cash. I kept my car, and he would keep his truck.

She continued, "There is also a note on your front door pinned with kitchen knives." My heart sank and curiosity got the best of me. The house was on my way to my office, and I knew, most likely, he had already left for work. I had to go see what that note said. His words were so frightening, I felt my life was in danger, so I took the note with me for evidence. It was embedded so far in the door with the kitchen knives that I had to carefully tear the note loose. The blinds in the living room window were open just enough for me to look inside. I gasped when I saw the condition of the house inside. I still had my house keys but didn't dare go in. I knew I needed backup and rushed to work to call my dad. At lunch break, he met me at the house. Upon entering, we stood, astonished at the sight we saw, as we opened the front door. The sofas had been ripped to shreds, with stuffing lying all over the floor. Mirrors were shattered. Plants had been thrown around the room, leaving potting soil everywhere. The worst part was seeing my grandmother's paintings with the canvases sliced open - corner to corner – with a sharp knife. They were completely destroyed. These paintings were my deceased grandmother's creative artwork of beautiful country scenery. The cherished memories I had of her. He had no respect for that, nor any material thing left in that house. Every object was sliced or shattered into pieces, damaged beyond repair. I just remember Dad's trembling voice saying, "Oh my God, baby daughter this mess could've been you!" I didn't have the heart to tell Dad about the many times, it was me. Not to the extent our belongings endured, thankfully, but I knew about this angry temper. I didn't want to burden Dad with the visions of being abandoned on dark streets in the middle of the night. I didn't want him to know I was kicked and slapped on many occasions. I did not share with him the daily jabs of verbal abuse that I withstood for eight years.

After taking photos of the house to my attorney, he was shocked and dismayed. He advised that since there were no longer any personal items to negotiate, the required waiting period was all that was left to endure until I could sign the final decree of divorce. I agreed to cut my losses on the sale of the house with just enough to pay off the mortgage. No chance of any extra money in my pocket. The motorcycle was too damaged from him running over it with his truck for any chance to make a profit. But I was finally free from a life of abuse. I had nothing but hope for the future. I now lived back at home, where it was safe, until I was ready to find my TRUE love. I was blessed with a "do-over." I could close this chapter of my life with little scarring and pretend it never happened. I still had a chance to plan that beautiful church wedding one day, after all.

Truth be told, I was nowhere *near* ready to find REAL true love in my condition. I was still wrapped in a web of lies that the enemy had tightly woven within me from the time I was a small child. I was still very young when I left this marriage. The only purpose for me I knew was to be SOMEONE's wife. The night I went to the dance hall with my co-workers was the very first time I had darkened the doors of a club, as a single person.

Later, after divorcing Rob, I had fantasies of finding my "Prince Charming," in this new world. I dreamt it would be like the happy endings of romantic comedies I loved to watch. I was clueless to the trickery that lay ahead. I was single alright; but I was definitely NOT free.

To summarize, the enemy had me believing these lies about myself by the time I was 23 years old:

1) I wasn't planned so I don't have a purpose; 2) I was no one unless I was associated with someone; 3) I wasn't smart enough to get a formal education to support myself financially; 4) my only purpose and identity was being someone's wife.

I loved Jesus but was spiritually blind without KNOWING Jesus as my PERSONAL Savior and Friend. Subconsciously, I believed I was destined to be with a "bad boy" like those I was attracted to in junior high school. I thought this was the only type *I* attracted. It was going to be ok though. I could fix them. I could help them become better versions of themselves. Mom always taught us to look for the good in people. I became a master at looking PAST the bad and only seeing the good. My only deal-breaker would be he has to be a believer and he has to want children. All other flaws can be fixed with me and Jesus in the mix. Like I said, I was so very young and naïve.

As I embarked on my new normal as a single girl in my 20's, I was on the desperate search to find my identity and believed that was only possible, through another man. I had no idea my Heavenly Father spoke me into existence and wrote in His book for MY revelation, that I was fearfully and wonderfully made. He was my Rock and my shelter where I belonged. All I had to do to find the answers to all of my issues, was pick up the book sitting right in front of me on the coffee table – The Holy Bible. I was raised to think it was just a nice decoration and declaration that we were Christians. I had no idea it was an actual playbook by which to live my life.

To rub salt into my wounds, Satan still had one more sinister plot up his sleeve to take me down during this phase.

I have to explain one more story and it may seem redundant. You will understand the purpose in telling it at the end. To back up just a bit, about a year before Rob and I divorced, my boss at work invited me to come sing in the choir at her church. She was the organ player and explained they needed more sopranos. I was intrigued because I remembered how much I loved singing in the choir in junior high and high school. I hadn't darkened the doors of a church in years, but I felt led to accept the invitation.

I'll never forget the first day I walked in the small church with a beautiful sanctuary. Every window was decorated with stain glass pictures of Jesus in different settings. I mostly remember the overwhelming sense of peace and safety I felt. My nervous shyness was quickly diminished by the loving arms that reached out to hug me as I met the other choir members. I never felt so much love and acceptance before. It felt SO GOOD to be in church again. I had not been in church since I had started dating Rob at age 15, other than for my sister's wedding.

I knew deep inside this is where I belonged. This is where I could run to hide when I was afraid. This is where my Shelter from the storm was located. This is where Jesus lived and He was luring me into His everlasting arms, safe from harm. Every time I entered that church I didn't want to leave. I became a regular by singing in the choir. I soon became a member and volunteered in other areas, like filling in for the nursery, when needed and helping with the Youth.

Rob was never interested in going with me. In fact, he teased me a lot in different ways about my faith. At Christmas time, the choir director had asked me to sing a solo for one of the songs in the Christmas cantata. I was SO nervous! I practiced the song over and over at home. Each time I would rehearse it, Rob would mock me "in fun". As I practiced the high notes, he would imitate me with sarcastic high vibrato and laugh. It only added to my anxiety.

When I left him for the separation period, he suddenly had an interest in church. He went to my Sunday School teacher and asked her to talk to me. It didn't work – she had no idea what she was asking of me when she tried to convince me it was God's will for us to remain married. Rob finally talked me into letting my pastor provide marriage counseling for us. I only agreed to prove my point. Counseling can uncover deep dark secrets and I was willing to let them out to make my case. I had no intention nor desire to save the marriage. My pastor convinced me I might regret giving up without a fight and talked me into "a 3-month commitment" of marital counseling to at least say I tried. With each session, my pastor sided with him in oblivion to what I had endured. That was because Rob was on his best behavior, which was a complete act. Little did he know, I gave up my fight long before; but I agreed to try. I knew I would only be going through the "3-month protocol" to finally be paroled from my 8-year prison sentence.

The sessions proved to be useless. The pastor would ask hard questions and I would answer with hard truth. They were transparent and seemed cold-blooded. I would openly admit I didn't love him anymore – while STILL keeping his secret of abuse hidden. Nothing that was said changed my heart, nor my mind. I was done. Finally, during one session, which was the last session, Rob showed his true colors. It was only about a month into the quarterly commitment. Out of frustration from my honest answers to the hard questions, he suddenly jumped out of his seat and literally threatened to "bash my face in". I saw the pastor's mouth drop.

The secret was out. I tried protecting him, but he exposed himself anyway. With a stunned look, my pastor changed his role to protector and escorted Rob out of the building.

When he returned, he sincerely apologized for pushing me through this process. He had no idea. That was my fault for never telling anyone. I unloaded all of the darkness for his ears to endure. He convinced me I needed extensive counseling by myself and for myself to heal from years of abuse. Since I couldn't afford a therapist, he agreed to counsel me with his educational training in psychology.

Little did I know Satan had a more sinister plot.

The sessions started out therapeutic and helpful, as I began to slowly recover. I was young and naïve, thinking I was perfectly safe in God's house of refuge. This is why it never dawned on me it was not appropriate for me to be alone with him. Another female believer should have been present at every session.

One night my free pass for counseling ran out.

The session was conducted in a "new technique he wanted to try". He placed our chairs facing each other and so close together, our knees were practically touching as we sat face to face. He told me to imagine him as my "alternate self". He instructed me to describe what I would "tell myself", about my experiences of abuse. In other words, my "free self" was supposed to talk to my "bound self". Instead, it was more like my "broken and confused self" searching for what to say to her double. The fact I had to look straight into his eyes and "imagine it was my alternate self" made the situation extremely uncomfortable.

I had NO IDEA what he was getting at. My maturity level was stuck at age 15. I had been under the control of one man who never let me think for myself. I had no idea what to "tell myself". It became awkward and not therapeutic at all. I began to feel more uncomfortable and had enough sense to say I needed to end the session with a made-up excuse. As we both stood up, he grabbed me and passionately kissed me. Stunned, all I could do was run out the door. I never felt more disgusted in my life. Awkwardness quickly grew into deep shame. This incident needed to be kept a secret. The only way I knew to cope with it, was to forget it ever happened. The more I tried, the more bound I became. To make matters worse, he called me at work "on the sly" one day; and even professed his attraction to me during a Youth lock-in. Thankfully, there were other adults at that event to provide a safety net. The situation was a self-loathing nightmare.

I tried going on with my normal routine of singing in the choir. Every time I looked at him preaching and his sweet wife sitting on the front row with admiration, I became riddled with guilt and shame. The enemy turned up his lies telling me how dirty I was. This happened *to* me. I did NOT ask for it. Yet, *I* was feeling like the perpetrator.

It took me YEARS to realize and admit I had been molested, and fell victim to spiritual authority abuse. Great counseling . . . where I endure even MORE abuse in the worse form. I still have rarely told anyone about this. So, now I'm blowing the doors wide open in hopes to rescue someone else from a possible plight.

I ended up leaving the church soon after the incident and I didn't darken the doors of another church until many years later.

Satan was very timely in pulling his sinister plot in destroying my only sense of peace and safety. He took my faith in God and my trust in a church family and turned it into a disgusting lie that I did not belong in church. I felt too ashamed to run to my Savior for healing.

So, instead I headed to the bars to find my man-savior.

CHAPTER SEVEN
My Wilderness Experience

"And your sons shall be shepherds in the wilderness forty years, and bear the fruit of your infidelity" ~ Numbers 14:33

The 14th chapter of Exodus describes how God split the Red Sea to lead the Israelites out of generations of slavery from the Egyptians. To their surprise, there was a wilderness on the other side. God told them He was going to lead them to the Promise Land – yet all they saw was a deserted wilderness. At first, they didn't care – they sang "the song of Moses and Miriam" (**Exodus 15**) and danced praises to God for rescuing them from their hard life of labor serving cruel masters. In a quest to get to the Promise Land, their journey through the wilderness lasted 40 years. If you are not familiar with this story, here's a fun fact. There was a quick and direct route to the Promise Land that would have taken only eleven days to travel. Instead, God told Moses to lead them "the long way" – to dry places where they would have to search for water, etc. God's people were issued a single instruction from the Lord to put them to the test. *"If you listen carefully to the Lord your God and do what is right in His eyes, if you pay attention to His commands, and keep all His decrees, I will not bring on you any of the diseases I brought on the Egyptians, for I am the Lord, who heals you."* (**Exodus 15:26**). This "test" in the wilderness lasted 40 years, because of their disobedience to God's instruction. Because of their acclamation to a certain way of life, it took a PROCESS for God to lead them out of their slavery mindset.

They needed to learn to trust a LOVING Master, who had their best interest at heart. Instead of keeping their gratitude and obedient hearts, they began to complain about the living conditions and even more tragically began to doubt God. They soon forgot the incredible way God led them out of slavery with a supernatural occurrence! They even started saying they wanted to go back to that kind of life, because it was familiar, even though it was not good. God's intention was to heal their broken souls, so they could know how to steward well all of the blessings of the Promise Land. During this process, they became fearful of the unknown because they didn't trust God. They even became rebellious against God. At one point, out of fear and impatience, they decided to make their own god, a golden calf molded from melted jewelry. They began to worship it. So, in other words, they rejected the one-true God who delivered them out of Egypt. The One God who had all the answers to their struggles. They began to depend on their *own* capabilities to survive in the wilderness. They took matters into their own hands apart from God's provision and protection.

Let me repeat. God knew He couldn't lead them straight to the Promise Land. They needed a wilderness experience first to grow their faith in their God of Abraham. They couldn't even imagine a place where they could be free to live without a slave master. So, they clung to their old habits and lifestyles.

My wilderness experience lasted several decades, too. Like the Israelites, I was guilty of rebellion. I worshiped idols in the form of a man-god. Being someone's possession was familiar to me and I started yearning to go back into that bondage.

The next three years of my journey in my desperate search to find my identity – in my next husband – can be described best with an analogy of a Merry-Go-Round.

Picture me, all dressed up, sitting very lady-like on the decorative bench of the merry-go-round. The bench had room for one more person to sit beside me. As the ride slowly begins to take me in circles, there is a crowd of different men encircling the entire parameter. They all have different personalities, physical traits, and unique styles. The one thing they all had in common was their search for their next conquest, to put "a notch on their bed posts". On this merry-go-round, Satan is riding on his black horse behind me and as we pass these men, one is highlighted as Satan whispers, "Let him on the ride - he's the one." The ride would stop, and the man would hop on and sit beside me. Sometimes the ride with the new prospect was quite long, until he decided he wanted off. Then Satan would highlight another one and fool me into thinking "This one is SURELY the one" and the ride would be even shorter, before he would bail. On a few rides, I even yelled, "Stop this ride!" and *I* would kick *him* off.

The single scene in bars was full of smooth-talking "gentlemen" professing their sincere adoration for me. They claimed they were looking for their forever love in a wife too! That declaration scammed me every time. This merry-go-round analogy was a depiction of my life. Living in an endless circle - busy, busy, looking for a man or ANY man who would have me. I didn't know to WAIT and trust Jesus to bring me THE man He had hand-picked for me. I was looking for love in all the wrong places. I had found the bar scene. There were plenty of those "rule-breaking" boys I gravitated to in these places! The possibilities were endless! The courtships began by dancing the "two-step" to country songs, in a circle, like the merry-go-round. They swept me off my feet with questions like, "Do you believe in love at first sight?" I was so green from being with one man since the age of 15, I had no idea it was just a pick-up line. "Love at first sight" would fade to an "I'll call you" or "It's not you, it's me." You think I would learn after the first time, but the "pool was packed" with "different type of fish," each having a shiny, new lure on their line and hook.

I was blinded by my LACK of SELF-LOVE. I didn't believe that I deserved to be cherished, respected, and pursued. I was still bound by a slavery mentality. I thought I was property to be used for the pleasure of a man. That's all I had to offer. Otherwise, I would be forever overlooked, in the crowd of prettier women they could choose from. I didn't know then that with each "quest for Mr. Right," I was giving away a piece of my soul to someone's future husband. My own shattered soul was all that remained to offer to my future husband. I didn't realize I was supposed to save ALL of me for the wedding night of my forever love.

Let me not paint the picture, too bleak. I didn't "hit the bars" *every* weekend, and some of the romances lasted longer than a night. However, the outcomes were all the same – a dead end with no happily ever after. Many weekends, between short-term relationships, I would sit at home, watching romantic comedies. This was my favorite past time. I would fantasize that I was the girl in the story, and it would be my reality, someday. My favorite movie, *Fools Rush In*, was one I never grew tired of watching. It was about a couple who had a one-night stand. She realizes later that she is pregnant, and when she tells her "Short-lived Romeo" that he is going to be a father, they fall in love and live happily ever after. I allowed that story to dictate my story. I became a fool who always rushed in. I was in love with the *idea* of being "in love."

Romantic comedies, along with a majority of cable TV today, are some of Satan's best secret weapons. They romanticize sex outside of marriage. The world has grown insensitive to the reality of sexual sin. Media portrays it as being "Ok, because everyone is doing it" and makes this sin look romantic, exciting, and have a happy ending – every time. Before I finally learned, "don't fall for it" . . . I ALWAYS fell for it.

Satan was back for ROUND TWO casting the very same doubt he used on Adam and Eve in the Garden. *"Lisa, Did God really say"?* Except the lie I heard, had a different twist.

"The Bible doesn't mean you have to be LEGALLY married with the license and ring. You just need to be married 'in your heart.' If you are in a committed relationship and planning to marry one day, that's ok. That's not fornication." Growing up in religious pluralism taught me that my right can be different from the kind of right written in God's Word. I thought it was subjective instead of infallible. I believed the lie that sexual sin out of the confines of marriage was ok if my heart had good intentions. This is the most dangerous lie of all. There are NO various forms of right apart from God's word!

Every time I jumped in, I expected it to become a committed relationship. Some did, short-term. One relationship lasted two years and I truly thought I would marry him. I was willing to stay with a guy even in the midst of seeing the same abusive signs I endured in my first marriage! It was "familiar" and therefore it felt comfortable – just like the Israelites and Egypt. One sobering event ended the relationship after he beat me up so badly, I literally had to flee for my life. My dad ended that one abruptly and permanently, with one phone call. Dad angrily warned him to stay away from me or he would go to jail. I wasn't mad about Dad's ultimatum, but instead, relieved and grateful. I was getting better, no longer protecting my abusers. I saw those same red flags of control, isolation, and manipulation, but it took a terrifying night resulting in bad bruises, to wake me up. In no way was I ready to be in any relationship with a man. I needed to care for myself and discover why I subjected myself to toxic relationships. In my desperation to find my identity, which I thought was to be someone's wife, I continued to travel this path blindly. I just started walking a little slower with more caution.

My pastor, Michael Willard, once gave a powerful sermon on this subject. Pastor Willard doesn't mince words when it comes to real life struggles and teaching what God's Word says about them. He said it like this [and I paraphrase], "Casual sex is never casual. That's a cultural principle, not a Kingdom principle. The word casual means relaxed and unconcerned. The world view of sex will tell you that having casual sex will cause you no concern in life. The Kingdom view will tell you the truth. Sexual immorality which is any sexual act outside of the confines of marriage between a man and a woman, will spiritually and emotionally BIND you to that person, even if you are not consciously aware of it." He went on to provide an example. "Let's say you have "casual sex" with someone who suffers from clinical depression, apart from your knowledge of this. You have never struggled with depression, but years later, you could find yourself struggling with depression. You cannot explain why, since it is not something that runs in your family. It could be because of that act of sexual sin with that person." **1 Corinthians 6:16**

(NKJV) says, *"Or do you not know that he who is joined to a harlot is one with her? For "the two,"* He says, *"shall become one flesh."* The Bible warns us this can happen whether it is one night, or one year. When you commit sexual immorality by having casual sex with someone who is not your spouse, you literally become "one flesh" with that person, and this creates a soul tie. As Pastor Willard went on to explain [paraphrased], "This is why you may "feel" like you are married to someone whom you are not but ARE having sex with. Once you create that soul tie, you feel committed to a person even outside of a marriage license." In other words, this creates a toxic stronghold where you are "one flesh" with that person. This is why it was almost impossible for me to leave an abusive marriage. The sinful soul tie had already been formed. Google "Soul Ties" if you want to know more. Be sure to choose a Christian website on the subject. It is a real and serious trap, but it can be broken off through prayer and declarations.

It is very difficult to break an emotional stronghold of bondage, even when you KNOW it is very toxic and not where you want to be. It's certainly not where God wants you to be. I will provide you with a real-life example to illustrate Pastor Willard's teachings in Chapter 12.

CHAPTER EIGHT

From The Merry-Go-Round to the Roller-Coaster

"Direct my footsteps according to Your Word; let no sin rule over me." ~ Psalms 119:113

That two-year "rerun" of being with an abusive man threw me into a holding pattern on relationships. After being "beaten into a reality check" I was so turned off by men and was ready to just focus on work. I started putting in long hours at the office. By this time, I had moved up on the institutional ladder at the college, once more. After the incident with Mary, I was commended by the administration for my courage and integrity. Irony, good timing, and an admirable work ethic eventually awarded me a promotion as administrative assistant for Cheri, Vice-President for Student Services. We had formed a special bond from that experience. She was working on her doctorate degree and pursuing her dream of going up the administrative ladder herself. Today, she has fulfilled that dream as the President of the college, for well over 20 years.

My only career goal, as I searched for my husband, was to be her assistant and meeting *her* needs in support of *her* goals. We spent many evenings and weekends together in the office, while I earned extra money. She was paying me out of her pocket to type her dissertation while she pursued her doctorate degree in education. When that was accomplished, her destiny to one day, be College President, inched closer, as she was promoted to Assistant to the President. I moved up alongside her, promoted to executive secretary to the President, as well as to her. My "excellent multi-tasking skills" were tested to maximum capacity. I had a new purpose that I took very seriously. It kept me very busy, working long hours and out of trouble. A common saying goes, "you find love when you least expect it." For the first time in my life, I wasn't looking for love, but love found me.

Backing up a bit in my story, love did find me when Cheri was still pursuing her doctorate which took up all my free time. My weekends consisted of late Friday nights and all-day Saturdays, assisting her in meeting the deadlines of her dissertation. My job was to produce an error-free, type-written paper that met all the criteria for each stage of her submission. This task took up my entire summer, but the bright side was, it was keeping me out of the bars and putting extra money in my checking account. I was thankful for both.

My friend circle consisted of the same single ladies I worked with in the department where I was first hired. Josie and Dora were my closest companions, as we all bonded over the incident with Mary. On weekends, they too, were looking for *their* Prince Charming. They were on the hunt for their happily-ever-after. They were also deceived into thinking that the bar scene was the best place to find the perfect man. With my workload, I welcomed their stories every Monday after their weekend journeys of meeting new men. It was my social relief from work, living vicariously through their single-life excursions.

Eventually, Josie started dating a guy who was co-owner of a country-western dance club, the town's most popular hangout. Josie's new beau also played lead guitar in the house band every Wednesday, Friday and Saturday night. Her regular routine was to frequent the club on weekends, to be with her man. Soon after their love affair began, she started insisting that I meet the new drummer in the band. Week after week, I would hear more about this drummer every time during those morning coffee breaks. "He had moved here from Tennessee; he is extremely funny with an amazing personality; he is incredibly talented; he has a singing voice that quiets the room and melts hearts." Josie would go on and on, but all I heard was the teacher in the Charlie Brown comic strip, "wah, wah, wah" as I tuned her out. I was more interested in hearing about HER love affair, not about another guy in a bar. That didn't amuse me whatsoever. She always added, "The best thing, Lisa . . . he has the exact same sense of humor as you, girl. I just know you two would hit it off." Jo would insist each week, "You've GOT to meet this man!" It would go in one ear and out the other.

After about two months of badgering, I finally caved. To shut her up, I agreed to go with them to the club on a Saturday night to meet this "dream guy". It would be a pre-destined introduction, knowing they had been talking me up to him, as well. However, on this particular Saturday, work changed my plans. Cheri and I had a difficult day with technology and getting the work done needed to meet the deadline of her next dissertation chapter. What should have been a 4-hour workday turned into a 10-hour nightmare instead. When 7:00 p.m. rolled around and we could not see hope of finishing, I called my parents, who I was still living with. They had planned to go to the club with me. This was a popular club that attracted adults of all ages and many of their friends were patrons as well. My parents' main motivation, however, was to check out this new guy in town that seemed so "perfect" for me. I always shared everything with them over dinner and told them about my conversations with the girls. Mom reminded me one day in our conversations, "Don't forget your sister met her Prince Charming in a bar – it doesn't always turn out bad."

On this day, I gave them the bad news on the phone, "I'm not going to be able to make it tonight. We still have so much work to do. You guys go ahead though. I want you to meet this dreamy drummer man and explain to him why I couldn't make it. Check him out for me and give me a report in the morning. I may beat you home, but I'm going straight to bed if I ever get out of here tonight."

The next morning at breakfast, Mom and Dad could not stop singing his praises. I heard all about his outgoing personality, southern charm, amazing talent and great sense of humor. They reported that he sat with them at every break to visit with them. Calvin won their approval hands down, which isn't easy to do with Dad. Mom is a push over for any well-mannered gentleman, but Dad is more of a skeptic.

I knew he had his "baby-daughter radar" on high alert after my last fiasco of a courtship. One potential "Dad-strike" against Calvin could be the fact that he was seven years my senior. My protective father was going to need some convincing, for obvious reasons.

So, when I heard *DAD* going on and on about this new guy, I thought it had to be a sign from God. I went from skeptical and not interested, to intrigued and curious to meet him. Still, with much caution.

To ensure I wouldn't get caught working late the following weekend, I agreed to go with the girls to the club the following Wednesday night, for a couple of sets. I reasoned that a weeknight was safe in case I didn't find him as charming as everyone else did. I could use the "gotta-get-up-early-in-the-morning" excuse and gracefully bow out. As we walked in the front foyer of the building, which was out of sight from the main room, I heard the most incredible singing voice. My initial thought was "Oh the band must be on a break. They are playing recorded music." As we sat down at our table near the dance floor, I see this tall, curly-headed man on stage with a golden tan and big hands, singing like Ray Price while keeping perfect rhythm on the drums. I have a thing for hands. It's always the first thing I look at in a man. To me, strong hands stand for safety and comfort. I was immediately attracted. I soon discovered what all the rave was about with this guy. He could play the drums with excellent precision, while singing his lungs out, with his eyes closed. Josie didn't lie. He *did* have a singing voice that could melt a glacier. My stone-cold heart toward men began to melt, beating harder and faster the closer it got to break time.

I will never forget his words as he walked up to our table. The girls introduced us, and he smiled, looked straight into my eyes jokingly saying with his southern accent, "Well, if it isn't the infamous Lisa Dee. You actually are a real person." I immediately felt a spark and sense of belonging. Our conversation flowed with ease as it quickly became obvious, my friends were right. Our personalities clicked in perfect timing, like his drumming. Knowing he moved from Tennessee, I asked him the usual casual-conversation question, "What brought you here to Texas?" I was surprised and taken back by his answer, "I think to find you." I was so flattered, but my defenses IMMEDIATELY went up. "This guy is full of sweet talk." I had heard good one-liners in the past. It was a very familiar sound. I had grown and was not easily fooled anymore. I was still licking wounds from my previous 2-year abusive relationship. I was a hard nut to crack.

After a great conversation and a few dances with him, it was time for him to go back to work for the 2nd set. Before leaving the table, he asked, "Do you want to go get some food when I'm through tonight?" The invitation was tempting but I declined. I explained in *long* detail I wasn't ready to jump into another relationship. His reply was short and to the point, "It's just food and a cup of coffee, not a marriage proposal." He once again made me laugh, but when I kindly declined again, I'll never forget his next punch line. "Ok – but just know I'm not going to wait for you forever, butthole!" laughing out loud as he got up from his chair to walk back on stage. "Butthole? Really?" I was deeply intrigued. I had never been exposed to southern charm before. I was used to cowboys with very few words. Our conversation flowed as if we were two lifelong friends. In a few short minutes, I felt like I had known him all my life. No man had ever shown that much interest in me from the first introduction. I knew my heart was in trouble. I also figured I had thwarted him off for good with my reservations.

The next day at work, I was really taken back when I heard his voice on the other end of the line of the department phone. He had taken the initiative to find out how to reach me, even when I didn't give him my phone number. Our courtship started out with a few lunch dates until I finally felt comfortable in accepting his invitation to the club to hear him sing on a weekend. Cheri's dissertation was finally complete, and I had my weekends back again. On this occasion, the plan was to ride with the girls and let him take me home afterward so we could talk some more. By this time, I had moved into a cute one-bedroom rent house close to campus. It was time for me to move out of my bedroom at home and be on my own. His warm personality made anyone feel safe, but my fear was "How far will this charm go when he takes me home?"

To my pleasant surprise, that experience was magical. He was a perfect gentleman. We rode straight to my house and sat in the car, parked in my driveway, exchanging our favorite jokes and talking for hours. We also exchanged stories about our past relationships. He had been married once before, too. He and his first wife had been married for twelve years and had no children. He wanted children, but his wife had health problems that resulted in a hysterectomy early in their marriage. His divorce was very new and was the driving force to start a new life in Texas.

I learned he was born and raised in Georgia and was the youngest of four children. The best part was hearing that he was raised in a Christian home where they were devoted members of a Pentecostal Church; and he loved Jesus. I was still a Presbyterian at the time and had no idea what a Pentecostal Church was, but all I cared about was how he loved Jesus. So, on our very first date, he already checked off both of my boxes in the beginning of a long conversation. No deal breakers yet – he wanted children, and he loved Jesus. I TRULY was in trouble.

That night, I also learned that he started his singing career at age 16. His family struggled financially, and he grew up in a very modest environment. He shared that they didn't even have indoor plumbing for several years in his childhood. Seeing an opportunity for him to make good money, his parents allowed him to quit high school after his sophomore year to tour the country with a popular Gospel music recording group in his region. Despite not having a high school diploma, he managed to be successful in other things besides music. He was a talented auto transmission mechanic as well. He could fix any model on the market. He worked under his uncle and learned the trade with excellence. He was living proof that a formal education is not always necessary for a person to become successful.

His common sense was admirable. He was a prolific money manager. Being raised in a poor family taught him to value every dollar he earned. He was also gifted in fixing about anything that was broken. My dad was also a mechanic. He could also fix everything from cars to factory machinery. They were going to bond instantly, no doubt.

He was the only one in the Gospel group who was under-age. The other members were at least 15 years older than him. When he turned 18, he found the country-western scene after the gospel band quit touring. I learned that the drums were his second-favorite instrument. His true love was playing bass guitar. He had more natural musical talent in his little finger than most people had in their entire body. I remember walking into my house, saying, "Thank you, God. You have finally brought me THE man." We had our first kiss "good night," and it sealed the deal. I fell head over heels in love with this man in a very short time.

The first few months of the courtship were nothing short of Heaven. My family loved him, my friends loved him and the more I came to know about him, the more I loved him. One fond memory was the first time I accepted his invitation to go eat breakfast, after the club had closed. In the middle of conversation, I was puzzled as I started to see tears well up in his eyes. The conversation had been lighthearted. When I asked him what was wrong, his answer both comforted and confused me. "I don't know, I'm just experiencing Godly sorrow right now." I had never heard that term before and asked him to elaborate. "Godly sorrow – you know, conviction from the Holy Spirit," was his reply. Holy Spirit? Did he mean the Holy Ghost my ritual songs in church mentioned? "Glory be to the Father and to the Son and to the Holy Ghost. As it was in the beginning, is now and ever shall be, world without end, Amen, Amen." That's the only time I had ever heard the Holy Ghost mentioned in my upbringing. When I described my church background in detail, he jokingly replied, "You would be scared to death in my church then." He began to tell me stories of people dancing on the pews and "falling out on the floor." He was right. It did scare me. It also intrigued me to see a grown man talk about his faith with so much passion and conviction.

As time went on, I became more and more amazed at Calvin. For instance, he was extremely tidy. The first time he invited me to his apartment for dinner, I was surprised at how clean and organized it was. I remember laughing in amazement when I first discovered he folded his *dirty* clothes in the hamper. "You can fit more in that way," was his rationale. Another fond memory was the first time he came to eat at my parents' house. My mom was so tickled at his tendency to clean any area that needed a "tidy fix." He was standing in the kitchen talking to me and Mom while we prepared the side dishes. Dad was outside, tending to the steaks on the grill. Mom kept a bowl of Dad's favorite nuts in the shell and hard candies, on the kitchen counter. It had a lot of empty nutshells and candy wrappers, as Dad always cracked the nuts and just threw the shells and wrappers back in the bowl. Tidying up seemed to be second nature for Calvin as he was talking non-stop to Mom. He was telling a story, while sorting out the shells and candy wrappers from the bowl at the same time. Mom and I looked on with amazement while snickering to one another, without his awareness. By the time he finished his story, the bowl was neatly sorted with only shelled nuts and unwrapped candies. The trash from the bowl was put in its proper place, in the trashcan. When Calvin left the kitchen to go see if he could help Dad, Mom leaned over to me and whispered, "If you don't marry this guy, I'll divorce your dad and marry him myself!" My dream guy was friendly, tidy, old-fashioned, Christian, and family-oriented. What more could a mom want for her child? Josie was so right about this one.

Senior-citizen, dancing couples who frequented the club, had the exact same opinion of him. Calvin loved visiting with the older generation and hearing their stories. He would make the rounds at every break, greeting people and making them feel welcome. He became the "talk of the town" with his talent and southern charm. I felt extremely proud to be his girlfriend. I came to know the wives of the other band members and was immediately accepted into the group. We would all sit together at the club, watching our men entertain the crowd and get together for Sunday afternoon barbeques. The bass player, J.R., had known Calvin for a long time, as he was from Tennessee and had played music with Calvin for years. He was the connection in getting Calvin to come to Texas. His wife Linda and I became instant best friends. She was a jokester just like Calvin. She always had a joyful disposition, and she was pregnant at the time with their second child. Family time was important to *this* band, and it changed my whole perspective of the stereotypical musician.

However, one typical trait remained.

It is no surprise how easily I was lured into trying out my first marijuana joint with Calvin. I felt safe and secure with this older man who had the opinion that it was a much healthier buzz than alcohol. I was soon convinced he was right. Just a few puffs put me in a state of euphoria. We would laugh for hours, and I never felt a hangover the next day. Even though none of the other wives took to the drug, they did take a liking to alcohol. I discovered Linda was the biggest drinker in the bunch, soon after their baby boy was born. She had abstained from alcohol during her pregnancy, and I remember being thoroughly entertained by her buzz the first time I saw her intoxicated. She was even funnier, as the little bit of inhibition she had, was numbed by the Jack and cokes she liked to drink. It wasn't long after, I was introduced to the drug the band wives *did* like. I thought I would never lay eyes on, much less partake in cocaine. The band and their wives seemed to handle this indulgence with dignity and respect. It was never to be done on a weekday and never in front of the children. I soon discovered many "respectable" people in our community indulged in this party drug as well. Doctors, lawyers, businessmen and women all partook in moderation. Once I was introduced to this community, I was conditioned to think the drug itself was respectable. My need to fit in told me, this was ok.

I didn't really like the effects though. It made me feel shaky with heart palpitations. The last thing I needed was something to cause more anxiety. Pot suited me better, as it helped me to chill and relax. My main attraction to coke, however, was its ability to curb my appetite. I was obsessed with keeping a slim figure, after being criticized by Rob for years for being chubby. Right before I divorced him, I went on a liquid diet and lost 35 pounds. I was determined to keep that weight off! A little indulgence in moderation, with this new remedy, was just the key. It also kept me alert if my drinks were too stiff. If I started feeling too intoxicated, just one "little bump" would sober me right up. Problem solved. I now look back and realize how fortunate I was that I didn't find cocaine very enjoyable. I've seen how addicting it can be for others.

There I was at age 26, introduced to a whole new world of how to "enjoy" myself and still function as a productive member of society. It was reserved for weekends only. I still felt completely in control. I discovered marijuana agreed with my body. I was always one to "listen to my body" for any signs of illness or disruption to my bodily systems and I found no red flags with marijuana. "It was a plant God created, so it couldn't be too harmful," I would reason. It seemed like the perfect indulgence to relax and have fun with friends. It greatly helped in managing my anxiety and depression and helped me to relax and be sociable, so another win-win. I thought I had found my perfect man and my perfect remedy to stay happy the rest of my life. Unfortunately, my utopia soon began to show signs of decay.

One night is forever etched in my memory. It was the first storm that hit my new-found paradise. We were about six months into the courtship and life could not be any sweeter. The club where Calvin worked decided to host an event to bring in revenue on a night when the band wasn't playing. The owners booked a "Ladies Night" on an off night and hired professional male dancers for entertainment. The rules were "Ladies Only" from 6:00-9:00 p.m., before they opened the doors to the opposite sex. The house band was hired to help with waiting tables and bartending. Calvin was assigned to the lower-level bar that was on the opposite side of the front door.

At that time, I was serving as cheerleader sponsor at the college, for extra money. I was required to attend a basketball game that night in my role of supervising the cheer squad. Calvin was bummed when I told him I had to work that night. It would've been a perfect time for us to spend together when he didn't have to play or sing. I could've helped him behind the bar.

I felt like my lucky stars were lined up that night when I was pleasantly surprised how fast the game ended. Our team ran away with a high score victory. I was out of there much sooner than I expected. I was going to be able to make it before doors were opened to men.

I could not drive fast enough to the club to surprise him. It was destined to be a great night hanging out with him, after all. When I arrived at the club, a line of women extended out the front door and halfway around the building. As I approached the long line, I was pleased to run into one of my closest high school friends, April. She and I stayed close during my early years of courtship with Rob. She was not aware of the abuse I took from him. I had not seen her in years, as she had married straight out of high school, and started her own life with her new family. Her husband had given her the night off to go enjoy "Ladies-Only" time. We had plenty of time to catch up as the line moved slowly to the door. She was shocked and sympathetic when I explained why I had divorced Rob. I was so excited to tell her about the flip side of my story - my new love I had found, in Calvin. I had time to give her the long version of how I had finally met the man of my dreams. He was a perfect gentleman and after kissing a lot of frogs, I had finally found my prince. As we continued to inch our way to the door, I could not stop telling her about all the special moments in my romantic love story. She was so intrigued and anxious to check out this dream guy. When we finally made it through the front door, I could not wait to take her to the lower-level bar to introduce her to my Prince Charming.

As we approached the lower deck, I was suddenly punched so hard in the gut, it took my breath away. It wasn't a physical punch, but it hurt as if it was. To my astonishment and embarrassment, the story of how perfect he was, suddenly became a fairytale. He was standing by the bar with his arms wrapped around another woman.

↑ Don't Fall For It ↓

He didn't see me at first and so I stood back to gaze at this unbelievable sight. "Surely I've just walked in on an innocent hug and there is a good explanation." But the embrace kept lasting longer and longer, with a few kisses and lots of laughter. Realizing this was not an innocent friendly hug, I finally walked closer. I'm sure my eyes were glowing with anger. When he turned his head and saw me, his mouth dropped wide open. I was sucker-punched like I had never been before. April was sympathetically embarrassed for me, pulling me away to go sit and console me. As I walked away, he called my name to come after me, with an explanation. When I turned to glare at him, eye to eye, he knew any explanation would be blatantly rejected. So, he returned to his place of frolicking.

My immediate reaction was to leave. I told April goodbye, and we parted ways as she found some friends to sit with and I headed for the front door. Something within me stopped and my stubborn, rebellious side, took over. "No! Why give him the satisfaction? It's Ladies Night and I'm not going to let him spoil my fun." I went and sat with April's friends as the other band wives were conveniently sitting at the table next to us. It was obvious to them what was bothering me, and they confessed, they had observed his shenanigans all night. He never attempted to talk to me the rest of the evening and instead, I got to observe him dancing with this mystery girl, all night. I tried to pretend I was ok, as I started taking one Tequila shot after another, with no regard for the busy workday I would have the next day. I was doing anything I could to numb the pain.

To this day, I cannot recall how long it took, but he finally convinced me of that old cliché', "She means nothing to me." He blamed it on alcohol. "He had been drinking before I got there, and he began to drink excessively after I caught him in the act." He blamed it on his first wife who always made him feel unattractive. He blamed it on his upbringing that caused a low body image, due to his adolescent weight problem. His family and friends teased him with a nickname "Healthy." He gave me the sob story that he was not used to girls coming on to him until he moved here, and he didn't handle it well. He begged and begged for a chance to prove to me that's not who he was. I was already so deeply in love; I couldn't resist the temptation to let him off the hook and forgive him.

I, at least, had enough common sense to realize, he was still hurting from the fresh wound of a recent divorce. I had three years over him to heal from my wounds and I realized he needed time and space to allow his wounds to heal as well. It was obvious he was not ready to settle down into another committed relationship. So, I agreed to forgive him on the condition that we would take a step back, remain friends and allow time for both of us to heal from past hurts. I didn't want a man who was curious about other women, so he needed to go "find himself." If he was meant to be with me, he would come back.

He was thankful for the nugget I offered and was adjusting well to this new arrangement. I made it very comfortable for him. I stayed home night after night while he continued to play the field. I would recite a poem every night, laying on my pillow, as I pined for him. "Love is like a butterfly. If you let it go and it comes back, it's yours forever. If it doesn't – it never was."

We had mutual friends that would keep me informed of his latest exploration. I was always happy to hear the news of another dead-end tale, when he quit dating them. These reports kept me hopeful and uninterested in looking for another man to be in my life. I was convinced if I allowed him his space, he would eventually see that I was, for sure, his forever. I just needed to let him "sew his wild oats."

Unfortunately, allowing him space sent the message that he could "have his cake and eat it too." I was not strong emotionally nor grounded in the truth that I am a child of God, only deserving the utmost respect. Instead, I was a co-dependent, blind child who thought I had to submit to whatever was in front of me. This man, with so many amazing qualities, *plus* an issue with temptation, was what I had in front of me. He couldn't resist the numerous other single ladies who admired his qualities as well. If I wanted to be a part of his life, I would have to weather the storm of his excursions. Many times, the other women would flaunt it in my face with

↑ *Don't Fall For It* ↓

blatant, flirtatious competition. I didn't realize I deserved so much better. He won me back after every incident with charm and empty promises to keep me holding on tight to his short rope.

To make a long story shorter, our two-year courtship consisted of good times and not-so-good times, when I would catch him seeing other women. The good times overshadowed those bad times. He would be so faithful for a good stretch before temptation would get the best of him. After enough of his excursions to break me, I gave up on our happily ever after. I broke up with him and started going out on casual dates again. No more sitting at home, waiting for him to see the light. His dark road of exploration outlasted my patience. Calvin did not take me dating other men well at all. It was his wake-up call. He came to me on bended knee and tearfully professed that he was through with other women. I *wanted* to believe him when he said I was the only woman he would ever want. We agreed on being an exclusive couple again. He even started joining me for Sunday morning church services. He suggested I move into the same apartment complex he lived in, so that we could be close neighbors. So, I found an apartment that was just around the corner from his. Life had calmed down to a steady life of fidelity, mutual respect, adoration and love for one another. That only lasted about six months.

The "honeymoon" ended on his 34th birthday. I decided to throw him a surprise birthday party at the club on the night of his birthday. Because he had to work, I also planned a *small* get-together, after the club closed, at my apartment. The guest list included him, the band members, their wives, and a few other close friends. I left the club early to prepare for the guests to arrive. The plan was quickly altered, as people from the club heard the "buzz" that there was an "after-party" at my apartment.

The small get-together turned into a crowd so large, I could barely move around. I lost sight of where Calvin was. A while later, I began to scan the room and found him nowhere in sight. I asked some of the other guests if they had seen him. One guest told me he was seen walking toward the master bedroom. As I approached the bedroom, I could hear voices coming from the adjoining master bath. The door was shut and when I tried to turn the doorknob it was locked, so I decided I needed to listen on the other side to investigate. I heard whispers of his voice and a female's voice. As my heart began to beat out of my chest, I knew I would "blow my top" if I stayed there and waited for them to come out. I didn't want to cause a big scene in front of the other guests. I even reasoned, "It's not what it looks like. He would not do this to me on this night, especially in my own apartment." I decided to just join the others at the party.

Several different conversations filled the living room, and I was being pulled from one to another. I had a hard time focusing as I watched for Calvin to re-enter the room, but I kept getting distracted with forced conversations from guests. Sometime later, the crowd began to thin out, and I figured Calvin, and the mystery girl were still in the bathroom. I went to investigate again, only to find, the bathroom was empty. I came back out and asked if anyone had seen Calvin. That's when I was blindsided with the news that some of them had seen him leave with "Melody."

"Melody" was basically my "nemesis-turned-new-best-friend." We had a history during my "three-year search for love" of dating the same men, thus becoming rivals in the dating pool. "J.J." was a past heartthrob I dated briefly, but he broke up with me and started dating her. They became seriously committed to one another. So, I had a streak of jealousy toward her. Later, after she broke up with J.J., she took an attraction to a guy I was dating, although we were not serious. She developed a jealous streak toward me. It soon developed into an unspoken rivalry. Then, sometime later, we became friends and agreed to put our differences aside as we began to discover why we liked the same men. We found we had a lot in common and began to become close friends.

My so-called "close friend" had just left the party with my boyfriend. History was repeating itself. There I was, sitting on my couch in a pool of humiliation, as others tried to console me. I was furious, heart-broken and embarrassed, all in one breath. I still wanted to believe he just gave her an innocent ride home. Luckily, I knew exactly where she lived. I couldn't keep myself from driving over to her apartment, just to see what I might see. I saw and heard all I needed to. They were sitting on her 2nd floor balcony, which gave me the advantage of getting close enough to hear their conversation without being discovered. The gist of the conversation was Calvin, convincing her that we were not exclusive, and it was ok for her to go out with him. That's all I needed to hear. I would leave, go home and wait to hit him with his own words when he returned. I drove back to my apartment. It was obvious to everyone else the party was over. When the last guest left, I sat for hours on my couch, thinking he would be coming back over. I dozed off and when I woke up, the sun was barely coming up. I walked over to his apartment and my heart sank when his car was not there. I knew what I was in for but had to go see for myself. I drove to her apartment with just a glimpse of hope that I was not going to find his car at her apartment. That hope was completely shattered as I turned the corner and found his car in the exact same spot as the night before. He had stayed the night. I was not going to let myself reason it was something innocent, any longer. I knew what I had to do.

I broke it off with the intention of never looking back. The head basketball coach from the college had formed a platonic friendship with me and had heard many stories about my struggles with Calvin. He had tried to talk sense into me on several occasions that I deserved better, but I always made excuses and took up for Calvin. So, I was finally able to give this coach the satisfaction that he was right, at work that Monday. He and I became close friends, but never developed an intimate relationship. We were just buddies who liked to hang out. Calvin kept an eye on this developing friendship from a distance and his jealousy drove his determination to win me back. This new guy in my life was viewed as a true threat to his ultimate plans. He persisted in his pursuit to win me back by pulling out all the stops of his natural charm. My cold heart grew weaker and weaker. I missed him and wanted to forgive him but was fearful of being hurt again. That fear and a cute male friend/companion kept me strong enough to hold out long enough to convince him he had finally gone too far. It felt good to make *him* jealous, for once. My head kept telling me to move on, but my heart kept wanting to see him again. At my weakest point, Satan moved in and set up a group lunch date. It is such an ironic and funny story; it is a forever memory of our story.

I agreed to go to lunch with Linda at our favorite Chinese restaurant that the four of us frequented when I was with Calvin. Little did I know, it was a set-up, as J.R. and Calvin "conveniently" ran into us and asked to sit with us. Linda and I were already sitting across from each other in a booth. So, it only made sense for J.R. to sit next to his wife, leaving the only empty place available for Calvin to sit, next to me.

So many mixed emotions were flowing through my mind. I immediately figured out this was pre-planned. I was determined not to cave in. I tried to hide my shaking hands as we ate. I made a concerted effort not to look at him for the entire conversation. If I wasn't looking down, I kept my eyes on Linda only. I remained quiet and just listened to the three talking. Several times, Calvin would cut one of his funny jokes that he knew I would normally laugh at. I managed to react with only a semi-smile. Then, something happened that shattered my cover.

As we finished our entrées and the fortune cookies were served, I couldn't believe the red writing on my little "fortune." I could not help but giggle under my breath. My restraint almost made me choke on my last bite of broccoli. I looked again, closer, just to make sure it actually said what I thought I read. Everyone else was taking turns, sharing their fortune. When Linda signaled it was my turn to share, she silently chuckled in a curious way, as if she read my mind. My look said it all. I was given a good one. She began to chuckle under her breath, as she read my lips mouth the words, "Don't ask. Just move on." That only heightened everyone's curiosity, urging me to share. This wasn't going to end, so I finally handed the little slip of paper to Linda to read. She couldn't control her boisterous laughter as she read the message out loud, "Someone close to you is seeking reconciliation." The outburst of pent-up laughter caused other heads in the restaurant to turn and look toward our table. That ice breaker began the journey back to reconciliation. That small window turned into a wide-open door for him to walk back into my life. What are the odds of that relevant "fortune"? I resolved it must be fate... and so it was.

Calvin convinced me, we needed to move in together. It was his declaration that he was going to be completely committed to me. He would have no freedom to do anything secretly behind my back. He was fully ready for a serious, monogamous relationship. I fell for it hook, line and sinker. My two-bedroom, two-bath apartment was the obvious choice. He gave up his one-bedroom and moved in with me. We settled into a calm existence of doing life together, being in love, like any normal "newlywed" couple. I brought study materials home from the college for him to prepare to take the GED exam and finally get his high school diploma. I knew he could do it because he was naturally intelligent, regardless of his limited education. He passed with flying colors. He was so proud of himself, and we celebrated his accomplishment. We started to make future plans. He now had the "ticket" to pursue other careers besides singing in the bars. Life was good once more, for about 4 months, until I had to take a 4-day business trip.

When I got home, I was sucker-punched once more with news from a close friend that she had seen Calvin with another girl. The story was validated by another close friend – my own mother. I was so shocked and infuriated! It was the only straw I had left. I proceeded to throw him and his belongings out the front door, while vowing I never wanted to see him again. No chance for lame excuses and empty promises. I just needed him out of my life. He had finally broken the camel's back. So, I thought. To break a camel's back you have to deal with two humps. I still had one hump left.

My lingering anger kept me strong for several months. The band wives told me that he had secluded himself in a large storeroom, in the back of the club. He made that his new home. A storeroom. He was in a deep state of depression and displaying other bizarre behaviors. I acted like I didn't care, although I couldn't help but worry. On one hand, it gave me a false sense of satisfaction, while on the other, I was deeply concerned about him. The rumor in our circle was that he was using cocaine, more than just recreationally. His life was a shipwreck, as he sailed dangerous waters with his own navigation. Friends would burden me by saying "I was the only one who could rescue him". That only fed into my tendency to be a fixer. I was so conflicted. What about *my* feelings? I wasn't strong enough to carry his burdens. I had enough of my own. Simply put, I could not keep riding this endless roller coaster with him. I chose to stay away and let God have him. Later, I learned he finally moved out of the storeroom and found a house to rent. I also heard he was still seeing, "on occasion," the girl he was caught with that caused our breakup. Nothing had changed. The worst part was that my heart for him had not really changed either.

My heart and head were in constant battle. I knew he wasn't good for me, but I couldn't stop yearning for more of those good days we spent together with amazing conversations. All the good times would play on repeat in my mind. Like the spontaneous trip we took to Dallas to attend the State Fair, one night after the club closed. We had decided to just get in the car and drive all night to make it to the Fair the next day. We were like two kids who were carefree. Nothing to hold us back. Another good time was a planned trip to Nashville and Chattanooga to meet his closest friends. We were like a newlywed couple, seeing all the sights and visiting his past. When the times were good, they were REALLY good. Full of fun and laughter and romance. When times were bad, they were the worst and my heart was constantly bruised from disappointment. Those bruises kept me strong for a long time to resist the strong hold he had on me. I was determined to put it all behind me and move on.

A few months later, a surprising moment of weakness came over me when a visitor walked through my office door one day. As Executive Secretary to the President of the college, Dr. Riley and to the Assistant to the President, Cheri - my work environment was very formal and professional. Personal time was frowned upon during business hours. My office had an outside door that gave visitors who had an appointment with the President, easy access to our office suite. Calvin would use that backdoor entrance every time he would pick me up for lunch, when we were together.

I was sitting at my desk this unsuspecting afternoon when I heard the door open. Luckily my bosses were behind closed doors in a meeting, which minimized my awkward embarrassment. I looked up to see Calvin, walking through the door, with tears streaming down his face. Before I could ask, "What are you doing?" He knelt by my desk, sobbing, and pleading with me to take him back. I immediately suggested we go outside and talk before he caused a scene in the office. As we sat outside on a bench in the campus courtyard, he poured his heart out, confessing he could not live without me, while sobbing uncontrollably. I could not get him to calm down, so I agreed to go to his house after work and talk. It was the only thing that would suffice for him to leave and let me get back to work before I got into trouble. Luckily, I only had to wait one more hour before quitting time. It was a losing battle in trying to concentrate on work. Instead, I rehearsed over and over in my mind what I was going to say when we continued our conversation. I took mental inventory of all the girls he had been unfaithful to me with, to show him why I could never trust him again. Heart in check, I had my speech prepared and ready to deliver as I pulled into his driveway.

As he met me at the front door, I could not deny the fact that it was good to see him. His usual southern charm was at full throttle. I couldn't help but crack a few smiles at his jokes. He pulled out the hospitality card, offering me an after-work cocktail to take the edge off. I was shaking like a leaf, so I accepted that tempting offer to help my beating heart relax. As we sat down at the kitchen table, I started the serious discussion. I was not going to let him off the easy hook with humor and light conversation. No more sugar-coating his trail back to my heart. "So, I'm here and I'm listening. What were you trying to get across to me at my office before I stopped you?"

He began his long and familiar plea to have one last chance. It was woven with several more serious promises and explanations for his season of sowing "wild oats." The effects of the alcohol started breaking down my walls. That's when something happened that I was not ready for. He got down on one knee, took my hand and began to repeat his stories in depth of all the struggles with low self-esteem, when he was a teenager. I could certainly relate to that. He continued sharing all the emotional and spiritual struggles he had experienced since he had moved to town. He confessed that he had always thought I was too good for him. He was desperately looking for comfort in other women as a defense from potentially getting hurt by me. I was getting ready to give my rebuttal, when he said those words that took me to the core of my yearning. "Lisa, I'm asking you to please marry me. I promise you that I AM a faithful husband. I was married for 12 years and never once cheated. I believe in marriage. I promise you; I am a much better husband than I have been a boyfriend. You deserved so much better, and I want to spend the rest of my life making it up to you. If you will have ALL of me, I promise I will never hurt you again." It's all it took for my heart to melt, but with conditions. I knew I was in trouble because I wanted nothing more than to be married; and *this* man had a hold on my heart that I couldn't shake.

After a long pause and internal battle, I finally responded, "I need you to hear me, Calvin. I still love you, but you need to hear this condition and believe how serious I am. One time, Calvin. Only one time, or even one SUSPICION of infidelity and there will be a divorce with no chance for reconciliation. I've already given you all the chances I have in me. This IS your final one. You will not get a second chance. I am out of second chances. So, if you can live with that promise from me, then yes. I will marry you based on my promise from you."

He immediately flung to his feet, picked me up and whirled me around the kitchen in celebration. We immediately started making wedding plans. All my fears and concerns turned into elation, as we planned that church wedding I always dreamed of.

↑ *Don't Fall For It* ↓

The most difficult time of my life suddenly became the most joyful time in my life. My family and closest friends celebrated our engagement, even though they had walked through the valley with me in my 2-year courtship with Calvin. They still believed in our union as much as I did. Mom told me about an experience she had and it really "sealed the deal" for me. She shared that on one of my darkest days and in her sadness over our struggles, she was sitting out in the backyard one morning, praying for the both of us. Suddenly, she had a vision in her mind's eye of Calvin and I, kneeling side by side and a light was shining down on us. She suddenly saw God's arms wrap around the two of us. "I have been wanting to tell you that for a while, Lisa, but I knew it would only make you feel worse. I truly feel like it was a sign from God that you two were meant to be together," Mom explained in all her heartfelt sincerity. We tearfully hugged and thanked God for that vision. I needed that confirmation that I was making the right decision!

We decided to plan the wedding quickly. I had not met any of Calvin's family, since they lived so far away. His oldest sister and brother-in-law were planning a trip to come visit around Labor Day. Although that was only a month away, we wanted someone from his family to be at the wedding, so we got busy. We planned a church wedding with all the frills in about two days, with the wedding date set in one month. We took my grandmother's wedding set she had left me when she went to Heaven. We had a jeweler melt the gold and diamonds into our own custom-made, matching wedding bands. THIS is how much this man meant to me.

I still remember the yellow summer dress I wore to the club just a few nights after the proposal. I never felt more beautiful. My parents and close friends sat with me at a long table as Calvin announced from the stage before he kicked off the first set, "I would like to dedicate this first song to the love of my life – my Fiancé, Lisa Dee – she has agreed to marry me, and the wedding is in one month." The crowd cheered and clapped for us. I felt like a princess. I had never been a "Fiancé" before and the sound of that was blissful. I had only been "the girl to marry in ten minutes at a JP's house." Calvin's song he dedicated should have been "I Can See Clearly

Now" because all the bad feelings had disappeared. There was that rainbow I had been praying for. Suddenly, a little black cloud approached me and tried to rain on my picnic.

A woman I knew only casually, walked up and knelt beside me. I knew enough about her to know she, too, had been married to a musician and was now divorced. "Lisa, I don't want to dampen your night, but I just feel so moved to warn you to please be cautious in this decision. Life as a wife to a musician is not easy. There are a lot of lonely nights and daily struggles. They are a different breed." I politely thanked her for her concern but quickly brushed it off. I told myself, "Her story will not be my story." I reasoned, her husband was probably not a believer, so that's why they had their problems. We have already weathered the storm she's talking about. Life for us will be a great love story, with God's blessing. I never felt surer of that in my life.

Looking back on that night, it is obvious now, that girl was possibly an earth angel warning me, instead of a "Debbie Downer" trying to ruin my party.

The wedding plans were smooth sailing. The church was available. My Pastor was available to marry us. I found the (almost) perfect dress that was able to be altered in time. I was in bridal bliss. I was finally going to have my church wedding, although small, intimate and tasteful for two people getting married for the second time. With only one attendant each, J.R. stood beside Calvin. Mom, my best friend, was my Matron of Honor. Calvin's motivation for asking J.R. was for another reason, besides being his closest friend. J.R. was part of a surprise Calvin had planned for me at the altar. At the appointed time, J.R. grabbed his guitar to accompany Calvin while he sang to me, "Walk Through This World With Me" in front of a church full of witnesses. Besides my tears, the sound of sniffles among the guests filled the air. I still remember walking back down the aisle hand in hand, while the women clapped and the men "high-fived" Calvin. When we entered the private prayer room, I'll never forget how Calvin wept joyful tears. We laughed and cried at the same time, out loud, with no apology. Then, we knelt at the altar of that room and thanked God for reuniting us. Mom's vision in the backyard that day of God holding us both was now a real picture. Our nightmares were finally over and nothing but a life full of happiness was ahead of us.

Our reception looked like a scene from the movie "The Urban Cowboy" because we decided to celebrate at the club where we met. The wedding was early enough to have a private party at the Club, before it opened to the public at 8:00. The party continued after the club opened and the public poured in on a Saturday night while Calvin went to work playing in the band. I stayed in my tea-length wedding dress and Calvin stayed in his ivory tuxedo. The wedding party and guests stayed in their wedding attire too. We all stood out from the normal "cowboy" apparel of regular club patrons. We kept our reserved tables on the lower level, next to the dance floor and continued the celebration until closing time. Ironically, the lower-level bar went from being the site of my worst nightmare that one fateful night I caught him being unfaithful to now being the happiest night of my life. Life travels in full circles.

During the evening, I encountered two girls who had dated Calvin before. They were two of the worst "antagonists" back in those days. As they entered the front doors of the club, I was walking toward the restroom and bumped into them, face to face. It was obvious by their surprised looks, they had no idea about a wedding, until they saw my dress. It was a "poetic-justice" moment when simultaneously, Calvin offers a toast to his new bride over the microphone on stage. I looked back at those girls with determined eye contact, as I noticed tears swelling up in one of them. They both forced the best smile they could muster and congratulated me and walked out of the club. Their Saturday night plans were obviously shattered in that moment. I felt like the demons had finally been defeated in my love story.

I look back on that moment today and wish I had known then, what I know now. Those girls were not my enemy. They were just as broken as I was, desperately searching for their sense of purpose too. I know they, too, had fallen victim to Calvin's southern charm.

I could've told them in a spirit of forgiveness, they were beautiful and deserved to find their true love. This is how we defeat Satan in his game of hate. The Bible says we are to love our enemies. Love conquers all! I also could have told them; I had spared them from more heartache by taking their heart breaker off the market.

We left the next day for a week-long trip to San Antonio with Calvin's sister and brother-in-law. It was their first time in Texas, and we wanted to show them the heart of Texas culture. That morning before we left, I will never forget when Charlotte, his sister, entered my room to have a heart-to-heart talk. The one sentence I remember in her speech was, "Whatever you do Lisa, don't let Calvin get away with his tendencies. You stand your ground. I know he loves you a whole bunch, but you keep him in check." I was taken back because I didn't realize she knew about our past struggles. I assumed Calvin must have filled her in and I was touched that he told her the whole story, not just his side. Little did I know, and come to find out years later, she didn't know a thing about our story. She was talking about his behavior in his first marriage. She could've exposed the lie he gave at the proposal about "being a better husband than a boyfriend" had I probed her a little more. Being oblivious at the time, I took her warning lightly and the four of us had a wonderful trip on our honeymoon.

"Teach me Your way, Lord; lead me in a straight path because of my oppressors." **(Psalm 27:11)**

IF ONLY I knew Jesus back then like I do now. He sent me so many warning signs to direct me down the right path. I could've saved myself a lot of heartache, if only I knew how to listen to His voice. Instead, all I knew was to listen to my emotions. Irrational thinking formed by toxic and abusive relationships, was my only guide. On the other hand, God still had a Divine purpose for our marriage anyway. I ponder today that He sheltered me from the true intent of Charlotte's words to keep me peaceful and emotionally stable for the next season of my life. The most important one.

Just a few weeks after the honeymoon, I noticed I would immediately get nauseous at the smell of second-hand cigarette smoke. Next thing I remember, was taking an in-home pregnancy test a couple of weeks later. We were pregnant! We were both ecstatic! I was 28 years old and felt my biological clock ticking away. Calvin was 35 and thought he would never get to be a dad. Another reason to celebrate and the best reason EVER!

It was hard enough adjusting to life together in a new marriage, so being pregnant just added fuel to the fire. We didn't really argue, but my emotions were all over the place and Calvin proved his words to be true. He was an amazing husband, so much better than he was as a boyfriend. He would wait on me hand and foot and do most of the cooking. My house was always spotless because Calvin would never sit down. He was always cleaning something. To fill up his days off from the club, he decided to take on a part-time job at the college, working in food service. He enjoyed the work as his co-workers took an instant liking to his humor and his work ethic. The food service director was thankful to have him around. He was completely different from the usual caliber of employees she would hire. He never took any breaks or idle time at all. He completely reorganized the stock rooms and continuously cleaned the kitchen from top to bottom. He did the same at our house. He was a deep cleaner. When he ran out of spaces to clean, he would pull the refrigerator out from the wall to mop behind it. He was tireless in making sure the house was in order. Our spice cabinet had to be alphabetized with all the labels facing the same way, for ease in finding the right one. I was not aware at that time of the signs of obsessive-compulsive disorder. I just basked in the glory of a built-in cook and housekeeper. His job at the college allowed him to be home much sooner than my position at the same college. He would always have supper waiting for me in a spotless house. Life couldn't be better.

Calvin's obsession for cleanliness and order made for a sanitary home for the little feet that were going to be waddling around soon. We kept the news to ourselves until we were sure the pregnancy was viable and to protect our privacy. We were excited and ready to settle down and raise a family, so God wasted no time in His plan. He is still the God of forgiveness who saves, redeems, restores, and has a mighty plan for our future. Besides, we were not getting any younger and God saw fit to give us a child while we were still at the child-bearing age.

My pregnancy was easy. The slight nausea and fatigue from my first trimester had diminished and I didn't have any complications of any kind. I still remember the very first time I felt the baby move. We happened to be lying in bed and we both got to experience the first kick together. We laughed and we cried. Due to my crippling fear of becoming fat, I did not love being pregnant because of the way my body was changing. However, my joy and anticipation of becoming a mom overshadowed that struggle. We had decided to tell the doctor, "Don't tell us what we are having - we want to be surprised." I already knew that if it was a boy, his name would have to have "Cody" in it somewhere. My entire life, as I would dream about my future children, I could only imagine boys. I figured, it was because I was a tomboy myself and mostly played with boys on my street, growing up. I could never imagine having a girl. So, a girl's name was more of a struggle. I had my heart set on Cody as a boy name, when I would dream about children. It was a good ole' "West Texas" sounding name and was becoming the new trend in boy names at that time.

Some nights I would go for the 1st set to hear Calvin sing and leave before the crowd arrived and the smoke started filling the air. My parents would go with me every time to drive me home. I will never forget a certain night. The mood in the room was calm and quiet, with just a few tables occupied. The four of us were having a great conversation, until it was time for Calvin to take the stage and the band to start their first set. The band kicked off their opening number and a rhythmic country song filled the air. That's when something incredible happened. I started feeling the baby kick to the beat of the drums. In astonishment, I exclaimed, "This baby is kicking to the beat of the music!" My dad was the first one to say, "Welllll – you're probably feeling the vibrations from the floor" in a skeptical tone. I challenged him to that theory by inviting him to put his hand on my tummy. The timed kicking started again, and his eyes lit up with amazement, "You're right! Mama feel this." Mom tested the theory and was convinced, too. We agreed I was carrying a natural musician, just like his/her dad.

Friends and co-workers also looked skeptical when I would tell that story, until a few years later when this baby started playing drums, at age 2. As time got closer to the due date, Calvin couldn't have been a better partner in life. He made sure he was home as soon as the very last song of the night was played. He always eased my mind that he was only working and not lingering to talk to anyone.

I still remember the conversation we had when we were trying to think of names. Again, a girl's name was just not coming to us, but he liked the name Cody too. If it was a boy, I wanted to name him after his grandfathers and if it was a girl, after her grandmothers. Rita Barbara had a nice ring. I was bent toward John Cody Joseph for a boy. Calvin wasn't convinced. He didn't want to offend either grandparent if their name didn't go first. So, for a compromise, I suggested we name a boy Jay Cody, and the Jay would represent both grandfathers.

Calvin always had a dream of making it big, in the music industry. He most-definitely had the talent; he just needed the opportunities. He seemed to dream vicariously through this new baby. Every time we would brainstorm about a name, he would test it out to see if it sounded right as a stage name. Most names were quickly rejected with no "catchy ring" for a show introduction. So, when I suggested Jay Cody, Calvin did his usual thing, "Ladies and gentlemen, please welcome to the stage – Jay Cody Carnes! Yep, that's it – that's a stage name." We just put the girls' names on hold – for good reason we didn't yet know.

Jay Cody was born on March 25, 1989. Little did I know, the conversation between his parents that day was prophecy. When Cody was a toddler, one of his favorite things to do during playtime was to put on the black leather Fedora hat my grandfather gave him. Cody called it his cowboy hat. When we had company, Cody would grab his hat, and his toy guitar and go in the back bedroom while the adults sat in the living room. Then we would hear in that cute toddler voice, "Present Me!" That was our cue to say . . . "Ladies and Gentleman ... Presenting – JAY CODY CARNES! YAYYY!" Cody would run out to the middle of the room and put on a show. He always would have a captive audience of admirers and it was always a sure thing to receive laughs and applause.

Cody is now in his thirties, and he provides for his own family by living out his calling. He is a professional worship leader/song writer under a well-known record label. Cody doesn't enter a stage today with a formal introduction. He humbly walks on stage in the dark to pick up his guitar. As soon as the stage lights come on, he begins leading the crowds in worship of Lord Jesus. He never introduces himself. He only introduces Jesus as the main focus of the gathering. God, in His infinite wisdom and protection, leaves me speechless with gratitude as I look back at how Cody's life began and where he is today. He was conceived in love and born to two parents who absolutely adored him at first sight. However, his two parents were lost in a world of issues. Emotional instability, drug addiction with victim mentalities and immature spirituality short-changed Cody from being raised in an in-tact, Christ-centered home. We were trying to DO all the right things, but we were not dependent on the One Who already did it all for us and to walk in His light. We still liked doing things our way, just like the Israelites. We continued to build and worship our own idols that the world offered.

Shortly after Cody was born, strife began to surface, as my resentment grew towards Calvin. He was still allowed to enjoy the nightlife in his job as a musician, while I was left at home to care for a newborn. The heart of the matter was, I didn't completely trust my husband. Some nights he didn't come home until long after the club had closed. I would ask him to explain his whereabouts and it was always the same story. He had to help clean up the club before clocking out. It was a reasonable excuse but something in my spirit didn't sit well. I could sense he was keeping secrets from me.

Our arguments became frequent, so Calvin decided to quit the nightlife and take a position working at a factory where Dad worked. Life began to settle into a typical American family. We went to work, we came home, we cooked supper, did the chores and were raising a beautiful baby boy. All the pieces to a happy marriage were there, except for the most important one, the very last piece of the puzzle to make it complete. Where was Jesus? We were not a family that prayed together, nor attended church regularly.

Once we got married, we fell into the habit of backsliding, simply because we couldn't find a "happy medium" in the wide pendulum of our worship preference. Calvin attended my super-formal religious church, and it was that church where we got married. Worship became mundane and ritualistic for him. He would jokingly scrutinize with this question, "If Jesus were to show up in the flesh in the middle of your service, would He be allowed to speak when He isn't listed in the program?" He was, in no way, used to the ritualistic, "follow-the-program" type of service, that started and ended promptly on time. His question had a sobering point.

On the other hand, I got a taste of Calvin's upbringing when we drove to Georgia for his mom's funeral, when Cody was first beginning to walk. Pentecostals were wild, in my opinion. Even at a funeral, they took the opportunity to have a day-long service of worshipping Jesus with loud voices, falling out on the floor, dancing on the pews and speaking in tongues. I had only witnessed this once in my life. It was way back in my childhood when I spent the night with a friend, whose family were members of Assembly of God – Pentecostal, Holy Ghost "wild" worshippers. Compared to the solemn, rule-driven, ritual style of worship in my church, I found myself hiding under the pew, in fear. This funeral experience practically had me doing the same thing. So, it became a silent agreement to avoid church altogether since we couldn't appease one another with our preference in worship style.

Despite the dilemma, we were both becoming more convicted that Cody needs to be raised in church. We searched and found a perfect compromise in The First Church of the Nazarene. The worship was calm enough to appease me, yet contemporary enough to appease Calvin. Some people raised their hands. Others didn't. I soon became accustomed to this new way and found myself lifting my hands as well. We also found a new group of friends, who were not patrons of the nightclub scene, nor partakers of illegal substances. They embraced us and we settled into a life of church, with fellowship in the form of potluck gatherings and card games. Cody was dedicated to the Lord in the First Church of the Nazarene. The congregation embraced us and appreciated Calvin's talent, as he began to serve on the worship team. Life could not have been sweeter.

The one bitter taste that Calvin could not stomach, was his job at the factory. He grew more dissatisfied and aggravated by boring tasks and disgruntled co-workers. Calvin was constantly dealing with strife on the job, because he was more talented as a mechanic. Men who had a long tenure felt threatened by him. It was a complete contrast to the jovial atmosphere at a nightclub where there is laughter and dancing. It was wearing him down and me as well. Our daily conversations centered around his misery at work. We finally saw a glimpse of hope for a happier situation when Calvin received a phone call one night.

A long-time musician friend from Tennessee, who was well-known for his banjo-playing, called to invite Calvin to be a part of a new opportunity for musicians in the Smoky Mountains. Live-show theatres were beginning to evolve and Pigeon Forge, TN was expected to be the next Branson, MO. Well-known artists were beginning to open these theatres, hiring singers/musicians to perform in a family-friendly atmosphere. Mel Tillis was one of those artists who had just acquired a struggling theatre in Pigeon Forge. He had big plans that would turn this theatre around. Calvin was invited to come audition as a regular musician/singer for this venue. We saw this as a promising break in Calvin's musical career. He had been playing/singing in the nightclubs since he was 18 and now in his mid-30's, he was finally seeing hope of being discovered for his incredible talent. It was a huge leap of faith, but we decided to go for it.

He went ahead of Cody and I to audition and ensure employment, before I gave my notice at work. Not only was he hired to be in the show, but he was also chosen to be one of the lead singers. He had to report to work right away, so he stayed in Tennessee to find us a place to live, while I gave a 30-day notice at the college. On July 4, 1990, with Cody in my arms, I ventured into the unknown for new beginnings. As soon as we landed, we were whisked off to an outdoor show where Calvin was singing and playing, at a park in downtown Sevierville, TN, our new hometown. The thing that stuck out in my mind was the wholesome, friendly and family-oriented environment. It was like being at a huge family-reunion picnic. Children were playing, while adults lounged in their folding chairs or blankets. I received a warm welcome from those associated with the band. The other thing I was amazed at was the weather. In Texas, July 4th always meant desert-hot scorchers. The temperature in this atmosphere was in the mid-70's, with no strong wind. Being raised in windy West Texas, it sure felt foreign. Only a calm breeze in the bright sunshine kept the outdoor accommodations at just the right temperature. As I sat there, with my baby in my arms, watching my husband amaze the crowd with his incredible singing voice, I thought to myself, "This is what Heaven is going to be like." I was never more thankful to be where I was than in that moment. We were far away from the bar scene, the drug-infested environment and from my worries of other women who were constantly on Calvin's temptation radar.

There are so many fond memories of that summer of 1990 in Sevierville, TN. We lived in a very small two-bedroom apartment. Calvin looked diligently for a CLEAN apartment for us and was sold on a particular one. It was newly built, and we would be the first occupants. To Calvin, that meant not dealing with someone else's dirt! It was in a quaint apartment complex that looked more like a motor inn. It was a single-story structure, with only 20 units. Our new home had the clean, fresh smell of new paint, new wood and a friendly vibe. Our neighbors consisted of young couples, with small children, too. Cody had plenty of friends his own age to play with, in the small playground that was provided, on the premises. Cody made instant friends with Ben, whose mom was a stay-at-home wife and mom. She was the perfect solution to our "sitter" needs, if Calvin had to leave Cody for a while, when I was at work. Our opposite work schedules allowed us both to be his main caregivers. Soon after settling in, I got hired in the Human Resources department at Dollywood in Pigeon Forge because of my computer skills. I loved going to work because there was never a dull moment.

Most typical weeknights, Cody and I would go to the show theatre with Calvin to watch him perform in the repetitive, well-rehearsed show. The theatre was set up exactly like a movie theatre. I would grab myself some popcorn and a soda at the concession stand before finding a place to settle with a toddler. It was always early enough to grab the seat of our choice at the front of the big auditorium. I would get situated and ready to give Cody his bottle. His feeding schedule was timed purposely to keep him occupied and quiet during the show. We never got tired of the repetitive show, especially when they would introduce Calvin before his opening song. Cody never fidgeted watching his daddy perform on stage. I don't remember ever having to take him out in the lobby to avoid disturbing others. It was as if he was taking notes in his mind about his own future. Although the show was the same, the crowd was always fresh. We would witness the same reactions to his singing, each night, from a new set of spectators.

A common response from the audience was laughter because of what Cody did, EVERY time his dad would walk out on stage. Cody sat face-forward in my lap, taking his bottle. That was his routine. The show would start at just the right time, when Cody had enough milk in his belly to take a breather. As soon as the introductions were announced and the lights illuminated Calvin's face on stage, Cody would pop that bottle out of his mouth and yell, "DADDYYYYY!!" The crowd would laugh out loud every time and Calvin would usually crack a joke about it. It always got the entire show off to a great start. The director always welcomed the endearing interruption, seemingly as part of the show. I felt like I was living out Groundhog Day. Night after night, the same routine would take place right on cue. I never grew tired of those moments. Although we didn't have a lot of money, getting by with bare necessities, I felt like I was the richest woman on earth.

↑ *Don't Fall For It* ↓

Then, Fall came, and the fall happened. My world full of sunshine and rainbows was suddenly overshadowed with a storm. Mr. Tillis announced the show theatre had not turned around as quickly as he had planned and was losing revenue. So, he decided to close the theatre and Calvin was out of a job. I had cashed in my pension from the college to provide a little nest egg. We tried to put that money aside for any emergencies but instead, were forced to use it to live on. My meager salary at Dollywood helped us get by while Calvin desperately looked for steady work. In the meantime, he was able to find a gig here and there to keep food on the table. He was quickly reminded why he had moved to Texas. Texas night spots paid three-times better than the heart of country music, in Tennessee. The state was packed with talented musicians, all competing for the same gigs with the sole purpose in mind to be "discovered" in the industry. Competition was fierce and the pay was minimal. Musicians back then would play for practically nothing, just to be recognized. Calvin finally landed a steady job as a musician in a world that was going to stretch his comfort zone.

He was hired by a rock band in Knoxville, about 40 miles from Sevierville. The job would require him to be gone, three nights a week. The biggest challenge for Calvin was learning to play rock music. He was strictly a country boy with a country-music upbringing. This was a whole new world he had to discover and adapt to. The songs he was asked to lead were way above his range and he was constantly having to work on his falsetto. I remember him listening to the practice tapes and getting so frustrated. He would yank off his earphones, extend them to me and say, "Would you listen to this and see if you can make out these lyrics? I can't understand a WORD they're saying!" I would always giggle at his southern accent and old-fashioned taste. We didn't have the luxury of the internet that would've allowed us to "Google it." The new challenge stretched him, but he soon prevailed and began to attract new fans, belting out songs on the charts like, "Hot Legs" by Rod Stewart. His talent took him to a whole new level of singing . . . and other things.

I was thankful we had a decent income again. I was not so

thrilled that our past life had suddenly replaced my wholesome Utopia. Thankfully, I had befriended a lady at work who was a trustworthy sitter to keep Cody on occasional nights I went to Knoxville with Calvin. Cody loved going to stay with our new-found, surrogate family. They treated him like a grandson. She and her husband always greeted us at the door with their pet pick-a-poo, their young children to play with Cody and open arms, ready to give him a big hug. It soothed my maternal instinct to feel good about leaving him well cared for and accomplished my mission to keep Calvin under my watch. I felt pulled to go scope out any kind of possible threats to my happy marriage. Those familiar fears were back in my spirit. I needed to stay connected and on guard.

The atmosphere was so familiar; a dark, smoky nightclub setting with flowing alcohol, and musicians taking breaks between sets, outside. That meant a few tokes off a joint and other substances as well. Our past demons came back to play, and we fell right into the devil's game. The drug of choice in that town was a diet pill that had the same effect on the body as cocaine. It gave you the same rush but lasted longer and was much more affordable. Reasoning would convince me to indulge in the "less harmful", mind alteration. It helped me keep my figure, kept me alert, and kept my man interested in me. Desperate to keep any hedge from coming between us, I became a "party wife" those nights, along with the other wives, so that I would be accepted in Calvin's new world. As usual, we were able to manage our new form of recreation, still being responsible parents to our son. However, the draining routine soon became less and less fun. I DID grow tired of THIS monotonous routine, hearing Calvin play his same few lead songs, each time I went with him. I only went on occasion. It never felt right to leave Cody with a sitter, more than occasionally. Those nights home alone with my baby boy were bitter-sweet. I always felt a great sense of belonging by staying home and looking after my son, but a constant thought occupied the back of my mind. What woman was Calvin talking to? Will he come straight home, or will he linger? Will he be sober enough to drive home or will my worst nightmare happen?

↑ *Don't Fall For It* ↓

Life soon spiraled quickly into a constant state of depression for both of us. Calvin felt like a "fish out of water" in the rock music scene. I was back in the constant routine of living with the struggles and worries of other women tempting Calvin. That word of warning from the woman, the night of our engagement announcement, had come back to haunt me. I was living that life she predicted. The fear was worsened by the fact that he worked 40 miles away so that traffic could serve as an excuse for getting home late; and the club was in a hotel. I don't need to write the obvious fears I had about that. I found myself missing home. If I was going to have to relive this type of life, I wanted to be near my momma. Mom and Dad were missing Cody. I wanted to go home and so did Calvin, but we didn't see a window of opportunity to do that. Then one day my phone rang at work.

Cheri was on the other line, "I'm sorry to bother you again but we need your help." The girl they hired to replace me at the college was not exactly working out. This was the third time Cheri had called to get my guidance on previous projects I had done, which were now the new girl's responsibility. This phone call was God's perfect timing. She called when I was really missing home and just needed a little nudge to get up and go. After I was able to answer her questions, she repeated some of her frustrations with my replacement. When we were about to say our goodbye, she said, "Is there any way we can talk you into coming back?" That was music to my ears. The gate was wide open to unload my burdens of homesickness. That's all Cheri needed to hear. "Just come home, Lisa. We will find you a position." The next thing I knew, I'm hired over the phone by one of the other Vice-Presidents, who had an opening. Within two weeks, we packed up and headed west to Texas. We had all our belongings in a moving van, towing our family van, with Cody snugly secured in his makeshift "pack and play." We laughed and sang all the way home.

It felt so right being back home at the college. All my previous co-workers welcomed me back with open arms. My parents were elated we were back as well. Our old house was still available. Mom and Dad owned the home and had allowed us to rent it before. They didn't sell the house when we left, but instead rented it to my uncle. The timing was perfect, as he had planned to move out of town at the very same time we were coming home. Every piece of the puzzle was falling in and fitting perfectly. There was only one piece, that last piece of the puzzle that was always dropped on the floor, making the puzzle flawed and incomplete. Calvin accepted the club's invitation to go back to work, singing and playing in the band. I reasoned; it was better than the situation we just left. He is still playing in the bars, but now he is 5 minutes away from home and I have hometown people in my corner, for support.

Life quickly became as though we had never left 9 months prior. We settled back into the routine of Calvin keeping Cody in the daytime, while I worked my 40-hour/week job. I had Cody on my own for just the 3 nights a week, while Calvin worked his night job. Once again, he was very respectful in satisfying my need for him to keep us first on his list of priorities. He would be home 5 minutes from the time the club closed. My husband was doing everything he could to relieve any insecurities I had about his love for me. He promised there would be "no repeats" of the late nights, working past club hours.

All the benefits I was enjoying in my marriage caused me to overlook the danger signs of what was down the road. I began noticing when Calvin came home from the club, it would take him a while to go to sleep, even when it was 2:00 am. He was the type that had to have someone to talk to. I was always barely awake, just long enough to welcome him home. He would get on the phone and call a friend from "back home" in Chattanooga, TN to talk for hours before he would come to bed, about the time the sun would come up. At first, I accredited it to just the adrenaline of excitement of being in a "party atmosphere." Soon, my eyes started waking up to the realization that Calvin was using cocaine again. The temptation was as strong as the supply was available, within the environment he worked in.

Life became more stressful as his habit returned. It put him in a whirlwind of indulgence, extreme guilt, emotional distress, declarations of quitting, then back to another hit. The cycle would repeat. He became emotionally draining. He frequently called me at work; and always when I was the busiest. As soon as I answered, I would hear startling panic on the other end, saying "I'm having a bad day! You've got to cheer me up!" It became exhausting and burdensome. Thankfully, Mom was able to be Cody's full-time daycare provider, so I didn't have to worry about him being alone with an addict. It was a perfect situation because Mom was employed at the college as the women's dorm supervisor. She and dad lived in an apartment in the dorm, and I could walk across campus at any time to tend to Cody, or just go for a visit. It was a perfect situation for Cody too. He had about 150 "big sisters" who were always anxious to play with him. Obviously, my parents didn't know what was really going on at home. I made excuses for Calvin like any good, co-dependent wife was supposed to do.

Calvin started coming home, later and later, from work at the club. When I questioned him about his whereabouts for the delay in getting home, he would have a good excuse ready. The longer this routine went on, the more suspicious I became. The more suspicious I became in my interrogation, the more defensive he became. He would explode in offended anger for my accusations, and I would retreat apologetically for doubting him. This vicious cycle finally came to a head where I put my foot down about him staying at the club too long after closing time. We came to a truce, and he vowed the late nights would stop. That lasted no time.

I remember the night of the final blow to our marriage like it was yesterday. It was a Saturday night and while he was getting ready for work, the phone rang. From his end of the conversation, I could make out that "J.J." was on the other end, inviting him to an "after-party" when the club closed that night. I always marveled at the irony of J.J.. As I mentioned earlier, J.J. was the heartthrob I dated briefly back in my "looking for love" days in my early twenties. As fate would have it, he had now become friends with Calvin. We attended barbeques at his ranch on several occasions. J.J. and his brother attended our wedding. Your past can always circle around to look you in the face, when you live in a small town.

As soon as Calvin hung up from his conversation with J.J., I presented him with a stern ultimatum, "You can go to that party and come home to an empty house, or you can come home at closing time to your family. Your choice." There was no denying what I was sensing in that conversation. He took my warning very seriously and promised me with every sincere bone in his body that I had nothing to fear; he would be home. I felt so confident in his promise that I didn't bother waiting up to watch the clock. I knew I would feel him climb into bed around 2:00 a.m. To my shock and horror, I rolled over in the middle of the night to find his side vacant, and the clock was shining 4:00 a.m. I shot out of bed as if I had heard a gunshot go off. I did hear one, but only in my heart. When I discovered he wasn't anywhere in the house, I couldn't believe it. He broke his promise KNOWING how serious I was! Does he take me for that big of a fool? I paced around my house for a while and decided I had to follow through with my threat. I put an escape plan together and began to execute.

I went in and packed Cody and I an overnight bag, but I didn't leave the house yet. Waking up a baby at this time of day did not feel right. So, I began to plan a strategic plan. I wanted Calvin to see my face before I walked out on him. I sat on the couch while I let Cody sleep soundly, snuggled in his bed. I watched the clock strike 5:00 a.m., 6:00 a.m. and the black sky was beginning to turn a lighter shade of grey. I finally heard the back door open and shut ever so gently, as if he was trying his best not to wake me up. His surprised, guilty expression with wide-eyed dilated pupils, told me all I needed to know. I was sitting on the couch with my suitcase beside me.

"What are you doing up?" he tried with a nonchalant greeting.

"What are you doing breaking your promise?" I fired back. As he started in with his list of excuses, I let him get through the list and then hit him with a bombshell. "Well . . . sorry you had such a long night, but you had better get some sleep. The baby should be getting up around 8:00, according to what time he went to bed." I grabbed my bags and walked out of the house. He didn't even try to stop me. He knew he had no recourse. He may have been in a slight state of shock that I followed through with my threat this time.

As soon as I got into the car and drove out of the driveway, I called Mom and Dad to let them know I was coming over and I spilled the ugly truth about our circumstances. I knew Cody was going to be safe long enough for me to get there and then send Dad over to retrieve Cody, before he woke up. My well-thought-out plan to protect Cody from being in the middle of a tug-of-war battle was executed with great success. I was expecting the worst and strategized accordingly. I wanted to give Calvin a wake-up call to remind him, he is still a dad with responsibilities, and he is not exempt from that just because he decides to party all night. I wanted him to panic even though it would be for a very short time. Dad confirmed my plan had worked when he was back with Cody in no time, still sleeping in Granddad's arms. I knew Calvin would not try to cross my dad. He reported that Calvin was SURE GLAD to see him, eagerly and thankfully handed Cody over to him, with a look of relief. I'm sure he was fearful of being in charge in the state of mind he was in.

However, Calvin wasn't relieved at the note Dad was instructed to give him, as he left with Cody. Dad said Calvin's face dropped as he handed the note to him, but Dad did not stick around to witness his reaction. A very concise message was written in my handwriting, "We are now officially separated. You have until 5:00 p.m. today to get yourself and all your belongings out of my parents' house. Lisa."

Calvin obliged my demands and left the house with a peaceful retreat. As he stayed with Linda and J.R., I remained in the home we had set up for Cody. We strived to keep things as normal as possible for Cody to remain in a stable environment. Calvin and I celebrated Cody's 3rd birthday as a separated couple, but ever-present parents at his party. As a three-year-old, Cody had only enough realization to ask me on the other days, "Where's Dad?" That small question stabbed at my heart every time and all I could muster was, "Dad's working." I knew that this toddler was smarter than my excuses and my answer was not going to suffice for him long.

It was one of those times I look back on today and realize Jesus was so close in ordering my steps, teaching me how to protect my son. His divine plan had me working closely with the Dean of Counseling, Harvey, at the college, during this season. In prior years, Harvey and I were co-workers in the same division, and we developed a bond. He was like a second dad to me and a great mentor. I had known him for many years, since he was also my high school counselor. With a Master's degree in psychology and a licensed professional counselor, Harvey was well-known as the "one to go to" for free counseling, among all the staff at the college. His warm and welcoming demeanor always made a person feel safe and free to unload their burdens, for his expert advice. I don't know how I would have managed my life at that time, had I not had Harvey to lean on. He gave me such great advice. He taught me the stages of childhood development and how to use the right words to help Cody cope with the situation. So, I began to answer Cody's question with, "Daddy is close by and he loves you so much."

Years later, I eventually went to work in the counseling area and remained there, after receiving my bachelor's degree, working as an academic advisor under Harvey's supervision. It was obviously God's Divine Plan to keep me close to Harvey for several years, as he helped me navigate through some of the roughest seasons of my life. God strategically placed Harvey in my life for the emotional health of Cody and my future child. Harvey was my cheerleader and was very instrumental in encouraging me to go back to school. He was my parenting coach and was one of my very best friends, who always had a listening ear and words of extreme wisdom. One piece of advice he would emphasize almost daily was extremely valuable. "Whatever you do, Lisa, NEVER criticize your boys' dads in front of them. Children do not need to be involved in grown-up affairs. Let them be children and no matter what the dads throw at you, you take the high road. When the boys become adults, they will figure things out themselves and they will have so much respect for you when they realize you protected them." Harvey could have had his own talk show way before Dr. Phil came on the scene.

The tragic ending to my love story with Calvin was inevitable. We tried separating and sharing Cody in two different households.

We tried working out our problems with the hope of reconciling, but the problems only multiplied. I truly thought that in giving Calvin a "wake-up call," he would finally realize how much he had hurt me, by staying out late. I knew he wasn't being unfaithful, but the party life, without me by his side, was disrespectful and inappropriate. That's all I was trying to get across to him. The more we would try to talk things out, the darker things got, with no light at the end of the tunnel. Bottom line – Calvin was still using drugs. That root problem was in the equation and there seemed to be no hope for a solution. Cocaine alters a person's brain, personality and reasoning. It had to be dealt with first, for any possibility of a reconciliation. However, he remained in denial and, therefore, we remained separated.

A small town has its perks, and it also has its downfalls. The biggest downfall is the "grapevine." Everyone knows everyone else and their business. The town started buzzing as soon as word got out that we were separated. I started getting one shocking phone call after another, along with comments from mutual friends who I ran into. "I'm so sorry to hear about you and Calvin. I guess you finally found out about him and (insert a different girl's name)." With each phone call or personal encounter, I would get an unsolicited report of him being with a different girl. I wanted to scream, "NO! I DIDN'T find out, until now! He was just staying out too late, that's all!" I was now dealing with a familiar demon, infidelity, to pile on to our problems. I would confront him with each claim, and he would blatantly deny it every single time.

A particular girl kept coming up, in the flood of reports. More than just a few people knew about her. I finally decided to confront him about it, one night when he came over for family time. After Cody was asleep, I explained my latest conversation with reports about this girl. He denied it again, claiming she was just a friend and respects my marriage. I knew that was a lie, when I saw the look on his face as I offered my rebuttal. "Ok, I will let this go, after she confirms that to me," as I walked toward the telephone. Back then, we had the luxury of phone books, where residents' phone numbers were listed. I could see the wheels turning in his head, trying to figure out how to talk himself out of this one. He stood over me as I picked up the phone, dialed the number and waited for her to answer. She remained silent as I told her who I was and why I was calling. I made it clear I was not calling to make threats or to blame her in any way. I made the sincere plea to her that I just needed the truth, to know where I needed to go next. I explained my marriage was at a crossroads and I needed help deciding which road to take. My plea touched her compassion. When my speech was over, she replied in a meek, sympathetic voice, "Yes, Lisa, it's true. We have been having an affair, but I can assure you he loves you. There is just some kind of void he is trying to fill." It was the bombshell I dreaded and hoped would be disarmed with a different answer. As my heart sank, my anger rose, and my expression prompted Calvin to snatch the phone receiver from my hand. He began to shout obscenities at this girl, accusing her of being a liar. It did not calm the burning rage in me. Any shred of doubt I was hanging on to, about the rumors, were completely ripped from my grasp. I couldn't even speak as high amounts of adrenaline ran through my body. I could barely whisper the words, "Get out. Just please get OUT!" As Calvin left the house in compliance, I couldn't even comprehend the words he was saying as he walked out.

I felt my legs buckle underneath me, the moment I heard the back door shut. I literally slid down the wall until my butt hit the floor. All I could do was stare out into the darkness, through the bay window of my kitchen. The wall kept me propped up as my "sleeping bunk" in those sleepless hours. It felt like only a few minutes had passed when I saw the sun breaking through the horizon. I suddenly realized I had been sitting on my kitchen floor, staring out the bay window all night long, in shock. The life I had dreamed of and thought I was living, was now officially over. I had to keep the promise I had made 4 years ago when I accepted his proposal. He blew the final chance he didn't even have. I filed for divorce the next week.

The next major event in our saga was Calvin declaring he would get clean and checked himself into a very well-known drug rehabilitation center in south Texas. I was very grateful for that

↑ Don't Fall For It ↓

decision, but I was not budging from my decision to end the marriage. I had too much anger in me to let him off the hook that easily. I was on my rampage of revenge. He was destined to hurt as much as I hurt.

About two weeks into Calvin's recovery program, I got a call from his sponsor, urging me to come to the week-long family counseling session scheduled for his final week in the program. I agreed to go but made it clear, "I am in full support of Calvin's sobriety for the sake of our child, but the divorce will still take place." To my humble surprise, my words were soon my supper. The 5-day "Family Week" proved to be extremely therapeutic for me as well as Calvin. We received 40 hours of extensive counseling, and I was able to work through MOST of my anger and mistrust. By the end of the week, I agreed to put the divorce on hold and give our marriage another try. We left there hopeful, but I had some very high stipulations Calvin was going to have to meet in order to keep me as his wife.

It did not take long for the hidden wounds to surface. The same arguments became the topics of our conversation, night after night. Calvin attended AA meetings while I went to the adjoining Al-Anon meetings for the family members of the addict. It was a pleasant little routine, but it didn't offer the extensive therapy we needed to put our marriage back together. We certainly didn't seek the ultimate Counselor, the Holy Spirit, whom we needed most, as an opportunity for Him to speak from the heart of God. The Holy Spirit's invitation to guide our union would've been a HUGE game changer! Unfortunately, neither of us thought to ask our Helper for the help we desperately needed.

We grew more and more angry at one another and even more tired of fighting. Our flesh had full control and so we feasted on each other's resentments. The argument that sealed the deal was a heated discussion about Calvin going back to work, at the club. I was against it, knowing what the recovery program had taught us. The addict needs to stay away from triggers in order to keep from relapsing. There would be triggers all around him in that environment. I was worried about the female triggers more than the drugs, in all honesty. In the heat of the argument, I demanded that if he went back to the club, I was going to get a job as the host at the door. Cody could stay with Gigi and Grandad on the weekends. His response was all it took for the final curtain call.

"If you think I'm going to come sit under your thumb every break and not make my rounds at the tables, you are mistaken!"

The truth was I wanted him under my thumb, in my constant sight and to spend the rest of his life paying for breaking his proposal promise to me. We both were so emotionally damaged. There was just no glimpse of hope in having an emotionally stable reconciliation. We finally gave up and I reopened the divorce proceedings. It was a very tumultuous divorce. Calvin was getting to drink the bitter taste of "Kharma", as he was forced to watch me march in my parade of getting even in keeping my promise of an instant divorce.

Calvin wasn't the only one I was furious at. God was hot on my list of foes. How could He let this happen? I'd been a good wife and an even better momma! I felt like I didn't deserve this storm. What I didn't realize then was that church is just a building you go to. It is called the House of God, but you'll never sense His presence, if you're not talking to Him during the week. We can be just like the Israelites. We can get so far from Who we should worship. We tend to grumble in our sense of entitlement, trying to depend on ourselves and worshipping idols. My idol was finding a substitute for Jesus. I thought a man was my only hope to experience love, joy, peace, kindness, goodness, patience, faithfulness and most of all self-control!

God inspired the Holy Bible as our true compass to live out our life in accordance to His word and then He gives us free will to make decisions for ourselves. So, in the midst of my sinful nature, my beliefs were in error to think that it was God's will for me to be with a partner who used street drugs and slept around. God's will was put on the back burner in a relationship where we never opened the Bible, except at Church. At home, Jesus was just the topic of a FEW conversations during our courtship and marriage. EVEN STILL, when we choose the wrong path, God is FAITHFUL to take what the enemy meant for evil and turn it for good. God had a good plan for my union with Calvin. He created Jay Cody, and our lives were sanctified through his life. God, in His infinite wisdom, already had a plan to bring Cody into the world. This world needs more Jesus-loving Cody's, and no matter how determined we were to ruin our own lives, God's plan to use Cody for His glory would not be stopped.

Coming out of that hurtful ending to a tumultuous marriage, you think I would have learned to make better decisions. Not yet! I was still a "stiff-necked" believer. This is what God called the Israelites. History was repeating itself with God having to deal with me in the wilderness too.

I was no different. I knew all about church, but I had no idea who Jesus really was. I would go to church to check off my Christian box. I should have listened more closely to the sermons, instead of daydreaming about my love life. If I had taken church seriously, I might have heard that in this world, I would have trouble and Jesus is the One Friend I could have run to with all my hurt, anger and pain. Instead, I rebelled against God and chose to go my own way – worshiping a golden calf in the form of my next expedition in finding the man of my dreams. All the while, I kept wearing the cloaks of anger, mistrust, and revenge.

Once again, the town was buzzing with the latest episodes of our saga and my divorce continued to be the topic. I was still getting many phone calls, but this time there were frequent ones I welcomed from one particular person.

CHAPTER NINE
A MAD-DASH INTO REVENGE

"For the anger of man does not produce the righteousness of God." ~ James 1:20

As soon as our divorce hit the gossip fences of our small town, I began to get frequent phone calls from "J.J.", the heartthrob I mentioned in the previous chapter. My past was now calling *me* to party with him, *instead of Calvin*. J.J. grew up in my hometown. He was from a well-known, multi-generational ranching family, raising cattle and leasing land for oil production. J.J. was labeled in the single circle as "the most eligible bachelor who was impossible to snag." To say he was "a looker" (West Texas term for handsome) was an understatement. He had piercing ice-blue eyes, brown wavy hair, a muscular build, and a gentle demeanor that made every girl swoon. I was introduced to him in my early twenties, following my first divorce. His stepmom was my "wing man" as she was my supervisor at the college, for a short season. She was married to J.J.'s father, his second wife, and they were convinced J.J. needed to settle down and it needed to be with me. I was the "perfect match" in their eyes, to tame the "wild" in J.J. and make him more responsible. After only dating for a short time, J.J. decided "I was too good for him." I think that was his nice way of saying, I was too boring for him. I was still very "green" from living 8 years in a controlled environment with my abuser. J.J. was much more worldly and liked living on the edge. He dated several women before, and lived with a few as well.

↑ Don't Fall For It ↓

I had only been with one man during this time. He was also a party boy. Our differences were too great for me to be able to convince him to settle down.

What a difference a few years on a long journey can make.

During Round 1 of our courtship in my earlier years, the road he was on was alluring to me. It looked glamourous and FUN! That glimpse was enough to intrigue me to go and see what this "party life" was all about. This is why it was easy for Calvin to lure me into trying marijuana and cocaine for the first time. It seemed harmless when done in moderation. That "dabble" into darkness sent me on a journey that would take me right back to J.J.. This time though, I was more seasoned to be his type. I, too, had "partied like him" before. I wasn't so green anymore. I was a mom now and I soon found out he was on the sideline watching throughout my marriage with Calvin. He observed, through the lens of friendship, seeing that I had become his perfect balance. He saw that I was a responsible mom and loyal wife, but I also liked to have fun when given the perfect scenario. NOW, I was finally the kind of girl J.J. went for. The timing of him wanting to settle down, while I was now a little more exciting to hang with became the perfect scenario in our eyes.

Ironically, when I met Calvin, he and J.J. had become running buddies, as stated earlier. Calvin knew I had dated J.J. several years prior and I almost felt as if Calvin was "keeping his enemies close." I detected a streak of jealousy when J.J.'s name came up, but Calvin is the one who kept him in our circle of friends. Back then, it never crossed my mind that one day, I would be dating him again. J.J. was the perfect antidote for my burning anger toward Calvin.

Back to current events. My heart would pound every time I heard his voice on the other end. In the initial conversations, he would tell me he was so sorry that I was going through a tough time. He would emphasize that we were friends before Calvin was ever in the picture, so his devotion leaned toward me. Although he was the one who invited Calvin to his party that fateful night, he had no idea of the marital problems we were having. He swore Calvin never brought other women to his house and if he had he would have kicked them out. J.J. was a serious person and I believed he was telling me the truth. He offered any support I needed to get me through this valley of heartache. Eventually, he started inviting Cody and I to come over for dinner, and other times to join him with friends who had children Cody's age, to play with. They began as friendly outings of support. The grown-ups would play our favorite boardgame, "Wahoo", while the kids would play in their own child-friendly space. I would watch and admire how J.J. interacted with Cody. He beamed with adoration as he talked about his dreams of having a son of his own, one day. The friend zone soon began to narrow into the courtship path. One profound statement he made one night sealed the deal. "You know, when I watched you walk down the aisle to marry Calvin at your wedding, I realized at that moment I let the right one get away."

So, in the blink of an eye, my divorce was final with Calvin, and I immediately went on my first official date with J.J.. I took no time, nor gave myself room to grow and heal from my recent divorce. This was a much safer and more familiar road, for the time being. I wanted the microwaved meal of healing, instead of the slow-baste, worth-the-wait, tasty meal that would TRULY satisfy my hunger. I gravitated toward another man, instead of the Son of Man.

As I've said, in those days I was only a believer, not a true follower of Christ. I had no idea that I could've run straight into the arms of my Savior to give HIM all my hurt and anger. Instead, I rebelled against God, and ran straight into the arms of a man that my flesh could not resist. I ran with my big bag of expectations to put on him, too. He now had the job to "fix broken Lisa" and make her perfectly happy. It has always been a big job for all my men. They had to be substitutes for Jesus. BIG SHOES that were impossible to fill.

If I had been on the Dr. Phil show, I would've heard that famous question, "So, how did that work out for you?" I certainly wasn't showing a lot of wisdom in most areas of my life. However, the one area that was incubated with protection from the Lord was with Cody. I am thankful God put earth angels in my path to help me navigate through my issues and make good decisions when it came to my son. I am so, SO thankful for my village at church and my workplace that ministered to us both.

The courtship with J.J. began a bit slow, but we eventually grew closer and began dating exclusively, almost three months into our relationship. I soon discovered that J.J. had a completely different side to him than what his "playboy" reputation depicted. J.J. was pretty much a homebody. He loved to cook, and he loved to entertain friends. To my surprise and delight, he wasn't one who liked to frequent the local nightclubs. His idea of a good time was hanging out with family and close friends in a house, instead of fighting large crowds in a loud bar. So, our social life centered around house parties where there was entertainment for all ages. The adults would play cards, board games, and enjoy "adult beverages", while the children played together in their designated play areas. Everyone enjoyed staying in and keeping the kids close, rather than going out and dealing with babysitters. I was starting to see a promising future with a man who displayed strong family values. The fact he was drop-dead gorgeous was a huge bonus.

It was not a perfect picture by any means, but at this time, I thought it was close. Our life was simple, steady and beginning to look more and more like a married couple. We never talked about marriage, but my days became predictable, with him frequently inviting Cody and I over on weeknights for dinner and some television. His guest room began to transform into Cody's playroom. The routine continued every weekend, hanging out with his close friends and siblings with children. Life was fun. I was dating the "heart throb of the town", and Cody was getting to play with kids his own age. We were plunged into this circle of affluent families, big homes with expensive taste and tasting the "good life."

J.J. and I were becoming very close friends, but something was missing. We weren't getting to the point of saying, "I love you." Our conversations remained on the surface, with superficial topics. J.J. was a hard nut to crack. He didn't like expressing his feelings or he didn't know how to. So, his true feelings for me remained a mystery for the entire time of our courtship. We were content with our "fun friendship, with benefits." We had lots of fun if we were with a group of friends. Alone time became awkward and silent. We struggled with conversation because J.J. was a man of few words. He tended to be moody as well and I soon realized he suffered from depression.

Eighteen months flew by, and I began to wonder if the relationship was really going anywhere. I began to consider the possibility that maybe this wasn't exactly where I should be. Party time had been fun, but I was over the feeling of wanting to get revenge on Calvin. I started entertaining the idea that it was time to call it quits on this relationship where marriage was never discussed, Jesus was never the topic of discussion, and the "L" word was never spoken. It was becoming the mundane world of convenience, without any depth. I began to plan the conversation in my head on how I was going to break it off. I felt it would be a mutual and amicable breakup as I assumed he felt the same way I did.

Instead . . . another wave of change headed for my boat and changed my direction. I found out I was pregnant with our child. I had made a big bed for myself that I was now having to lie in, with another human life involved. J.J. had made it so clear how badly he wanted a child in previous conversations. He even tried to convince me to quit taking my birth control pills, but I wasn't convinced that was a good idea at all. Then, I came down with Strep throat and the strong antibiotic I was given interfered with the effects of the pill. So, here I was at the crossroads of my rebellion and not sure which direction was right. The only good side was that I had no fear whatsoever in giving him the good news. I was pretty sure he would be thrilled with the news and almost certain a proposal would quickly follow. I talked myself into putting a breakup out of my mind and was becoming excited about being a mom of two. Cody was growing out of the "cuddling" stage and my momma arms were beginning to ache for another baby to swaddle. To be perfectly honest, I wasn't as thrilled at the thought of becoming his wife. I knew I loved him, but this love felt different than the love I had for Calvin. However, this relationship was MUCH more STABLE than my relationship with Calvin. All I needed to fall deeply in love with J.J. was intimate conversations. Then it would've been a perfect situation. Infidelity was never involved, so I trusted J.J. completely. I was attracted to him; any right-minded girl would be. I reasoned that we could grow closer in time and have more meaningful communication that came so easily for Calvin and me. Like I said, J.J. was just not a big talker and Calvin didn't know when to shut up!

It was only two weeks before Father's Day when I took a pregnancy test and confirmed with a physician it was accurate. So, I thought it was a cute way to tell J.J. by asking him, "What do you want for Father's Day?" He looked at me with a puzzled expression. Then I pulled out the positive pregnancy test. He picked me up and whirled me around in celebration. It was another scene like one of those romantic comedies I loved to watch.

Then, dark clouds formed, and the rain came. When I asked him what was next, he again looked puzzled. So, I mentioned marriage in a round-about way. That's when thunder and lightning hit. His response was, "I am very excited we are having a baby, but I'm not so sure I'm ready for marriage." Wow. The answer I wasn't expecting but the answer I deserved after battling the very same feeling. The battle in *my* mind was already over and the idea of marriage had won. I did not want to be an unwed mother. I wasn't about to abort this baby either, so I was prepared to say "yes" to J.J.'s proposal. The joke was on me.

In those days, pregnancy out of wedlock was very much frowned upon and a popular topic for town gossip. My first and biggest fear was losing my job. I had recently been promoted to serve as Director of Community Relations at the college. I was the "face of Howard College to the public", as I was told in my interview. My duty was marketing the college and I was out in the community frequently. I would be representing a community college that is grounded in Christian values, as an unwed pregnant 33-year-old, who should know better. Talk about character assassination!

This is where my 16-month plot of revenge left me; stranded on a deserted island, having a baby outside the confines of marriage. Luckily, I wasn't a consistent churchgoer at this time (about a once-a-month Christian), so I didn't have to confess to a church family. However, I still had my own family and employer to break the news to. I felt like I was a pregnant teenager again, dreading telling my parents. Instead of facing them, I wrote my parents a letter to ease the blow with my uninterrupted thoughts, emotions, and apologies. I couldn't bear to see the look on their faces, even though I was living independently and free to make my own adult decisions. They were already not too thrilled about me dating J.J. in the first place. His playboy reputation from years back made them cautious. I will never forget the phone call from Dad after he read my letter. The caller ID machine alerted me that he was on the other end of that telephone ring, and I braced myself for the worst. Instead, I heard, "Baby Daughter (short pause) . . . I am SO PROUD of you for not choosing an abortion!" I had never felt so much relief in my life. Throughout ALL of my misguided decisions in my life, they never failed to support me through whatever pit I jumped into.

My supervisors at the college were just as supportive and I was assured my job was not in jeopardy, probably because it could have been a lawsuit. Then again, my supervisor and co-workers were like family too. Even with this type of unconditional love surrounding me, the heartache of putting my sins "more on display" with each passing month, weighed heavily on my emotions and my spirit. I imagined I was still the subject of whispers behind my back. I felt embarrassed and began to grow resentful for having to bear this burden alone. I felt so alone. J.J. could go to work on his family's ranch and never talk to anyone about our situation. Meanwhile, I was constantly on public display with an increasingly growing belly as my spotlight. I just buried myself in work and tried not to think about it. Luckily, this pregnancy was even easier than with Cody. I continued to teach step aerobics part-time, which was something I had done for years. Students could earn a 1-hour PE credit for taking my class at the college. My big belly fooled them into thinking I would go easy on them. I saw surprised faces of regret when I directed them into high-impact aerobics while performing high kicks and jumps, toting a baby in my belly.

Simply for convenience, J.J. was insistent that we move in together, but an engagement was still not in the plans for this new arrival. He was extremely protective over our baby, making sure I ate right and abstained from any kind of decision that could potentially be harmful. I began to feel more like a baby factory than his life partner and companion. Yet he still "courted" me, like bringing home flowers frequently and being a caring facilitator to any of my needs. I still couldn't shake the resentment toward him, refusing to make me an honest woman. I started making plans to leave him after the baby was born and we could work out a mutual agreement to co-parent our child, under separate roofs. We could just go back to being good friends who happened to have a child together. That was the obvious path to take.

I had just gotten used to that idea when J.J. "threw in a wrench" during my 2nd trimester. He started bringing up the subject of marriage, but not an official marriage proposal. By this time, my stubborn hard-headedness refused. "Let him taste his own medicine and see how it feels to be rejected". Living as a single mom afforded me the benefit of a substantial tax credit on my income tax return. So, my excuse was, I didn't want to mess that up by changing my marital status before the tax year ended. With reluctance on my end, we decided to get married on January 7th, a little shy of a month before the baby was due. I could have easily bailed and figured out plan B, but there was one thing that told me to say yes. Our child deserved to come into the world with married parents, where his name would never need an explanation. He deserved to have his birthright and my selfish decisions could not get in the way of his heritage.

At this stage, we knew we were having a boy and began to search for the perfect name for him. Unlike Cody's pregnancy, we *did* want to know beforehand. I still remember the day we had the sonogram to determine what gender the baby was. J.J.'s sister, Diana, was the nurse for the doctor who was caring for my prenatal needs. I remember her joking, "Come on and let it be a girl. Cody doesn't need any competition!" J.J.'s family considered Cody family, as if he were blood kin. When we found out we were having another boy, J.J. was beside himself. I've never seen a man look prouder and more excited. This new addition was going to be the first male child, born in the family's next generation. All other siblings, cousins, etc. who bore the family name, had girls. So far, this was their only hope to carry on the family name. The family realized he would probably be the last addition, since all the child-bearing relatives were quickly growing past that stage.

Even though there was not a "proposal" to remember, only a new topic of conversation, I do remember shopping for the 2-Karat diamond ring. That is a fond memory. J.J. had already bought a loose high-quality marque diamond and we went to a jeweler to design the setting it would go in. This was the first time I really felt like his fiancé. It was a special time selecting the perfect ring that would be one of a kind. J.J. had an artistic side to him, and it was fun creating together a masterpiece of the marque diamond surrounded with baguette diamonds in a raised white gold setting. It served as my engagement ring as well as my wedding ring and I wore it proudly. Finally, I didn't feel the embarrassment because strangers would see that I'm pregnant with a wedding ring on my finger. Life became easier in that regard. My anger subsided and my resentment vanished. I knew I was entering into a marriage of convenience where the "L" word was yet to be exchanged. However, I was starting to fall in love with J.J.; but I was too proud to say it first, not knowing how he felt.

I was eight months pregnant when J.J. and I made our vows before God and our immediate family, in the home of his big sister. The minister at our church was a very loving and gracious man. He conducted our pre-marital counseling and officiated a sweet ceremony. It was very intimate and full of loving affirmations from the people we were closest to. A reception immediately followed at the local restaurant that our closest friends owned. During the drive to the restaurant, we had our first meaningful conversation as J.J. kept calling me by my newly married name. "Lisa Dee Currie – that has a nice ring, doesn't it? Never thought I would ever get married and I'm so happy it's with you," were his sweet words of affirmation. An "I love you Lisa", would've made it even sweeter, but I never heard that.

Upon our arrival at the restaurant, we were greeted with a room full of supportive friends and extended family. It was a touching experience seeing my co-workers and our friends congratulating us with hugs and smiles. However, an uneasiness still stirred deep within me. I was able to hide my fear behind a big belly and a painted-on face. The more we were congratulated, the more my anxiety level rose. No matter how much you love a man, a "gunshot wedding" will still make you jumpy. I felt like a volcano, brewing for eruption. Eventually I found myself locked in the bathroom, breathing heavily into a paper bag to calm my anxiety attack. It was an episode completely undiscovered by anyone else. Our guests were oblivious to the fact that the bride may have been a runaway, if she only had herself and Cody to think about. The future still seemed very uncertain. It was obvious this marriage was founded on "fondness and friendship" and the mutual love for our unborn child. Was that enough to build a lifelong commitment on? I had serious doubts. I had no idea what I was in for. The road ahead was so unsure with this "heartthrob crush," who I wasn't convinced, was really in love with me. Is marriage without love enough? I wasn't sure this was God's will.

One month later, on February 2, 1994, Groundhog Day, William Jon came into the world. Much of my anxiety settled when we laid eyes on our eight-pound healthy baby boy for the very first time. His big round blue eyes and blond hair melted our hearts. My heart went from brim full to overflowing, now as a mom of two precious little boys I had always dreamt of. The first time Cody, at age 4, laid eyes on William will forever be engraved in my heart. He was so excited to have a baby brother to play with.

Will's entrance into the world also involved a miracle. This event also convinced me what a great dad J.J. was going to be. Our doctor was a close friend of the family, being the boss of "Aunt Diana" – J.J.'s sister. The whole town knew all the quirks about Dr.

Bruce Cox. We called him Bruce, as a close family friend. He had a very "crazy" bedside manner; very hyper and always cutting jokes more than giving medical advice, at least with us. He also had a reputation for being the most accurate diagnostician in the region. He graduated in the top 3 of his class in medical school. So, in other words, his brilliance made him exceptional with a personality to match!

J.J. was heavily involved in showing his club steers in the major stock shows circuit with his niece, Natalie – Diana's only daughter – all over Texas. It was in the heart of this season when Will was due. I was 2 weeks away from my due date, when J.J. left in the evening on a Sunday night to drive to Fort Worth. The best plan was to drive all night to get to the stock show yard as early as possible, to get in line for check in. That way, he could pick his ideal spot to prepare his steer.

Meanwhile, I had my usual checkup the next Monday morning. When Bruce went through his usual check-up routine, asking me several questions, he became UNGLUED at my answer to this usual question. "Is the baby moving and kicking good?" I replied, "Actually, come to think of it, he's been kind of still." He fired back, "WHAT?! What do you mean he's STILL? When is the last time you felt him move, Lisa?"

Me: "I think it was yesterday morning."

Bruce: "YESTERDAY MORNING???"

Me: "Bruce calm down, I'm sure it's ok! He's probably just settling into the birth canal!"

Bruce: (yelling loud enough for the entire lobby of patients to hear) "WHO IS THE DOCTOR, LISA? DON'T TELL ME TO CALM DOWN!! DO YOU WANT TO DELIVER A DEAD BABY?"

Wow. That surely got my attention. Bruce was extremely emotional because he had, in fact, delivered a stillborn just a few days prior. He demanded, "Don't even think about going back to work. You are going straight to the hospital to be put on a baby monitor."

I reluctantly agreed, thinking he was overreacting. Babies start getting less active when they are ready to be born, right? That's what I had always heard. Sure enough, when I was hooked up to the monitor at the hospital, it was discovered that Will was in fetal distress. His heartbeat was strong, but very unstable. The OB nurses concluded he was either laying on his cord, or it was wrapped around his neck. Dr. Cox immediately scheduled an emergency delivery for 7:00 a.m. the next morning. Today, I know it was Holy Spirit that guided Bruce to take this situation seriously. Will was laying on his cord, and if I had waited the remaining two weeks to deliver him, Will would not be in this world, or could've been severely disabled with lack of oxygen to his brain. Satan tried – God won.

Little did I know, during all the commotion, that J.J. was having a terrible day that Monday. The alternator in his truck died as he was sitting in line at the stock show yard, before the sun even came up. After checking in, with the help of other participants, he had it towed to a mechanic. It took them most of the day to get it running again and he did not get checked in to his motel room until around 9:00 that night. This explained why I couldn't reach him all day to let him know we were going to have a baby the next morning at 7:00 a.m. I called his motel room several times to leave a message, "J.J. – please call me back. There's been a new development and Bruce is delivering Will tomorrow!" I was beginning to worry about him as well, because I knew as soon as he heard that message, he would be calling!

When he did finally called back, he sounded excited, but also extremely exhausted, "Thank God for Bruce!" was his repeated declaration several times. J.J. was going on over 36 hours of no sleep. The original plan was to set up his steer, after being up since Sunday morning and then crash at his hotel room for a good long nap. His alternator spoiled those plans. That didn't stop J.J.'s determination to see his son being born. He got back in his truck to drive 4 hours back to our hometown. I remember him climbing into bed around 3:00 a.m. and it seemed like 30 minutes later when the alarm went off at 6:00. Luckily, Will's delivery was quick. Bruce induced my labor at

7:15 and Will was born around 10:45 a.m. J.J.'s adrenaline of being a new dad provided enough alert energy to get back in the truck around 12 noon, drive back to Fort Worth and continue his plan to compete in the Stock show. The man went about 48 hours with no sleep on this memorable week. This was my very first acknowledgement of J.J. being a tremendously dedicated and loving father to Will.

Life settled into a family of four and it was stable, predictable and comfortable. We bought a large house out in the country where the boys each had their own bedroom and a spare bedroom for overnight company. They also had 10 acres to run and play. On the anniversary of our 1st year of marriage, J.J. finally told me he was in love with me. I told him back. Ironically, this "most eligible bachelor and city playboy" proved to be the most faithful, trustworthy man I had ever been involved with. I never had to wonder where he was, or what he was doing, because he was always at home or at the ranch.

J.J. loved our home life and proved to be a faithful husband and dedicated father to both boys. He loved to play with the kids and dabble in his favorite hobby. He continued to raise champion show steers on the back of our 10-acre land to compete in stock shows every year with Natalie. He was an animal lover, so we always had at least one momma dog and several litters of puppies to give away. He embraced every holiday. J.J. LOVED holiday traditions. We had to find real Christmas trees still planted in a bucket of dirt every year to decorate and then plant it in our yard when the season was over. Easter always involved more than an egg hunt. We had to make sure we dyed at least two dozen eggs to hide (that no one ate) in the traditional Easter egg hunt. The dying process was the actual celebration – with lots of laughter with the boys and Natalie. The egg hunt was just an excuse to get together with friends and family. J.J. loved helping Cody with his Cub Scout badges and school projects, like building Indian tom-tom drums or matchbox cars for the Matchbox Derby competition.

Out of all that, what I'm most thankful for today was J.J.'s obsession for video-taping every moment of life that was possible. He literally followed the kids around with the camcorder or sat it on a tripod in the living room to capture so many precious moments. It was not limited to just special occasions. He captured normal days at the house, the everyday little miracles. These video tapes have been a treasure for reminiscing, now that Will is a grown man.

I wish I could now write "and we lived happily ever after," but sometimes love is not enough to heal deep depression, addiction, and broken spirits without the help of Jesus. We relied on our own strength to try to work through our issues. They were just too big for us, and we never knew to surrender them to our Big God where nothing is too big for Him.

The video obsession suggests J.J. knew subconsciously he would not be alive to watch Will grow past his elementary school years. He wanted to give Will the gift of watching his early childhood years to know how much he had always been loved by his family. J.J. passed away when Will was 11 years old, after suffering a LONG battle with alcoholism and an opiate addiction, from the side effects of depression. He became addicted to pain pills earlier in life, after a back injury from being thrown off a horse. The combination of these opiates with alcohol was a deadly poison to his liver. We had already been divorced for 7 of those 11 years. Thankfully, we remained good friends and compatible co-parents to Will for the entire 7 years.

The one GOOD thing that resulted from our divorce is that we know J.J. is saved. His divorce attorney was a very godly man who encouraged J.J. to attend a men's Christian retreat to help him heal from the divorce. He had always been a believer, but like me he didn't understand Jesus wanted to be a part of his everyday life. He was raised in a formal church too where his family attended occasionally. J.J. met Jesus on this specially-appointed weekend and rededicated his life to Him. He did everything in his own strength to follow Him afterward. Yet, he was very sick with the disease of alcoholism and drug addiction. Although it was too late to save J.J. from his illness, Jesus saved J.J. from eternal torment. We can rest with assurance he is in Heaven today. God has even allowed me to have dreams about him in Heaven. He is healthy and whole. We have had conversations in those dreams, and I know we will still be good friends for eternity. Unfortunately, J.J.'s life was cut short here on earth because he couldn't find the strength to fight his demons.

The following explains the details of the difficult and dark side of our story.

J.J.'s and My Battle

J.J. had so many admirable qualities for one human being. He was the type of person that would give his last shirt off his back, if he saw someone in need. Anytime he had the opportunity to do something nice for someone else, like cook a brisket for a grieving family, it would ignite his motivation while lifting his spirits. He was a believer in Jesus, and he had a heart like Jesus. He was tender-hearted and sensitive to others' pain, suffering, or loss. He had an overwhelmingly soft heart for animals. When he hunted deer on the family ranch, he always cried when he shot one. When he sold a steer at the stock shows, he always cried when he had to put them on the sale truck.

Bottom line, J.J. loved God's creatures, both two-legged and four. The only creature he did not love well was himself. He suffered from chronic depression and since he came from a multi-generation of "proud cowboys," he succumbed to the generational cycle of self-medicating with alcohol. "A stiff drink of whiskey will cure what ails you" was a common phrase in his family. His mother became a full-blown alcoholic after she retired from nursing. Many in his family line suffered from this cruel disease. The combination of a pain pill and a stiff whisky cocktail always transformed him from a quiet, distant, moody person, to highly motivated and ready for fun.

It was a "respectable addiction" in the eyes of society. It was prescribed and within the boundary of the law. So, it didn't have the same stigma attached to it, like street drugs. Unfortunately, J.J. became fond of the euphoria effects it had on his mood, as well as easing his pain. This "high" became harder and harder to reach as his body became accustomed to the dosage. He began to increase his dosage, without the approval of a physician. It's very dangerous to practice medicine without a formal education.

In the 90's, children were raised in a generation of adults who liked to "indulge in seldom pleasures." Affluent folks could afford the well-known drug, cocaine. Of course, I knew J.J. liked to indulge from time to time before we married. Calvin and I used to indulge with him on occasion. I knew what I was getting into. At first, it seemed harmless to me since it was reserved for special occasions only. Eventually, any weekend became an occasion for celebration. It seemed socially acceptable because there was never any evidence of this drug in plain sight around the children. The indulgence was privately kept in its place for secret consumption. So, it was possible to have a little "adult fun" while still being responsible caretakers for the children.

During this time in my life, I was a partaker of the problem instead of being part of the solution. I thought I was living the "glamorous lifestyle of the rich and famous." A typical week at our house involved a cocktail (or two) before dinner and the normal family routine. J.J. loved to cook and always had a gourmet meal on the stove, while sipping on a glass of wine. After dinner, then followed Cody's homework, the boys' play time, bath time and bedtime at 8:00 p.m. Then, we watched TV until we turned in. On the surface, we were like any other typical American family, raising children to be stable and responsible humans.

However, when most Fridays (not all) rolled around, it was time to have friends with children over to the house. Everyone would put the kids together in one end of the house, while the adults gathered at the other end to indulge in adult entertainment. Card games, adult conversation and adult indulgences were always on the agenda. Guests would bring their kids in pajamas. It was inevitable they would fall asleep before the parents were ready to wind down. The boys loved having the frequent slumber parties with their playmates.

We were very protective of the children with private adult matters. A line or a "bump" was only taken behind locked doors of a bathroom. As I stated before, I'm so thankful I never liked the effect of cocaine, after the first bump. Too much indulgence made my heart race something fierce and caused great anxiety. My routine was to just "fake a bump" when it was my turn to "go to the restroom", just to fit in with the group. Peer pressure, even at adult age, is still a real struggle. The worry of having to care for the kids the following morning kept me practicing moderation as well. So, I escaped from forming an addiction to this otherwise very addictive drug. Others in our group were not as fortunate. A very familiar situation with my time with Calvin.

However, I still had my own demon to wrestle with a preference to marijuana. It was my "miracle cure" to all my problems. It helped me escape boredom, anxiety and depression. Once Calvin introduced me to it, I never turned down the perfect opportunity, out of the kids' sight, to take a puff when offered.

Having a natural tendency toward anxiety and depression, this "natural, miracle plant" seemed to be the solution to calming those "episodes." Just a few puffs took the edge off when the kids were driving me crazy, or life was too hectic to handle, or I was just feeling a little down or irritable. I had a great routine that kept my secret habit from the children. Fanny packs were first introduced as a popular accessory in those days. So, it was a perfect "party pack" that could easily hold my "Walkman" portable tape player, a rolled joint, a lighter, along with breath mints and purse-size body spray. Living out in the country provided lots of secret hiding places behind trees, far from the house. I was an avid jogger in my day as well, as it provided an extra dose of dopamine release. When I knew I needed an "attitude adjustment," J.J. would watch the kids while I took my daily jog. I would find a tree to hide behind, take a few good puffs of my joint, put my earphones on and jog to my favorite jams for 2-5 miles, depending on the weather. When I got close to the house, I would take a couple more puffs to last me through the day, use my sprays to eliminate any telling odors, and get back in the mommy game with a new attitude, ready to care for my kids wearing "my cheerful, patient hat" again.

This chapter in my life taught me how to hide my 20-year

marijuana addiction from my children. I became a master at that.

Living with someone who suffers from depression can be a nerve-wrecking roller coaster ride. I recall day after day, week after week, a dreaded drive home from errands or shopping. The lengthy trip from town to our country home allowed time for my stomach to tie up in knots, wondering which J.J. was going to greet me at the door. Will it be the sullen, neglectful, on the verge of anger J.J.? Or the energetic, fun-loving, on the verge of a good buzz J.J.? It all depended on what was in his system.

Depression was a sign of weakness in J.J.'s family. He thought the only solution was to "suck it up" and self-medicate. So many conversations involved me pleading with him to seek professional help and the response was always, "I'm not crazy. I don't need a shrink."

It was a perfect storm with two people trying to build a life on a broken foundation. J.J. suffered from depression, with the side effects of addiction. I suffered from my own addiction, along with insecurity and no sense of identity or self-worth, so I was very codependent on him. My daily moods all depended on his moods. Many times, my moods were gloomy as I felt neglected, unappreciated, and unsafe emotionally. These battles prompted us to depend more and more on our "quick fixes". Even though they were quite young, I felt our children were absorbing the emotional strain we were both under, no matter how much we tried to shelter them from our issues.

Through all this turmoil, we still attended church pretty regularly. Unless there was a party going on Saturday night; our priorities were worldly, to say the least. We had a false sense of salvation thinking, "If we keep God happy with our good attendance, then we are covered." We were good to put on our Sunday outfits and our "happy mask," looking like any other well-grounded family, living a Christian life. He worked cattle at the ranch, while my work week consisted of all the chores left for a stay-at-home mom. I quit my full-time job at the college after Will was born because we couldn't find a suitable caretaker. I let go of my last shred of independence to be completely dependent on my husband from a wealthy family. I even gave up my sports car when we married, because the family decided we needed a family car for a safer ride for the boys. So, the *family* traded in my car for a "momma car" in the form of an SUV. The family signed the note. I didn't. I was basically driving a borrowed car from his family. The family also made sure I DID sign a prenuptial agreement to protect the family fortune. This family was careful to guard their wealth, strictly to be handed down to blood relatives only. No spouses were named as heirs to any part of the fortune, in any trust fund. So, I became financially AND emotionally dependent on my third husband, who often made me feel emotionally unsafe.

Thank goodness he did not have a quick temper and was not a "rage-aholic," so I never felt I was in physical danger. On the other hand, I WAS a "rage-aholic." I had suppressed all kinds of anger pent up from my past experiences. My quick temper would evoke a fight from him occasionally that would result in slamming doors and screaming in front of the children.

For the most part, we provided a stable home with its occasional storms. As time passed, the weekend partying became more of a routine than an occasional gathering. As the weeks and months passed, this routine was really starting to wear me down. Mainly because I was the sole parent responsible for caring for the kids, while J.J. slept it off the next day. The dreaded task of keeping my young boys quiet and to "not wake the giant" was daunting. J.J. would finally wake up in the middle of the afternoon, after I worked tirelessly to keep the home peaceful. He would still be very grouchy, and we had to walk on eggshells until his hangover subsided. His bachelor mentality in this area never seemed to wear off, even as a middle-aged adult. So, I felt constantly on guard, trying to keep some type of normalcy in our family. It felt more like a JOB than a life. I literally felt like a slave in a world that wasn't really my home. J.J.'s drinking was becoming increasingly frequent with large volumes. It was beginning to be apparent; he couldn't function emotionally unless he had a buzz. Yet he would never admit he had a problem that he couldn't handle himself. It was a vicious cycle of normalcy to dependency, day in and day out. Our stable lifestyle was becoming more and more unsteady.

Calvin was making matters worse, with his bitterness and emotional disorder as well. Although he was sober from going to rehab, he still displayed all the dysfunctional attitudes of an addict. Every time Cody came home from a weekend with Calvin, it was obvious my innocent little boy was being played as a pawn to get back at J.J.. It was never about what Cody said, it was the way he shied away from J.J. That in turn, caused J.J. to feel rejected by Cody. I knew Calvin was filling his head with suggestions that were putting my child right in the middle of a childish adult game. J.J. was no better. Instead of being the adult in the situation, he would get angry and lash out at Cody, as if J.J. was five years old too. I was stuck between a rock and a hard place. I strived to help my oldest child cope with a new family and a divorce from his own daddy, while trying to keep our current family happy and well-adjusted. I was worn out. I was nowhere near being well-adjusted myself. On top of all the issues I had to deal with in my surroundings, I was also dealing with my very own issues within myself.

Unfortunately, I began to get comfortable and make my home in this dark cave. As the months and years passed, the enemy had me bound in the belief that *this was all there was for me*. I had reached my destiny of being a wife and mother to other people, with no other purpose for my own life. I had to play the cards I was dealt with. So, I stayed and did everything in my power to make the best of it. The fact that I was still in love with my husband, and using marijuana to cloud the hard issues, made it easier. However, the marriage was still a constant roller coaster of highs and lows. I remember so many good times as a family. The good days were really good, but the bad days became harder to endure.

The frequent arguments finally came to a head, and we agreed to separate, to live in neutral corners and go to marriage counseling to try and find a more peaceful life. Luckily, the boys and I had a free place to go - the "bachelor pad". This was the house that J.J. had lived in for years before we married, and it was still owned by the family. All furnishings were still intact with no renters or other occupants. So, it served as a neutral corner for us to retrieve to in providing a full household setup.

Then, one of the most tragic and lowest dips of our marriage happened a few months later, one October morning. I got the phone call that our beloved Diana, J.J.'s older sister, had passed away suddenly at age 45. She was gone without anyone being able to tell her goodbye. She wasn't just a sister; she was a lifeline for J.J.. He was not just close to his sister, he adored her and depended on her for emotional stability. She was always a mother figure to him growing up. They were raised by an alcoholic mother and a workaholic father and so, his sister filled in as J.J.'s caretaker. That role never really faded as adults. She was a lifeline to me as well. Not only was she a nurse who oversaw our physical well-being, she also offered a comforting shoulder to cry on when J.J. and I fought. Surprisingly, she considered my side of the arguments and admitted J.J. could be difficult. I became dependent on her as well, as she was the glue that held our family together. Her sudden death was the blow that sent J.J. past the point of no return in dealing with depression and addiction. His drug use and alcoholism soared to a new level that made it obvious he was in danger of losing his life. The day we buried Diana, a big part of J.J. went to that grave with her. Our separation and family counseling were put on hold. I had no choice but to move back into our home to help him heal from this tragedy. Unfortunately, a broken person cannot help another broken person heal. J.J. only got worse.

After a few more months of dysfunctional living, I knew I couldn't stay a prisoner to this much longer. I felt so trapped and alone. I didn't realize at the time that I was NOT alone. My very Best Friend was always by my side, just waiting for me to turn to Him for help.

Finally, the day came. I eventually realized that by STUDYING the Bible daily, I had normally opened on Sundays only, brought me a sense of comfort, peace and hope on a consistent basis. The Word began to wash over me and provided me with my daily portion of refreshment. I began to depend more on the Word of God than the things of the world to satisfy my longing to be noticed, accepted and loved. The more I depended on the Word, the more my surroundings conflicted with what I was reading. Even though I was finding Hope in the Word, I was feeling less and less hope about my marriage. J.J. and I were fighting more than ever, as he was drinking more than ever.

I continued to study the Word and began to pray daily for God to either rescue J.J. from his demons or rescue me and my children from a very dysfunctional, unhealthy lifestyle. I knew I was misplaced. No matter how much I tried to reason, deep down, I knew this was not God's will for my life, nor for J.J., nor my children either. Unfortunately, he was so tightly bound in the only lifestyle he had ever known, he wasn't willing to come out of his familiar dark cave and live. He just didn't think it was possible. If something didn't change, my kids were in grave danger of being permanently affected by generational curses on BOTH sides of their parents' lineage. We both had a family history of alcoholism, and I was determined to make this generational curse stop with my children! I also felt that J.J.'s only hope for survival was a wake-up call.

One morning, the dawn finally broke through the grey clouds. I was right in the middle of my new routine of getting up extra early before anyone else, to study and pray with my morning coffee. Psalm 40 was the morning lesson. "*I waited patiently for the Lord and He inclined to me and heard my cry. He brought me up out of the horrible pit, out of the miry clay and set my feet upon a rock and established my steps...*" As I read the words on the page, I cried out to Him "Lord! Save me and my children! Show me what to do!" He began to lift me out of my horrible pit. For the very first time in my life, I heard God speak to me. It was so strong in my spirit; it was almost audible. Even though I had never heard that voice before, I immediately recognized it was Him, "Trust ME and go." I knew it was my Savior, but I had no idea how to obey Him. HOW was I supposed to go? WHERE was I going to go? The "bachelor pad" we once retrieved to was no longer an option. I had no job and no money of my own. I didn't even have my own vehicle anymore! Even if God

GAVE me a new dwelling, I had very few possessions I could take with me, that were my own. When I married into this family of wealth, J.J.'s expensive household belongings were much nicer than my discount furniture. I sold almost everything I owned when I entered this marriage. The only pieces I kept were the items I had for Cody's bedroom. So, I wouldn't even be able to adequately furnish a new home. My soul became conflicted, and my faith was very dim.

As the days passed, I could not get God's command off my mind. Unbeknownst to my spiritually infant mind, Holy Spirit kept whispering and leading me toward my escape, out of Egypt. I decided to take one step at a time. I went back to the college to seek full-time employment and I was hired immediately. That's God's guidance. The next big break was daycare for Will. The only caretaker we trusted, who kept Cody in his pre-school age, could now take care of Will, since he was old enough to comply with her license. That's God's timing. Sandy was a very sought-out licensed caretaker who worked from her home and the fact she had an opening was nothing short of a miracle. God had worked out the excuses. It was meant for me to go back to work. I started to feel more independent and less hopeless.

My new-found independence gained me more confidence and less dependence on J.J.. The fact was, I still loved J.J.. I just hated his lifestyle. Numerous attempts were made to try and help him to see the harm he was doing to himself. He was so terribly addicted to the buzz, he depended on it to help him cope with clinical depression. I finally had to start having the hard discussions with him to "choose your family or the bottle." It was an ultimatum he could not honor, so he amicably agreed that a legal separation was the only hope for our marriage to get our family back on track. Deep down I knew then it was his out to be able to drink in peace without having to answer to me. I had no idea if a legal separation would solve our problems. To be honest, I highly doubted it. All I knew was, I needed to find a way to place the boys in a more functional environment, absent of screaming parents with unresolved issues.

↑ *Don't Fall For It* ↓

By this time, I had been collecing my own paychecks and I deposited in my own private account to build my "escape fund." I began to research the options of rental property in the area. There was just no possibility in sight. Just like the Israelites when they came upon the Red Sea with Pharoah's army on their tail, my situation too, looked like a hopeless dead-end.

It was during one of my quiet times, when I decided to put the pencil to the paper and at least attempt at working out a household budget, based on my paycheck alone. I knew there was a good chance the family would not agree to pay me any type of child support, if I left their son under only a legal separation. This family was in denial that J.J. had a serious problem. I couldn't afford an attorney to fight for support. They could afford the best of attorneys. So, I knew I would be flying solo with no financial support. As I added up the expenses, they easily outweighed my income. My measly paycheck with only a high school diploma was no match for the pile of bills I would face each month. I put my pencil down with a defeated attitude. When I was about to throw in the towel, I heard God's voice even louder, "TRUST ME AND GO!" It almost knocked me of my stool I sat on every morning during my quiet time. This time it was more than just a suggestion. I knew I *had* to go. If I didn't go, it would be outright disobedience to God Almighty! My spirit knew my God was bigger than this obstacle. My mind just needed to catch up and *intentionally* obey! No matter what the natural world looked like.

Unbeknownst to J.J., the very next day I started searching for housing, just out of curiosity. Was it possible there was a rent house available that could fit my meager budget? My allowance for rent was a ridiculously low amount, so my hopes were, but a glimpse. BUT GOD! To my amazement, I found a house and the landlord was an old classmate of my parents! He was a kind, gentle, Christian man. Mom explained my situation and he agreed to rent it to me for the ridiculously low rent I could afford. That's God's provision. It was not a fancy house, but it was clean and well-maintained. We three would have our very own bedrooms and this angel for a landlord, didn't even require me to pay a deposit. His only requirement was that I pay on time and maintain the yard. I was FLOORED. Is this really you, God? He kept proving to me it was.

The next hurdle was to bring up the tabled discussion of legal separation again. I had to tell J.J. we were leaving, for real. I had no idea how that conversation was going to go and before I even uttered one word, I knew to pray for God to give me strength and courage and to give J.J. the right heart position to understand. The perfect moment came when J.J. was in a vulnerable state of mind, admitting his drinking was a major problem for our marriage. Surprisingly, it was a calm, heart-felt conversation and I explained what I had experienced in hearing God's voice. We were able to reason as mature adults and agree that something had to give. J.J. even agreed to seek a rehab center to find sobriety. That was only possible because Holy Spirit was right in the middle of our conversation. There is no other explanation. It was probably one of the most meaningful conversations J.J. and I had throughout our marriage.

We finally agreed on an "official" separation, not a legal separation on paper. It would be separate living quarters where we could work on ourselves separately and then try to figure out what we needed to do to mend our marriage. J.J. found a reputable rehab center. He agreed to seek that help while we go to neutral corners and rediscover our friendship and adoration for one another. Our current situation was making us enemies and we wanted to become friends again. I felt neglected and taken for granted and J.J. felt trapped in his deep depression, not able to be the husband I needed him to be. It broke his heart that he was slacking on being the father the boys needed him to be. He agreed we were at the fork in the road and promised to fight for his family. What we didn't realize at the time, was that the fight was going to be much harder than he could ever imagine. A multi-decade addiction doesn't just go away overnight or with the snap of a finger. The boys and I moved out very soon after that night and began a new journey that I was not exactly prepared for. J.J. was expelled from the rehab center after only two weeks because he had snuck in his pain pills and was caught. He just couldn't let go of his "safety net" and trust the

↑ *Don't Fall For It* ↓

professionals. My new-found freedom from adversity was quickly fading into more confrontations and obstacles. The mind of an alcoholic is very unpredictable.

As my moving-out plans developed, J.J. bounced back and forth from being understanding to being difficult. Every day was a "crap shoot" as to what the atmosphere would be. Some days he was obliging and other days he was angry and combative. One day, he decided if I wanted to move out and be on my own, then that is exactly what I deserved, with no help from him. I wasn't allowed to take any of his household items . The only items that were rightfully mine were the items I mentioned earlier in Cody's bedroom, a bunkbed, a dresser, a TV and recliner. What also kept me from moving was the fact I would not have a car to drive. His dad made it clear that family car was intended for THIS family and not for my escape.

J.J.'s family all had a mindset that anyone who married into the family were just "gold diggers." This was a sad and damaging mindset to project onto their children. It gave them the message they were not worthy of TRUE love. That's what I had for J.J.. TRUE love. I was raised in a middle-class family who lived a very modest lifestyle and that was good enough for me. Although J.J. was a very handsome man that attracted just about any woman he wanted, he was still very insecure in the subject of love and marriage. This insecurity stemmed from being raised in a loveless marriage where his parents only stayed together for the sake of the children. His mother's alcoholism caused his father to feel very neglected. Neither J.J. nor his siblings ever had the luxury of learning what a healthy relationship looked like. J.J.'s insecurity and other issues made this move an uphill struggle, all the way.

So, here I was, a mother of two young mouths to feed, with a job that paid a little over minimum wage. I took a lower-level position at the college with considerably less pay than my previous position. The only open position was a step back into the clerical arena. I had no car and barely enough money to pay the rent for a 3-bedroom house. A 3-bedroom house seemed useless with barely any furniture to put in it. I almost gave up on the idea of moving out. I could not possibly see how this was going to work out. BUT GOD!!

Within days, Dad came to see me at work and handed me a set of keys to a car, fully paid for, that he bought from a co-worker. This was no clunker either. It was a Chrysler LaBaron convertible, white, with maroon racing stripes and matching maroon, leather interior. Dad's co-worker had refurbished it and only drove it in the summer for spins around town on pretty days. It was in MINT condition with low mileage. He needed room in his garage, so he sold it to my dad for a ridiculously low price. My Dad LOVED to bless people. It made him happier to hand me the keys with no obligation, than it was for me to accept them. When God provides, He provides in style!

I was so blown away at this generous gift because it showed me, God was with me and for me. It gave me the confidence to take a leap of faith and move to our new home, even with only the bare necessities on hand. In no time, the boys and I moved into our new safe haven. I wasn't sure how I was going to feed them, exactly. I knew there were still plenty of battles ahead with only a separation from J.J. We had a long and winding road ahead of us in figuring out how to put our family back together. It was a scary time, but a peaceful retreat helped tremendously. I knew God was on our side. We were going to be ok – one way or another.

CHAPTER TEN

New Beginnings

"And my God shall supply all your need according to His riches in glory by Christ Jesus." ~ Philippians 4:19

"Momma . . . are we going to end up in the poor house?" asked my 4-year-old, as he looked up at me with his navy blue "puppy dog" eyes and his troubled toddler look.

"Honey, we already ARE in the poor house, and see? It's not so bad. We still have a roof over our heads, heat and air-conditioning and everything we need," I told him, as I bent down and gave him a warm hug that said, we are going to be ok.

"Really? THIS is the poor house? You're right! It's not too bad at all!" William Jon is my mini-me. Since he was old enough to put sentences together, he has been my over-thinker and my worrier. I knew now, what I put my own parents through.

No doubt, this new home was a step down from the 4-bedroom, 3-bath country home we had just left. This new home was not in the best part of town either. In fact, it was not even favorable to safely leave the kids to play in the front yard, without my supervision. The one thing this home had that the former lavish home didn't, was perfect peace. No more screaming, crying, throwing things or name calling in front of the children. No more drug dealers (disguised as businessmen) stopping by to make an exchange for the weekend indulgences. No more alcohol. No more breathing second-hand cigarette smoke and no other outward evidence of dysfunction. However, this home was not perfect either. In our new safe haven, I was able to hide my own secret addiction to pot in order to cope with the fears of having a one-parent responsibility.

We moved in with the only 4 items of mine previously in Cody's bedroom. We made it work! In Cody's new bedroom, I slept on the twin, top bunk and Cody and Will slept on the double, bottom bunk. I sat in the recliner in the living room to watch movies on the VCR with our only television, while the boys laid on a pallet of blankets I laid out on the floor. This pallet also doubled as our dining room table, as we had daily "picnics" in the living room. It was all we had, and it was all we needed to be happy. An empty house that is full of peace and joy is better than a house full of expensive furniture but empty of the presence of the Lord. The boys were perfectly content with our new surroundings, and I was grateful.

BUT GOD!!! He is our Provider who supplies all our need as His children. The Scripture says all our need – singular. It may not be perfect grammar, but it IS perfect theology. Our God supplies all our One need – Jesus is all we need. Singular. Every other need falls into place when we seek Him first. When we first obey and trust God, He is faithful to follow through in our needs to sustain us!

Less than one month later, I got a phone call from a friend who was moving in with her boyfriend, and she didn't want to put her household items in storage. "Lisa, could you use my household set up? I would rather you use them, than pay for storage." My mouth dropped to the floor. Next thing I know, God provided everything we needed, from furniture and appliances down to silverware and towels.

God told me, "TRUST ME AND GO!" I took that step of faith FIRST, when there seemed to be NO way. God provided a three-bedroom house that fit my budget. He completely furnished that house and provided a new, COOL car at absolutely no cost to me. That's MY God and that's YOUR God! He makes a way when there is NO way in the natural! We just have to take that first step of faith, and He carries us the rest of the way up the staircase to a better way of living.

Unfortunately, the one thing God did not provide, was healing and wholeness in my marriage. God is able to accomplish ANYTHING, but He chooses to give man free will. Our choices determine our destiny. Instead of rebuilding a friendship, our issues only worsened, and our separation became more treacherous. After an excruciating 11-month separation, our divorce was final. The only thing we had left to rebuild was our commitment to Will, to try and co-parent in the most amicable way possible. Thankfully, as time passed and wounds healed, we were able to do just that. We gained a deeper friendship of mutual respect for each other's role as parents. We were able to ban together in disciplining Will to avoid any confusion between our two households.

I had settled into my new normal of being a single mom, free to make my own decisions and run my household, according to God's rules and values. The freedom was bittersweet. I had to work extra hard in a full-time job plus extra odd jobs, to make ends meet. Additionally, I had restarted my pursuit of a college education. When J.J. and I were dating, I was able to complete my associate degree at the community college. Now, I had to travel 50 miles one way to attend the closest university, in order to achieve my bachelor's degree in psychology. So, I was juggling a full-time job, ¾-time parenting, and being a part-time student. I received some child support from my ex-husbands, but it wasn't enough to live a life the boys were accustomed to. In fact, that supplement provided "just enough" to cover all the living expenses with VERY little left over for luxuries, like new school clothes or entertainment. If an emergency arose, such as a blowout in my tire, the new tire would have to be bought with a credit card. Soon, I was burdened by yet another bill to pay, and I could only cover the minimum amount due. This did nothing to help reduce my credit card debt.

The weight as provider of the household took a toll on my emotional state. Although the boys and I had many days of joy and laughter in our new surroundings, I suffered through many dark, secret moments, of fear, anxiety and the lingering addiction I indulged privately, to combat those feelings. Running away from J.J.'s problem did not help in dealing with my own problems.

There was one more thing needed to make all this anxiety go away. All that was left for the Lord to provide for me was a godly man. So, I thought. Although I felt I had just crossed over from the wilderness into the land flowing with milk and honey, I still had my "Jericho" to overcome. (Joshua 1,2). I still wanted a "man honey." You can take a codependent girl out of the country, but you can't instantly take the country girl out of codependency, just by changing her surroundings. I had romanticized ideas of my "knight in shining armor" riding in on his white horse, just because I was now free and single. After all, that was *still* the only way to satisfy my sense of identity and make life complete; to belong to a man and be his wife. Even though God had performed miracles in my life, I still didn't get it that He was the only One who could make my life complete. I was still like one of those stiff-necked Israelites who forgot He parted the Red Sea for me. I envisioned new and improved suitors would be calling. I took matters into my own hands as I hinted to single men at work that I would be free for the upcoming weekend, while the boys were visiting their dads. I just knew one of them would be calling me for a date.

Never happened. Instead, I soon found myself DREADING those "free weekends" that became my prison. I spent my free weekends drowning in tears while watching romantic comedies. These "RC's" hurt the worst. Self-pity grew as I longed for a similar love story. Satan loved tormenting me on those weekends with constant lies, I soon began to recite. "Why am I kidding myself? No DECENT man will ever want a third-time divorcee with small children. **I am just going to die alone!**" This was my constant self-talk in my head.

The only time I didn't wallow in self-pity were on the weekdays and 2nd and 4th weekends when I had the boys. I looked forward to those weekends when we would go on family outings. Those outings always had to be a Christian gathering; not because I was so spiritual, but because I was so broke! Church functions never had a cover-charge and provided wholesome entertainment for the boys. There was an underlying motivation as well. I always fantasized that I would meet a single dad and it would be a romantic love story, like the ones I watched on the Hallmark Movie channel. Again, never happened.

Eventually, the excitement and newness of living single began to wear off and morphed into depression and despair. I was NOBODY since I belonged to NO ONE. The thought never crossed my mind that I belonged to Jesus and to cry out to the ONLY One who promises He is with me always. I look back now and realize I missed so many incredible moments I could have had alone with Jesus on those weekends to myself. Instead, I would turn to the one remedy that provided instant but temporary satisfaction. If I had the luxury of bumming from a friend, I would sit on my back porch, light up and puff my sadness away, trying to enter another fantasy of a future love story. The crippling fear of dying alone would diminish for a short time until my high wore off. Then, only deeper depression would set in. Finally, I saw some light at the end of my dark tunnel. The Lover of my soul arranged a divine appointment to pull me out of my pit of despair.

It was on a Wednesday night during choir practice at my church. I was sitting next to a lady who had known me since birth. She was a close friend of Mom's. In between songs, when others broke out in conversation, she suddenly turned to me and said, "Lisa have you ever attended a Walk to Emmaus?" I explained I had heard of it but didn't know much about it. I had never thought about attending. She explained that it was a 72-hour Christian women's retreat, designed to get us closer to God. I envisioned a crash course in Bible Study, and it didn't really appeal to me. Besides, there was no way I would fit in with that type of crowd. I was sure they didn't allow drug-addicted divorcees in a holy place like that. Then, she mentioned WHEN the retreat was going to take place. "It will be held on the first weekend of February, and I would love to sponsor you and pay your fee for you." All I heard was the FIRST weekend, when the boys would be with their dads. SIGN. ME. UP.

ANYTHING was better than 72 hours of pacing the floors of an empty house, with more wallowing in self-pity.

Little did I know at the time, that it was a set-up for an encounter with Jesus. On the 50th hour of that 72-hour retreat, Jesus spoke to me, so clearly it was almost audible, the SECOND time in my life. When I heard, "TRUST Me and GO!" several months earlier, I went with fear and trembling. This time, I was drawn in and overwhelmed when I heard these words during a chapel session, "Lisa, look around you. This is your new community, your FAMILY. See daughter, you are NOT ALONE. **You are not going to die alone!**" At that moment, I fell completely in love with Jesus! I instantly understood that He sees me and **knows my every thought!** He heard my thoughts on every one of those lonely nights as I repeated Satan's lies about "dying alone." I fell to my knees in repentance at the altar to give my life to Jesus. I had given Him my heart at age 12, but at age 38, I vowed to give Him my *life*. I never felt more ALIVE than in that moment.

I went home that Sunday evening with a whole new outlook that matched my new countenance, FULL of joy and hope. My boys instantly picked up on the change in me and were filled with joy as well. As we walked in the house, I immediately started playing worship music to fill the atmosphere with praise and thanksgiving. I wanted to continue my journey on this Walk to Emmaus where I now recognized Jesus. I remember Cody going into his room and returning with his Bible in his hand. At age 9, he sat down at our dining room table, opened his Bible and began quoting Scripture, Baptist preacher style, while I washed dishes. Life was going to be different from now on! My heart was filled with joy and hope, and I felt complete!! I felt so FREE and on fire for Jesus! I no longer needed pot anymore either. I had discovered that there was "No high like The Most High!" Now, Jesus was my source of joy and laughter!

He even arranged a *second* encounter with me that would happen later that same Sunday night; the first night of my new journey getting to know Jesus. Let me explain. On the application I had completed for this event, it asked one question that had me a little stumped. "What do you expect to gain from this experience?" I tried to think of a "Churchy" answer, to make me look the part. Nothing came to mind. Finally, I just decided to be honest. I wrote, "I just want to learn how to pray." You see, I knew OF Jesus, and I believed He was my Savior, but talking to the Creator of the Universe and the Savior of the World seemed impossible, since I didn't know how He thought. What do you say to someone like that? Thee's and Thou's were just not in my vocabulary.

Jesus "called me up" first on this Sunday night, to begin the conversation. In the middle of the night, I was suddenly awakened by a song sung on the retreat, playing on repeat in my head. It was playing so loud in my spirit; it woke me up as if it was playing on the radio. In that instant, I sat up in bed and started pouring my heart out to Jesus, telling Him all my doubts and fears, along with my hopes and dreams. I thanked Him over and over. No fancy church words. Just me, in my everyday language, as if I were on the phone with my best friend. After I was depleted of words to say, my body went limp. I sank back down in bed. As my head hit the pillow, I heard Him so clearly, "This is how you pray, Daughter. Just talk to Me." I haven't stopped talking to my Best Friend since.

With my new-found friendship with Jesus, I just KNEW He was going to give me the desires of my heart! After all, that is what the Bible says. *"Delight yourself in the Lord and He will give you the desires of your heart."* **(Psalms 37:4)** I was about as delighted as I could get! I just KNEW I was going to meet my godly man in the new Christian community I was now a part of. I should have kept reading the rest of that Psalm. In verse 7 it reads, *"Be still before the Lord and wait patiently for Him. . ."* I had already wasted too many years looking for love in all the wrong places. I had no TIME for patience! I was still on my "perfect-man" hunt, but THIS time I just knew I was going to find him in church, or some other wholesome environment. No more bar scenes! I found Jesus, but I still had Satan on my back, whispering the same ole' lies. He was still up to his same deceitful tricks.

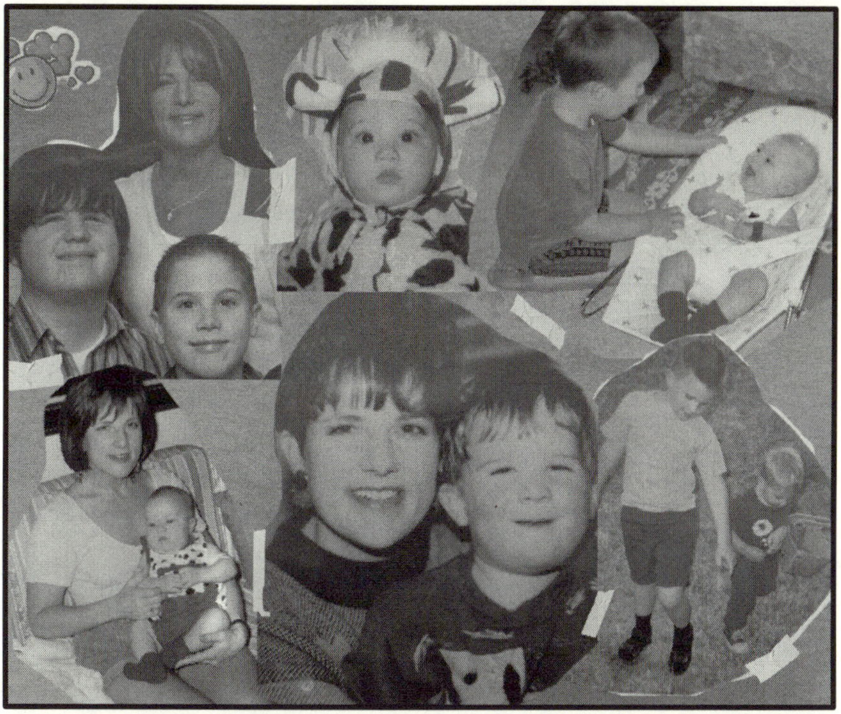

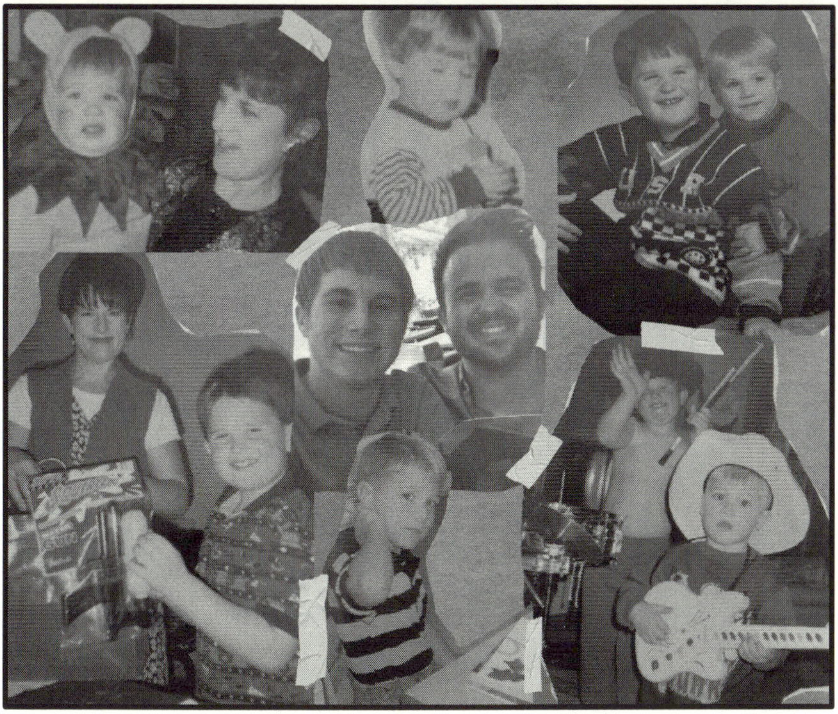

BEST FRIENDS FROM THE START
CODY, NATALIE, & WILL

CHAPTER ELEVEN

I Fell For It... Again!

"For such people are false apostles, deceitful workers, masquerading as apostles of Christ. And no wonder, for Satan himself masquerades as an angel of light."

~ 2 Corinthians 11:13-14

It was a little over a month since I had met Jesus as my Best Friend on that beautiful weekend called "The Walk to Emmaus" (a Christian retreat built around Luke 24:13-35). This movement has bi-annual retreats for men and women, and it was now time for the "Men's Walk #9." Each time a "Walk" is held, it is numbered so that the participants can identify their particular "Walk." My time was Walk #8. The number 8 in the Bible means "new beginnings". My new beginning was full of so much hope for my happily ever after. To my complete surprise, my own daddy decided he wanted to check it out. My dad was definitely a believer in Jesus, but he wasn't big on religion or church. So, for most of my life, we were occasional churchgoers. We would go through cycles of going every Sunday, but after a few months, we would miss one Sunday, starting a cycle of backsliding. Most often, Mom was the spiritual leader in our home, and she would take us, without Dad. After my first divorce, Mom, Dad and myself, became regular church-goers. Dad would go, as long as it didn't interfere with Sunday football, and he would be the first to get in the car after service. No time to stay back and chat with other members. He loved Jesus, but the

↑ *Don't Fall For It* ↓

Dallas Cowboys were #1 priority.

So, I KNEW it had to be God when, the very next Monday following my Walk, Dad walked into my office to have me xerox some papers for him. I went to work that day, still basking in the afterglow of the weekend and all that I had experienced. I didn't really say anything about the weekend to my co-workers, mainly because I had no words to describe it. Everyone around me could see a significant change in me though. So did Dad. As I went about the business of xeroxing his papers, I could see in my peripheral that he was staring me down. Finally, he spoke, "Daughter, how was that retreat of yours this weekend? Something SURE is different about you." My immediate thought was, *"How in the world do I explain this to him. There are just no words."* Suddenly, Holy Spirit placed a memory in my mind of my early 20's when I went on a church retreat with my parents. It was blatantly obvious Dad had an encounter with Jesus on that weekend and it was the perfect answer. "Dad the best way I can describe this weekend is this. Do you remember that retreat you, me and Mom went on at Lake Brownwood with the church?" He nodded. "Well, take that weekend and multiply it by 100 and that is what my weekend was like." It was the God-breathed answer that convinced Dad to go. I immediately knew it when he blew me away with his response, "I may just have to check that out." Anyone who attends one of these Walks to Emmaus will tell you, they immediately begin thinking about who in their circle to sponsor for the next one. You come away wanting everyone you know to experience it. My immediate thought was to invite Mom, and Dad was the LAST person I thought would EVER go. With still a little reluctance and coercion from me, Dad was soon signed up with me as his sponsor. Holy Spirit was the driving force, no doubt.

On the weekend of Dad's walk, the community gathered on Saturday night to worship and pray for those attending. As Dad's sponsor, I was expected to attend. I was so excited to be with this community again. It would be my first time to return to the very chapel where I met Jesus, face to face. To my shock and surprise, I ran into a man whom I had admired for years. We were co-workers on campus, but in different departments where our paths rarely crossed. I had watched him from a distance for several years, and always considered him a very godly man. I could tell he was an incredible family man who became my "model" for a man I was looking for. I first came to know him and his wife as they circulated through local churches with their puppet show children's ministry. At that time, I worked with the children in my church and got to observe them ministering with their puppet show. I saw what a godly marriage looked like and began to dream of having a marriage like that, one day. This was long before I even had children. Years later, the town was shocked to hear they were getting a divorce. The scoop was, he went through a hard time getting over the shock of her leaving. No family is off limits to Satan's attacks.

So, a few years later, "as fate would have it", we are both divorced and gathering to worship Jesus in this chapel. "God's timing is always perfect!" I had NO idea he was also a member of the Emmaus community, as he had gone on his Walk in a previous year. As he approached me, I know my mouth dropped at my surprise to see him and we embraced with the "appropriate church hug." Conversation flowed easily and when the announcement came that service was about to begin, my heart leapt when he asked me to sit with him. I was immediately smitten and one of those Hallmark movies began to play in my head. Could this be IT?!!

Well, to spare you more details of yet another familiar plot, I learned after dating him for several months, he was FAR from "It." Let's just say, I learned the hard way why his wife left him. Just because you meet a man in church doesn't mean he's exempt from the same issues you see in men at the bars. It's not a guarantee. Just because it looks good, doesn't mean it is God!

After that short chapter ended, I met another man. This setting was innocent as well. I wasn't even looking for a man. I was just going on my daily jog in my neighborhood one afternoon with a friend. This guy was sitting on his back porch when he jokingly yelled at us as we passed by, "Be careful! This isn't the best of neighborhoods!" I jokingly yelled back, "Why don't you come jog with us then and protect us!" I sincerely didn't mean it. I was just exchanging a friendly greeting. So, when we suddenly saw him jogging next to us, in his blue jeans, we became a little startled. As we continued to jog, we got acquainted and to our delight, we found him to be very friendly and polite. Our fear turned into comfort as we realized he truly wanted to come along, for our protection. His athletic build and outgoing personality cause me to not mind it at all!

Another long story short. He literally looked like Jesus. He was very handsome with long brown wavy hair and a fit physique. Turned out, he lived just a few houses down from me. He started pursuing me with friendly gestures of coming over and playing with my boys. He was just a few years younger than me and had a very playful disposition. That friendship grew into a courtship and once again I was thinking, I had found my forever guy. He started going to church with me and even singing in the choir. The boys loved him. I grew to love him and just knew God had sent him. It cannot get more innocent than finding a man who is a friendly neighbor.

Then the day came when I realized he had a hidden drug problem. He also had a temper and after showing it, I learned he had a history of assault in previous marriages. The relationship ended abruptly.

The one amazing story I can report is that I DID start paying attention to red flags that started appearing subtly. He started displaying some odd behaviors a few months into the relationship that made me pause. He also started insisting he wanted to marry me. Why the hurry? That made me pause as well. I will never forget the night it all came to a head when Satan reared *his* ugly head. Strangely, I had not heard from him in over a week. That was unusual. He worked as a carpenter and was always over at our house after work to eat supper together. Since no argument had occurred and I hadn't heard from him, I began to suspect I was in another dysfunctional relationship.

It just so happened I had been selected to work a Women's Walk that was coming up. On this particular weekend, the boys were with their dads. I had to attend a team meeting for the Walk on Friday night and all day, Saturday. The Friday night team meeting was powerful. We previewed some inspiring talks from other women on the team and had an incredible worship time. I was feeling so close to Jesus as I drove home. Still not hearing a word from my latest beau, I distinctly remember praying this exact prayer before I went to sleep on that Friday night. "Lord, if he is not the one, if this relationship is not Your will, PLEASE just slam the door on the relationship! Don't let me make another mistake!"

Jesus heard and answered. About 2:00 in the morning, I was startled as my doorbell started ringing frantically! When I looked out my peep hole, I could see him standing on my porch. Puzzled, I opened the door to find out what the emergency was. He walked right in the house without an invitation. His demeanor was completely different than I had ever seen. I began to get a little afraid, as he seemed angry. When I asked him where he had been, he became combative and rattled off a long story that made no sense. I started to see he was under the influence of something. As the conversation escalated, he started using profanity and used the Lord's name in vain. That's when I had enough! I told him he was not to use that language in my house and told him to leave.

As he angrily went to the front door, the last words I heard from him were, "You and your God can go to hell!" THEN, to my astonishment, he violently "slammed my front door" into the wall so hard that the doorknob left a hole in my wall! Did you get that? He slammed the door on the relationship. God slammed it with Satan's chess piece.

He left and I locked my deadbolt, my chain lock, my doorknob lock and even put a heavy piece of furniture in front of my door (not really- I didn't own a heavy piece of furniture, but you get the point). I was no longer scared though. That was just a precaution. Instead, I JOYFULLY skipped down the hall to my bedroom, constantly praising Jesus! That night could have turned out so differently! But I knew without a doubt, my Defender was with me, and He had summoned warrior angels to guard and protect me. He also answered my prayer with no questions asked!

It was another dead end in my search for Mr. Right. What I hope you can learn from my stories is this; I could keep searching and searching until my shoes wore out and I would NEVER find the perfect man to fulfill me. I even tried dating a few guys from church and they were as nice and polite as they could be. They still didn't satisfy my need to feel complete. Jesus was trying to get through to me that HE is the ONLY one who can make me complete. I kept attracting broken men because I was still a bit broken myself! Broken people gravitate to other broken people. The only way I was ever going to feel complete was to realize, everything I ever needed was found in Jesus alone! The only way to find a healthy relationship was to become spiritually healthy myself. The Great Physician was the only relationship I needed to pursue to become spiritually healthy and find true happiness and pure joy. No huMAN can ever supply that need, no matter how good they are. They are still human. They are still bound to disappoint if we try to make them our god.

He rescued me that night BECAUSE I ASKED HIM. The Bible says, "We receive not because we ask not." (James 4:2-3) If we ask anything ACCORDING TO HIS WILL, He is faithful to answer. You would think I was finally getting to a healthy place. It seemed like I realized all I needed to do was talk to Jesus about my relationships and He would guide me every step of the way.

Unfortunately, some of us are just very slow learners. It's easy for me to preach this today, now that I'm on the other side of that mountain. I circled around and around the same mountain for decades, looking for the Promised Land. Unfortunately, I was headed for the hardest lesson yet, bound in the most demonic stronghold of my life. I took my eyes off Jesus and even went "back to Egypt" to find comfort in my instant mind-altering, mood-boosting remedy leaf. Prayer takes discipline – pot only takes a lighter. So, I unknowingly invited the enemy in to have his way with me once more.

Fool me once, shame on you. Fool me twice, shame on me. The

↑ Lisa Dee Dunnam ↓

next relationship brought me PLENTY of shame on myself! To make me look even more foolish, I must confess, the next relationship I entered lasted EIGHT years! This time Satan brought a man disguised as an angel of light. This one turned out to be a mini-series saga, instead of a short story.

CHAPTER TWELVE

My Double Life

"If I go up to the heavens, You are there; if I make my bed in the depths; You are there"

~ Psalms 139:8

"Satan is the master of darkness. Doing things in secret can be an indication we are being fooled by him." ~ Lysa TerKeurst

I want to share some more insight from this favorite Bible teacher of mine, Lisa TerKeurst. I quote her wisdom:

". . . as long as Satan can keep us operating in our dark secrets, we'll stay deceived. We'll start believing the lie that what we are doing outside of God's Truth isn't that big of a deal. Then over time, **we will think it's impossible** *for us to escape the entanglements of sin."*

I have the perfect illustration of this truth because I lived it.

It all began at a time when I actually thought I was ok. *I thought I was content being alone in the world because I felt the companionship of Jesus. I wasn't in an earthly relationship, and I wasn't really looking for a relationship. I thought I was just waiting on the Lord in His perfect timing.* Waiting all by itself is not enough. Waiting on the Lord doesn't mean we just sit and wait idly by. Waiting on the Lord means ABIDING IN the Lord. Spend lots of quality time with Him. Study His Word and live by it. Talk to

Jesus every day, some days every hour, so that you will be equipped to receive His wisdom and discernment. Be a DO-er of the Word; not just a reader.

I can't say I was doing that. I was going to church, raising my kids, and spending quiet time with Jesus in the mornings. All the nice stuff. It became more of a routine I marked off my checklist though. I spent most of that time praying for my kids and very little time asking for His help with ME. I could've talked to Him about my desire to find a godly man. He loves to have real conversations with us. However, I had lost my zeal to seek Jesus with my *whole* heart. That's when I put myself in a vulnerable place for the enemy to lure me, once again, into a dark pit. If I had been abiding in Jesus, I could've easily seen this day coming when Satan would come calling. Instead, I was caught off guard and easily entangled.

It was a typical, uneventful Saturday. I was minding my own business, going about my daily chores. I was outside cleaning out my car when one of the boys hollered at me that I had a phone call. To my astonishment it was a man I'll call "Brian." I was acquainted with him when his wife had previously worked on campus in a different department. I knew her and I would see him pick her up for lunch from time to time when I was in her office area. Years later, I met him on a more personal basis through the man I dated for a few months. The man I wrote about in the last chapter - the "nice Christian man" I encountered at the Emmaus community gathering. While I was on a date with him one night, he took me to Brian's house since we were in the neighborhood. His wife was out of town. My first impression of Brian was he was handsome, successful, and incredibly funny. He was a "life of the party" kind of guy. He was very likable and happily married for over 20 years. There was an instant attraction that I quickly resisted. Again, he was a happily married man.

Here's another "again" . . . if I had been abiding in Jesus and living by His Word, I could've known from the time of our first introduction that he had issues too. We all had issues – him, my date that night and certainly ME. I was a blind sheep in the wrong pasture and did not recognize my Shepherd's voice. I discovered on this night we first met (several months prior) was that he had all the characteristics that attracted me to men. 1) He was musically talented. He couldn't sing like Calvin, but he was a much better musician on the guitar and mandolin. His musical talent intrigued me just like Calvin's did. He and other local guys had a country-western band where they played in local clubs and various special events in the area. Something that has appealed to me in my past. It was an atmosphere I was familiar with and drawn to. 2) Let's just say he was very comfortable financially. He had a very successful business that was oilfield related. Anyone who works in the oilfield during the oil booms is financially comfortable. He was a SMART businessman and money manager. His financial status was attractive. He was wealthy just like J.J.'s family, but he had created his wealth on his own, not from generational inheritance. That gained even more of my respect for him. His intelligence and wealthy independence were captivating. He also had those ice blue eyes and brown wavy hair that J.J. had. 3) He was athletic. It was obvious he liked to workout. That was the same trait that immediately drew me to Rob and my neighborhood jogger I dated for a short time. 4) He proclaimed his love for Jesus. He was raised in a very devout Baptist upbringing. His brother was a preacher. His father taught Sunday school. He knew the Bible. The icing on the cake! As I was on a date with another guy, I was taking inventory of this guy who checked off all of my boxes. I knew I couldn't have him, but I was sure fantasizing about finding one like him. My date that facilitated this meeting was clearly not "the one".

Hopefully you're starting to get the picture. Satan is not creative like our God. He will never be a creator like our Creator. He can only be a counterfeit and try to copy God. Also, he cannot create new ways to entrap God's children. He just repeats his same game, using the same playbook. He wraps it up in a shiny new package. He is so good at deceiving. He is cunning and sly and crafty at disguising something tarnished to make it look like it is shiny and new. I was one of his easiest targets. Even after all my failed relationships, I was STILL a gullible subject he liked to jack with.

The sneaky snake introduced me to a man that was one shiny package on the outside. At our first introduction, I was instantly attracted to the same traits that lured me into a covenant with my previous husbands along with their issues. On top of that, you can guess what we did for entertainment that night. We sat on his balcony, smoked a joint and sang while he played his guitar. Here we go again! This season is when I learned church-going men are not exempt from the devil's temptations.

That's the background of the story. Back to current events.

On this normal Saturday, about nine months later, I was perplexed as to why Brian was calling me. As I stated in an earlier chapter, phone books were a convenience. But they were also a possible nuisance. They made it easy for predators to call when your home phone was listed.

"I really need some advice. Do you mind if I lay some burdens on you? I just remember you last summer as being someone with lots of wisdom and I know you've already been where I'm headed." That was the line that hooked me. My heart dropped into my stomach.

He proceeded to tell me he had filed for divorce from his wife after finding out she was having an affair. I reasoned he probably knew I was an "expert on divorce" (according to my track record) and wanted my advice on what he should do. *Really dude? This is really why you're calling a woman you barely know?* That SHOULD HAVE been my reaction. If I had been abiding in Jesus, I would have easily seen the warning sign. Instead, I admittedly felt butterflies in my stomach with the idea that this man might possibly be in the single pool soon. I fought that thought with everything in me.

I put on my good, Christian woman hat and advised him not to go through with the divorce until exhausting all attempts to reconcile. I knew I had to follow Biblical principles to please Jesus. To be perfectly transparent, I was trying to appease Jesus, so that He would give me "the desires of my heart" with this "well-rounded" guy. I explained counseling could help reveal the reason for her infidelity and with prayer, they could get past it and rekindle their love. That was hypocritical of me since I never really tried that with Calvin. We never received counseling, other than what we got at the rehab center. I was definitely not the one he should be asking advice from.

That was the beginning of my next battle in the wilderness.

As the divorce continued, so did his pursuit of me with more phone calls. His charm was more captivating than any man I had ever encountered. He seemed like the perfect mate. I fooled myself into thinking it was ok to talk to him, even though he was only separated. The marriage wasn't officially dissolved yet. Emotional affairs are still extra-marital affairs. This was my sign from God to RUN THE OTHER WAY! I ignored the sign because again, I wasn't ABIDING in Jesus. I was more interested in pleasing my fleshly desires than pleasing my Savior and Friend.

The relationship started off slowly and innocently, as I continued to play the role of a trusted friend and confidant that he could vent to. Of course, we had to keep our conversations confidential. People might get the wrong idea. We were "just friends." Those conversations began to get longer and longer with more and more laughter and "innocent flirtations." Again, meaningful conversations were my love language. He had all the same perks that completely won me over, just like when I met Calvin.

So, to make ANOTHER very LONG story as short as possible, here is the breakdown.

We started a relationship that was grounded in sin, as we wrongfully developed an inappropriate friendship while he was still a married man.

That inappropriateness escalated into an emotional affair that escalated into a full-blown affair, because he was only separated. He was still a married man. Even if he had been divorced, we were still guilty of sexual immorality outside the confines of marriage.

I became entangled in an excruciating web of secrets, lies and confrontations with his estranged wife. Brian was actually jumping on both sides of the fence, keeping me and his wife on a string of lies and promises. His daughter was in no way thrilled with me either and never held back her disapproval. I had officially become one of those women I despised when I was on the other end of infidelity... a mistress. A homewrecker. A family divider. An intruder who had no rights to be there.

When the divorce was finally over, our relationship grew into a MORE excruciating entanglement. For the first year, it was a "blissful fog" with visions and dreams of a happily ever after. Eventually, I found myself *addicted* to a man, who fed my other addictions. He was addicted to marijuana too. He became my resource of abundant supply, only increasing my indulgence. The more I altered my mind, the more my common sense was dulled until I didn't know myself. Those amazing traits I saw in him in the beginning, began to morph into the reality that they were of the world. His Bible knowledge was instilled from a strict religious background that caused him to rebel as a teenager. He still claimed his Christianity, but I saw very little fruit of a Christian lifestyle. I wasn't any better. I wasn't living out my faith either. He was also a heavy drinker and I started to drink more than I ever had. I just wanted to connect with him and be a fun girlfriend that would keep him interested. We became functional alcoholics. Drinking excessively on the weekends we were together, but still able to function in our everyday responsibilities. He never missed a day of work – neither did I, and was still raising my boys.

I was destined to have to endure all the *dysfunction* in *all three* of my previous marriages wrapped up in one man! The only flaw he did not possess, thankfully, was the physical abuse I received from Rob. He never laid a hand on me physically. EVEN during one of my fits of rage where I put my hands on him! However, he got me back - his emotional punches hurt so much worse. No doubt there were MANY times he showered me with compliments and showed a lot of affection. But there was a dark side too. In a nutshell, his favorite "ego booster" was a practice of making me jealous and watching me go into a fit of rage. Then, he would call me psycho.

He made Calvin look like an altar boy when it came to affairs with other women behind my back. Many times, he even did it right in front of my face with his flirtations with other women. He didn't see anything wrong with it because he was not married to me. It was eight years of break-ups and make-ups, due to his wandering eyes and one-night stands. As my Pastor often says, "If he does it WITH you, he will do it TO you." I know today this was rooted in a lack of self-confidence on his part. He thought my jealousy would prove I loved him. Satan can really twist things into a nest of dysfunction.

This is going to sound strange, but the only sin that saved me from going completely under in my addiction and my sinful ways *was* my double life. My duties as a mom forced me to take days and weekends off from the party life. My sweet boys had no idea what a mess their mom was. It was definitely sin but I'm thankful it kept me on a thin rope of a lifeline. I was definitely a lost sheep that was barely hanging way out on a limb. The Good Shepherd left the 99 to come find me and rescue me . . . eventually.

Thankfully, I kept the lines of communication open with Jesus. Those were one-sided conversations though. I did a whole lot of talking and very little, if any, listening. For eight years, I whined and begged Jesus to just "fix it" and get me out. He needed me to learn to strengthen myself in Him. God is more interested in teaching us a lifelong lesson by going *through* the storm than just supernaturally transporting us to the other shore with an easy fix. He knew an easy fix would just keep me on this endless merry-go-around of dysfunctional behavior. He wants to create in us a sound mind and contrite (humble) heart. That doesn't happen with just an easy fix.

The one area where I did listen to Jesus was concerning my children. During the good times, I would fantasize about a day when Brian and I would get married. But I'm thankful that I had enough sense throughout the entire relationship to keep him separate from my children as much as possible. I knew he wasn't a good influence on them, despite them getting along with him the few times they were around him. The fact that Brian was not much of a family man helped with this arrangement. He was a loving and good dad to his only daughter, but he was not interested in going beyond the parameters of that to be a father figure to anyone else. So, we had a mutual agreement to keep our immediate families outside and away from our relationship.

So, when I was with the boys, Brian and I took a break from us and he spent time with his daughter as well, apart from me. I spent all my time and devotion to the boys. On weeknights and the weekends, they were home, it was all about a Christian atmosphere. We went to family-friendly outings, church, and watched movies; all the wholesome things I wanted my boys to be raised in. We prayed together and worshipped together. But when the boys went to their dads on the 1st, 3rd and 5th weekends, I became a party girl with an overnight bag, spending every hour with my new slave master. He didn't act like a slave master as Rob did. He was my emotional slave master. His prison was disguised as a happy place, where we partied, sang songs to his guitar on the back porch and laughed until our sides hurt. We even took several fun vacations. He was the first to introduce me to the sandy beaches of Mexico. This strengthened his hold on me, even when he would wander behind my back. Brian was perfectly happy with this arrangement with his "part-time soul mate". It gave him time to have his cake and eat it too. On our off weekends, he could go out and live his single life.

I could NOT break the chains he had on my soul.

Eventually, I grew more and more weary, deeper in depression and losing my identity as a daughter of Christ. I would spend those weekday mornings and "mom-duty" weekends continuing to beg Jesus to help me leave him. My words were sincere, but my actions debunked every prayer. Jesus wanted me to step out in faith just like I had before. THEN, He would take all the other steps. I just couldn't find the emotional strength to take that one step. The truth is, I enjoyed the dark side of my life. Satan makes sin fun. Otherwise, we wouldn't get caught up in it. I started to become someone I didn't even recognize. I was losing myself completely in the shadow of the most dysfunctional relationship of all time.

Don't get me wrong. I loved Jesus. I never stopped pursuing Him, wanting to get to know Him more. I never stopped believing in Him. I LOVED studying the Word. This is why I had such a conflicting battle going on in my spirit.

I realize today that I failed in *applying the Word* to my life because I never learned to be a receiver. I couldn't get to a point where I could fully receive His unconditional love. I could only see His love through the lens of my experience with humans. I knew He was God, but I couldn't fully grasp that He was my Heavenly Father, and I was His child that He adored, flaws and all. I couldn't fully grasp that HE was Who I was looking for! He was a perfect companion. He is my Comforter, my Provider, my everything I needed to fill the void in my life. Yet, I was like Adam and Eve, I hid from Him when I committed the same sins over and over. I should've run straight to Him, yet I would hide and try to cover up and make up for my rebellion.

I still couldn't grasp who I was in Him, so I tried to "work my way" out of my sin debt by being a good Christian mom on all the days the boys were in my care. This also caused me to parent from an unstable emotional state, instead of a consistent, loving authoritative state. I didn't always discipline the boys from a healthy mindset – lovingly correcting them for their own good. Instead, I either let things slide or punished them too quickly, based on my emotions – not necessarily their actions. I would try to overcompensate when I was feeling guilty; or would be impatient and harsh when I was feeling stressed. I failed in applying ALL of the Word to ALL areas of my life. I compartmentalized my walk with Jesus. That is SO dangerous! It's also ridiculous, since Jesus was my ONLY Friend Who knew me better than I knew myself! There is no pretending when it comes to Jesus. He already knows our innermost thoughts. Where we go, He goes.

Let's look at Psalms 139:1-18 [New Living Translation]

> *"O LORD, you have examined my heart and know everything about me.*
> *You know when I sit down or stand up.*
> *You know my thoughts even when I'm far away.*
> *You see me when I travel and when I rest at home. You know everything I do.*

↑ Lisa Dee Dunnam ↓

You know what I am going to say even before I say it, LORD.
You go before me and follow me. You place Your hand of blessing on my head,
Such knowledge is too wonderful for me, too great for me to understand!
I can never escape from your Spirit! I can never get away from Your presence!
If I go up to heaven; You are there; if I go down to the grave, You are there.
If I ride the wings of the morning, if I dwell by the farthest oceans,
Even there Your hand will guide me, and Your strength will support me.
I could ask the darkness to hide me and the light around me to become night –
But even in darkness I cannot hide from You. To You the night shines as bright as a day. Darkness and light are the same to You.
You made all the delicate, inner parts of my body and knit me
together in my mother's womb.
Thank You for making me so wonderfully complex! Your workmanship is marvelous—how well I know it.
You watched me as I was being formed in utter seclusion, as I was woven together in the dark of the womb.
You saw me before I was born. Every day of my life was recorded in Your book. Every moment was laid out before a single day had passed.
How precious are Your thoughts about me, O God. They cannot be numbered!
I can't even count them; they outnumber the grains in the sand!
And when I wake up, You are still with me!"

I should've started my day, each day, reciting these verses, until it was etched in my heart. That was my story. It is still relevant today but in different ways. If only I had clung to these words of King David. In case you don't know about King David, he committed adultery and murdered his lover's husband! But God STILL called David "a man after His own heart". David knew how to go to God for forgiveness and repent! God changed his heart when he did. So, if only I knew to be more like David, I'm pretty sure I would have a whole different story to write.

Instead, I was still tightly bound to the lie that my only sense of identity could be found in a man to belong to. I was still a slave to the fear of being alone. If only I had realized I belong to the One True Living God, Who supplies ALL of my need AND changes my desires to look like His heart. If only I had TRULY believed and received His promise when He told me "You are not alone, Lisa". I denied that promise in unbelief and I missed the mark. I didn't like being alone with me because I didn't like me. I had very good reasons not to like me.

It was during this time in my life that I broke God's sixth commandment 3 more times. I aborted two pregnancies with Brian and one with a man I dated very briefly years before I met Brian. It was more horrendous than the very first time, because this time I KNEW it was a life – not just a seed as I had been told as a teenager. I reasoned that bringing a baby into my dysfunctional life was only cruel and they would be better off staying in Heaven. It was the only false mindset that kept me sane. The truth was I was a selfish coward. It is NEVER ok. There is NEVER a good enough reason to play God and take a life that He created – no matter the circumstance. I've had to live with the guilt for years, and just recently I have been able to forgive myself even though God forgave me the moment I repented.

I know He has forgiven me because of my repentant heart, and He has promised I will get to spend eternity with my four other children, along with the two angels I did not abort. He has told me to name my other children. This is how kind our God is – He forgives and forgets our sins the minute we confess and repent. I'm still praying about their names. It is something that has to be deeply considered and not just randomly picked. It is still very painful to think my children lost their lives and that their purposes on earth were quickly snatched away at the hand of their own mother. As Holy Spirit continues to take me through the healing process, I know I'll be ready one day to give them their perfect names to call out to them when we are reunited in Heaven.

If you find yourself pregnant in a very unfavorable circumstance – please don't take the cowardly way out like I did. There are so many better alternatives. Find a "Life Center" or pregnancy help center of any kind that is PRO-Life. They are loving professionals who can help you with any roadblocks that are causing you to consider abortion. They can give you BETTER alternatives. Whether it is helping you navigate adoption for your baby or helping you with any need you have in order to raise your child . . . choose life – not death. God will bless you abundantly for taking the narrow road. His way is the narrow road. Satan's way is easy, and many take that wide road. Choose the narrow road! Otherwise, take it from me . . . you will live in the torment of guilt, shame, and regret for a long time. I literally killed the chance of being abundantly blessed by these lives HE created for a purpose.

When we take a detour from our God-given destiny, Holy Spirit will diligently work to show us we are on the wrong path. There are so many red flags He will raise, but if we are not tuned in to His voice, we will either miss them or BLATANTLY IGNORE them! Red flags with Brian were undeniable and I blatantly ignored them. Taking a journey with a worldly man will lead you down a path of unfathomable worldly decisions you can never take back.

Claiming to be a Christian without actually following Christ in all areas of your life is a dangerous tight rope to walk on. Salvation is not a magic one-time prayer that brings a "blanket of grace" to cover repeated sins over and over. Salvation comes from actual repentance and a relationship with Jesus. Repentance means to change your mind – to be truly sorry for your sinful nature and daily ask Jesus to help you change your ways – not just your mind.

I can't help but to think I was headed to hell before the day I fully repented. Jesus doesn't fall for lip service. He looks at the intentions of our heart and my heart was far from Him. I only played the part to appease my guilty conscience and to protect my children. It was only the beginning of the long journey I was on, being with a man who had a lack of respect for me. The reason I kept traveling down that road is because *I had a total lack of respect for myself*. When I would catch him with another woman, I would break up with him for a short time. I would date other men to pay him back. I would sleep with these men to pay him back. I ran the risk of getting pregnant again and facing the decision to choose life or death. I'm thankful that didn't happen, but God was trying to give me a wakeup call. I was so desperate to keep my secret life hidden, I am pretty sure I would have reverted to the heinous sin of murder – again. If God didn't intervene soon, no telling how far down I would've fallen. I kept ignoring the warning signs of a sinking ship until I almost drowned.

I convinced myself Brian was the only man I deserved. Good thing he was rich and good-looking. At least it made it a little easier to live in his prison. I kept trying to convince myself he was my soulmate because we had so many good times, coupled with the not-so-good times. I was just about settled into the agreement that I would spend the rest of my life with him, as soon as I get my boys raised. Finally, one day, while I was really seeking the Lord, he told me plainly, "Brian is your flesh-mate; not your soulmate." I was intrigued and bent my ear to listen and He continued. "Think about it Lisa, list all the things you love about your relationship with him and tell me which ones on the list are of Me." Wow – that really got my attention.

I could write about a million stories about this eight year walk in the wilderness. There were many valleys and mountains. It was treacherous terrain. I'll spare you the details; otherwise, this book would be about 800 pages. You've basically already heard it in my past relationships. Same plot and same outcome. Just different circumstances with more drama!

The truth was that I needed to STAY with fellow believers full-time and hold on to Hope. I needed to gain strength and remain in the greener pastures with my children, my church family, and my co-workers. I'll say it AGAIN. I pray this truth gets etched in your heart. The Bible tells us to ABIDE in Christ. Abide means "act in accordance with." We are likely to take on the characteristics of whomever we hang out with. The Bible says "Bad company corrupts good character" (1 Corinthians 15:33) Jesus changes our hearts and minds to love like He loves and to think like He thinks. Instead, my double life caused me to abide in Satan and all my friends and family who lived in the Light were oblivious to my other world. I was successful in keeping it a secret. **Satan's favorite tactic to keep us bound is secrecy.**

I was at least able to cling to my vocational destiny by achieving a bachelor's degree and moving up the ladder of success at the college until I finally landed the position I was meant for. I served my final 17 years at the college as an academic advisor and career counselor before I retired. I had a heart for helping young people realize their full potential in their dream career and to give them the academic map to get there. Little did they know, they were taking GREAT advice from a "woman of wisdom", who failed to follow it herself! My passion to help them was grounded in the truth that I wanted to spare them the grief I was currently in. To stay plugged in, I stayed active in church helping with various ministries. If this world ever clashed with my dark world, these people would not have recognized me. Nor would they have taken my advice.

I knew deep in my soul, if I continued, one day the two worlds *would* clash. I developed a deeper addiction to marijuana and became a master of hiding it from my children, my church and my co-workers. I was convinced it was the best medicine to control my constant state of anxiety and depression. Addiction surely entangles us and places a thick blindfold of deception over our eyes. It is not the answer, it's the root of our problems. It is a liar.

Looking back today, I am SO THANKFUL my two worlds never clashed into a scandal my family had to endure. I believe that was God's grace and mercy over my *children*. I, on the other hand, had to endure some consequences that stayed within my dark, secret world. I totally lost myself in thinking I had found my identity in this man who kept me in emotional bondage. It was THE most demonic stronghold of my life. Yet Satan disguised it as something good.

The worst part was seeing a change in myself that I truly LOATHED! As my jealousy grew into fits of rage, I saw myself turning into someone I didn't even recognize. This sin I couldn't hide. The fits became so violent when I was with him, he convinced me I was the problem. He even paid for me to see a therapist. During my appointments, he sat in the car or at a nearby bar! It never dawned on him he could use a little therapy himself. This is when I was professionally diagnosed with anxiety/depressive disorder. It was satisfying to see a label tied to my unhealthy condition. It was even more comforting to have access to medical treatment for it. This began a 10-year regimen on anti-depressants. The meds only treated the symptoms – not the root of my problem of being spiritually crippled. Conveniently, Brian used my diagnosis against me when it suited him. If I caught him "allegedly" cheating, he would call me psycho and ask me if I missed a dose. Brian nicknamed me "Lisafer" in reference to Lucifer. Oh, it was so appropriate. If I forgot to take my medicine, I would definitely act like this evil creature. Lucifer was behind every single incident and kept me bound in a broken soul. Mine and Brian's disagreements were never resolved with healthy resolutions, like prayer and transparent heart-to-heart conversations. If I was in the wrong, I would just work harder to please him. If he was in the wrong, he would use his wallet as a peace offering and buy me something expensive. There were never deliberate apologies and discussions on how we can completely resolve our issues. In Satan's world, you never say you're sorry, you just pile another sin on top to cover up the previous one.

BUT GOD! I'm so thankful He is MERCIFUL and loves me enough to not give up on me. I am forever thankful that He lengthened my days until I saw the Light. He finally got my attention and still teaches me how to choose Jesus, not the world – one day at a time.

I'm thankful today that Jesus redeemed my sin on the Cross, and I have received full forgiveness and mercy. Back then, during this time of turmoil – I just tried to "smoke screen" my sins and sweep them under the rug of my conscience.

However, this tragic love story finally came to an end, while we both have a chance to live a better life – apart - and we remain amicable friends today. We aren't close friends by any means as we do not communicate. We both have respect for the people who are now in our lives. Yet, through it all, I have forgiven him for all the hurt he caused me, and I hope he has been able to forgive me for the same. I hope I have not shed too dark of a picture of Brian. I believe *my* issues brought out the worst in *him* too. He does have many admirable qualities and I believe the Lord will bring him to full repentance, deepening their Father-son relationship, if He hasn't already. In fact, watching him from a distance, I actually do believe Brian has turned his life around. I can't know for sure, but from what I do see it's very different than when we were together. Ironically, we now both live in the same neighborhood, that requires me to drive by his house anytime I'm coming or going to my own home. His house no longer appears to be the same from the outside. When we were together, there was almost a constant party at his house. Several cars always parked there, with people coming and going to visit and hang out. Today, his house seems quiet and peaceful as he shares his life with only one girl and only their two cars are parked out front. She is a sweet girl who I know has always loved him very much. She is younger, and I'm sure she is devoted to taking good care of him. I'm happy to see him seemingly settled into a normal way of living, enjoying a quiet life of normalcy.

For his sake, as much as mine, but I'm also happy it's not with me! We were just too toxic for one another.

Our final goodbyes can only be explained by glorifying our Merciful, Loving Savior! Jesus still had my heart, but it was shattered into so many pieces. He never gave up on me though. He chose to **wait patiently on me to ask Him** to put me back together again.

I was so deep in my pit; I started hanging pictures and arranging the new furniture Brian bought me to make it more like home. I surrendered to the fact that this was my new normal and this was my permanent dwelling place. I was destined for a life of torment disguised as "just life".

BUT GOD came through again. He was not finished with me yet. Turn the page to learn about the final curtain call of this soap opera of a relationship. It's important to describe this incident, to help you understand an important lesson on the love of God.

CHAPTER THIRTEEN
My Final Exodus Out Of Slavery

"When I thought I lost me; You knew where I left me. You reintroduced me to Your love. You picked up all my pieces; Put me back together; You are the Defender of my heart... Hallelujah! You have saved me – it's so much better this way!" ~ (lyrics to "Defender" by John-Paul Gentile, Rita Springer, and Steffany Frizzell Gretzinger)

"I waited patiently for the Lord. And He inclined to me and heard my cry. He also brought me up out of the horrible pit, out of the miry clay, and set my feet upon a rock, and established my steps."

~ Psalms 40:1-2

Through all the constant chaos in my life, I still had a *shred* of common sense left to pray this daily request, "Lord, PLEASE do not let me enter into another failed marriage." God honored that prayer and never allowed Brian and I to be on the same page when it came to discussing marriage. In times when things were good between us, I know I would have eloped with him if he asked, but the subject was never discussed in those seasons. Other times, when things were rocky and he needed to lure me back in, he would propose marriage, but I was conscious enough to say, "No way!" I give God ALL the glory for the offset timing of those conversations! I was already married to him emotionally, but thank God there was no legal agreement that would have made it more difficult to break loose.

The years flew by, and it had been nearly a decade of this saga. My regular morning routine was still the same ole thing. Find a hiding place, take a toke, and run for miles to the beat of contemporary Christian music in my ears. Jesus had to listen to my whining from brain fog every morning, "WHEN Lord will you help me break free from this toxic relationship and bring me a godly man?" Even though I was still with Brian, I knew without a doubt we were both outside of God's will. It's comical to look back and admit I was asking for a godly man, when I was not exactly a godly woman, to say the least. The effects of the toke, would only take me deeper in my desperate cry.

You noticed my prayers were still centered around a man in my life? I STILL didn't get it that Jesus was the Lover of my soul, and He was all I needed. No man on earth could ever bring me the joy that Jesus can. Just as I told you about the Israelites and their 40-year journey in the wilderness - the Lord sometimes allows us also to go through LONG seasons of asking and waiting, while we are learning. But when He finally answers, He moves quickly. My Kairos moment happened when I least expected it. Kairos is the Greek word for *"strategic and opportune time."* My breakthrough didn't LOOK anything like I ever imagined it would.

It was a typical weekday, or so I thought. The day began with my usual jog and whiny prayer session with Jesus, followed by an 8-hour workday. A couple of hours before quitting time, I learned that both boys had after-school commitments. At that time, the boys were junior high and high school age. Cody had his own car and became the mode of transportation for Will on several occasions, as they became more involved in extra-curricular activities. Unexpectedly, I was blessed with 3 hours of free time to myself.

When I clocked out for the day, I didn't even take time to go home and change out of my casual business attire. I went straight to Brian's house to give him the good news that I could hang out with him for a while. This was a rare treat on a school night. When I got to his house, I discovered he and a few of his friends on the back

Don't Fall For It

porch, so I joined the party.

Instead of being the surprise, *I* was the one surprised as I learned that he had already made other plans. He abruptly informed me that I was not invited. It was "Boys night out" and therefore I did not qualify. In the back of my mind, I knew that girls were most likely in the plans as well. I had already sung many verses of that same ole' tune. I was so hurt that I quickly excused myself so he could carry on with his plans. As I was walking to my car sobbing, I said to myself "Fine! I'll just go find my *own* party!"

Satan thought he had his way with me once more . . . BUT God! Jesus came through with His sweet whisper as I turned the ignition to back out of Brian's driveway. "Hey daughter, why don't you just come party with Me on the mountain?" I am *beyond* grateful that I could hear His voice back then, among the angry chatter in my foggy head. Jesus meant a literal mountain. The state park in my hometown is an actual "mountain" (more like a very large hill) where locals hike and walk for exercise. Patrons can walk or drive around the paved road on the mountain and there is a bench on the very top that overlooks the west horizon. It is a favorite spot of locals to watch the sunset. I'm so thankful I accepted Jesus' invitation. THIS time, Satan wasn't successful in luring me into a worldly setting destined for revenge.

By that time, it was around 6:00 in the evening and the usual crowd of evening walkers were pacing the mountain trail. I slowly passed by several groups as I parked my car at the top of the mountain to sit on that sunset bench. I started my conversation with Jesus in the usual manner whining and all in my feelings of hurt and anger, "WHY Jesus? Why am I still with this man?" After several minutes of my pity party, suddenly, my countenance completely changed, and my petition became my battle cry. I literally stood up from that bench overlooking the horizon, dressed in my dressy blouse, capris pants and heels. I was a complete contrast from the walkers, drawing even *more* attention to myself. With my hands raised as high as my arms would reach, I began shouting from the top of my lungs!

"YOU HAVE GOT TO DO SOMETHING WITH ME,

GOD! I DO NOT WANT TO BE WITH THIS MAN ANY LONGER! **YOU** DON'T WANT ME TO BE WITH THIS MAN! YOU KNOW GOOD AND WELL THAT IF YOU DON'T DO SOMETHING WITH ME, I'M GOING TO GO RIGHT BACK DOWN THIS MOUNTAIN AND RUN RIGHT BACK INTO HIS ARMS, GOD! YOU'VE GOT TO DO SOMETHING! DO. SOMETHING. WITH. MEEEEEE!!" All the while crying crocodile tears and wiping snot from my face. I was *finally* at the end of myself, desperate and willing to look like a lunatic, in order to break free. I didn't care. All I cared about was moving the heart of God to save me. I literally went to war for my soul and my sanity.

Loud sobbing followed. I sat on that bench until the sun was kissing the horizon. I'm pretty sure some of those walkers told the park ranger there was a crazy lady at the top of the mountain. Shortly after my meltdown, he came to check on me. Thankfully, by then, I had calmed down to just a slobbery whimper. I apologized, convincing him I was not crazy but having a really bad day. *"No need to call the psychiatric hospital, Sir,"* were my thoughts and hopefully my subliminal message. His "wellness check" was my cue. It was time to exit and return to the safety of my home.

I'll never forget the overwhelming sense of peace I felt as I drove back down that mountain. At the time, I figured it was just a sense of relief by blowing off steam. It was deeper than that. Jesus had done a complete work in my spirit. My flesh just had to catch up.

I didn't break up with Brian (for the umpteenth time) immediately. But, over the next several weeks, I began noticing a strength in me that I hadn't felt in a very long time. Brian's hold on my soul began to loosen. I started to gain more and more respect for myself and determined to protect it. In other words, I stood up for myself and voiced my opinion when he hurt my feelings. This was a change from being quiet and submissive and just suppressing those feelings. My tenacity to break free continued to grow stronger. Today, I realize now that I was in a holding pattern. While waiting for the next incident to happen that would give me the perfect reason to leave for good, Holy Spirit kept speaking into me and drawing me closer to Him. Comically, I didn't see that I already had a million reasons collected in my jar to leave this man without incident. However, I began to understand more clearly, I deserved be loved the way God loves me. I became less tolerant of a situation in which I never felt safe. I even recall a day when we were driving to his lake house, and he said something hurtful to me. I looked straight at him and literally said, "Brian, I'm warning you. I'm about to bail and when I do, there will be no turning back!" He had seen me bail many times, but I don't think I ever made such a bold statement out loud. Still, he wasn't convinced.

One day, that reason finally happened, and it wasn't even a big blow. It was a typical reason that I had overlooked and forgiven a thousand times before. I caught him texting another girl, planning to meet up. As usual, he first tried to deny it. When I presented the evidence from his own phone, he minimized it with a "it's not what you think" story. I was finally done. I'm pretty sure he thought my abrupt exit was just another "lovers quarrel" that would buy him some time to go play before we made up again. In all honesty, so did I, deep down. I wasn't quite convinced that I was truly strong enough to finally break free.

But God. He said that it *was* the FINAL STRAW. I left his house for the very last time, never to return. God had INDEED heard my plea and had "done something with me". He restored my strength and dignity and led me back into a love affair with Jesus.

This time, the breakup period didn't have me sitting at home crying and waiting for him to come back. No. This time, I was feeling the urge to spread my wings like a FREE bird and fly! There was a new skip in my step and hope for my future. Finally, I was in a place where all I wanted or needed was Jesus. Another man never crossed my mind, nor did I have plans to search for one. My 8-year prison sentence was finally up, and Jesus paid my ransom once again!

By this time, Cody had graduated from high school and left home to go live in the Dallas metroplex area. Will was entering his freshman year of high school. Motherhood was quickly slipping away, and my "empty nest" years were quickly approaching. If Jesus had not brought my breakthrough, I know I would have been an easy target for Satan to trick me again with fear of being alone. Another one of his suitors could've snatched me back into bondage. Instead, for the first time in my life I was content with being single. No more fantasies about romance. I was SO DONE with the desire to try and find my "godly man" I constantly searched for. I had resolved to the fact that it was not in my cards. I settled into the mindset that "my picker was broke" and I probably wasn't meant to be married in the first place. The Apostle Paul was single. Jesus was single. Marriage isn't for everyone. That was FINALLY ok with me! I was in Good Company and ready to live out my days with the Lover of my soul.

CHAPTER FOURTEEN
The Key to TRUE Freedom

"Then Peter came to Him and said, Lord, how often shall my brother sin against me, and I forgive him? Up to seven times? Jesus said to him, "I do not say to you, up to seven times, but up to seventy times seven."

~ Matthew 18:21-22

This is THE MOST IMPORTANT chapter in my story and yours too, if your story is anything similar to mine. Ironically, I almost left it out. More ironically, Holy Spirit revealed my error in a Bible study called *Free Indeed*, held at a local church in my town. I was in the process of writing this book and I was actually celebrating in my spirit that night because *I thought* I had finished of my book and it was ready to be sent to my editor. As soon as I heard the words from the leader, "Tonight we are going to talk about forgiveness", the 100-watt light bulb went off in my head! Holy Spirit whispered, "Yeah . . . without forgiveness, your story is just another soap opera!" I love His sense of humor. God is STILL working on me, even in my old age!

No amount of therapy will ever work without forgiving your "enemies". Jesus told Peter he must forgive his brother seventy-times seven, which is 490 times. That's 490 times PER BROTHER! So, He was essentially saying "as many times as it takes". Jesus was pointing out that forgiveness is CRUCIAL for our own spiritual walk with the Lord.

I want to share with you some treasures found in our study guide that night at this Bible study. Thankfully, Holy Spirit had already walked me through these truths and was deepening my understanding of becoming "free indeed". The author of *Free Indeed*, Tom Vermillion of Mid-Cities Church in West Texas, explains the true concept more clearly than I can. So, when you see quotes, Pastor Vermillion gets all the credit.

First, we must define forgiveness. My own Pastor has drilled a good definition into our heads in many of his sermons. "Forgiveness means to lovingly, voluntarily cancel a debt someone has made against you." Pastor Willard has taught fervently that forgiveness does not require a physical reconciliation with that person(s). We are only required to reconcile the debt in our hearts – no matter the response from the other person. We are not even required to speak to the other person about it unless Holy Spirit tells us to. Forgiveness is for our own sake, not the other person's.

Pastor Vermillion says: "Unforgiveness is not an option in the heart of God. He wants us to develop the heart of Christ. Forgiveness trains us to TRUST GOD and allow HIM to be the judge."

This is what God says about forgiveness in His Word:

"Do not repay anyone evil for evil. Be careful to do what is right in the eyes of everybody. If it is possible, as far as it depends on you, live at peace with everyone. Do not take revenge, my dear friends, but leave room for God's wrath, for it is written: 'It's Mine to avenge; I will repay', says the Lord. On the contrary, if your enemy is hungry, feed him; if he is thirsty, give him something to drink. In doing this, you will heap burning coals on his head. Do not be overcome by evil but overcome evil with good." ~ **Romans 12:17-21[NIV]**

Wow. Those are strong words that seem humanly impossible to follow, right? They sure were for me. I had 5 men in my past who hurt me deeply. I was married to three of them and two were steady boyfriends. I never had to ACTUALLY "feed them or give them something to drink" and if I had read this scripture back in the day, I would have been tempted to feed them poison. Anger and bitterness were so deep that it took YEARS to sincerely forgive them. I've heard it preached many times that "unforgiveness is like drinking poison and expecting the offender to die." Unforgiveness unchecked will create a deep well of bitterness that will only affect YOUR life, not theirs. Notice that the Word says, "you will heap burning coals on his head" IF you respond to that person with kindness. LOVE CONQUERS ALL. Love is what Jesus means by burning coals. I like to paraphrase this passage as "kill them with kindness!" Anytime you choose to respond to hurt, bitterness and anger with the love of Christ, it will ALWAYS end in everyone's favor. Maybe not favor from that person, but always favor from God. That person may not accept your forgiveness, but it will still make an impression on their hearts, whether they realize it or not.

Here is another great quote from Vermillion's study guide. "As we forgive, we release the poison of our hurt and anger so that bitterness, self-pity, and vengeance do not take root in our own hearts. Eventually, the anger, bitterness, and resentment we hold toward others will spill over onto the ones we DO love and that can damage those relationships. As long as we keep the hurt alive [by refusing to forgive], *we tend to allow the one who hurt us to have some measure of control in our lives* because we will make decisions based on what he or she might think or feel about what we are doing, rather than what is simply in our best interest."

I emphasized that last sentence because I have a true story as a perfect example. I touched on it in an earlier chapter, but let's revisit to emphasize the importance of forgiveness. From the first day I found out about Calvin's multiple affairs in our marriage, bitterness took root, and it grew deep. Not only did I refuse to forgive him after his hundreds of pleas, but I also planned my counterattack to get revenge. I also became bitter toward God. Because of this bitterness, I decided to get even with Calvin as soon as J.J. started calling. This was my perfect opportunity to show Calvin how it felt to be betrayed. Although I was attracted to J.J., the main motivation to enter the relationship was revenge. Forgiveness was out of the question. I wanted Calvin to stew in his decisions and keep him on that hook of regret. I wanted him to feel the hurt he imposed on me with his extra-marital affairs.

It's never our job, nor our right, to be judge over someone, no matter what they've done. Again, God says in Romans, *"It is Mine to avenge."* If I had run to God with all my bitterness and anger first, instead of running straight to J.J., God only knows how my marriage with J.J. could have had a happier ending. J.J. was just as broken as I was. J.J. was, in no way, equipped to handle the heavy baggage I brought into our marriage. Had I gone through the process of forgiving Calvin, before I dated *anyone*, I would have been a whole person who could offer J.J. a complete partner, without bitterness and anger. Yet, God, in His infinite mercy, allowed me to learn lessons the hard way. He still gave me the most precious treasure in my second son, William Jon. However, Will and Cody both lived under the covering of two broken parents; dads who suffered from depression and addiction and an addicted mom with a deep root of bitterness, that influenced her feelings, words, and decisions. Our brokenness affected innocent children who could not pick their families. *We MUST love others as Christ loves us!* It's not an option, it's a command. If God Himself does it, so must we. It's the only way to live free.

"But God demonstrates His own love for us in this: While we were still sinners, Christ died for us." **Romans 5:8**

"He saved us, not because of righteous things we had done, but because of His mercy..." **Titus 3:5**

Another important truth from the study guide: "Forgiveness is ALSO a PROCESS. Our decision to forgive is an event that is an act of obedience to God. That first step of forgiveness is a decision of the WILL; NOT our EMOTIONS." In other words, forgiveness is a CHOICE; NOT a FEELING! My process has been LONG and HARD.

When I was on that women's retreat where I met Jesus, there was a talk from a preacher about forgiveness. We were allowed to submit anonymous questions to the speaker on note cards for him to respond to publicly. When the speaker came to my ANONYMOUS question, "Is it *true* forgiveness when I SAY I have

↑ *Don't Fall For It* ↓

forgiven someone, yet I still have a lot of anger toward them?" I believe at that moment Holy Spirit guided his eyes to look straight at me with the answer, as if he knew it was my handwriting. He advised me to commit to pray for that person (Calvin) EVERY day for 30 days and just see if the bitterness and anger went away. He explained that forgiveness is not even HUMANLY possible, but only possible with the help of Holy Spirit.

So, I took his advice and started as soon as I got home from that retreat. To be perfectly honest, the first day of that 30-day challenge was not a very nice prayer at all. It was short and to the point. "Lord, bless him" in a very sarcastic tone of voice. That was all I could muster up. If I went any further, it would've turned into a gripe session instead of a prayer. As each day passed in that 30 days, my prayers became longer and more sincere in asking Holy Spirit to help me TRULY forgive him. Holy Spirit started reasoning with me that we had a child together and I didn't want my bitterness to spill over onto Cody. I wanted us to find a way to co-parent Cody the Kingdom way, even in separate households. By the time the 30-day prayer commitment was complete, the Holy Spirit allowed me to see Calvin through His eyes. I grew more compassionate toward Calvin with each passing day, praying against the demons that had him bound. I saw his offenses against *me* LESS and the struggles *he* had more. My prayers to be able to forgive turned into prayers for him to be set free. the Holy Spirit – THROUGH A PROCESS – taught me how to have compassion for Calvin instead of resentment. I keep emphasizing "process" because I want you to give yourself grace. It's a very difficult task and God doesn't expect you to "just get over it". Depending on the seriousness of the offense, it takes time. How much time is different for everyone and for every circumstance. But if you're sincerely trying, there is grace for that. If you don't give up, you WILL accomplish true forgiveness!

I would be dishonest if I didn't admit I was *still* struggling with complete forgiveness while writing this book. Taking a stroll down memory lane caused a lot of ill feelings to surface from deep within my soul. I realize I still have deep anger and resentment toward Rob. I tend to include criticism of him, anytime I mention him in a conversation. I'm always claiming he was the root of my dysfunction. He wasn't. Satan was. Rob was just an unsuspecting chess piece the devil used to torment me. I believe one of the main reasons God told me to write this book was to continue taking me through the process of forgiving Rob. I thought I was past it all completely, but I cannot honestly say that. It's been more of an "out of sight, out of mind" situation. Soon after Rob and I divorced, his job transferred him hundreds of miles away where he made a new life for himself. I've never seen him since. Looking back now and revisiting a very hard time in my life has opened some deep wounds and caused lingering bitterness to surface. Forgiveness is the hardest command from God to obey; yet it is one of THE strongest commands in the Word. The Bible clearly states if we don't forgive others, then our Heavenly Father will not forgive us! THAT'S HARSH! God is not playing in how He feels about us holding unforgiveness in our hearts. I believe it's because it is for *our* good! He wants to get our attention because He loves us. It's also a perfect way for God to prove Himself to us. With God, NOTHING is impossible!

It's taking me years to go through the process, and I know I'm getting better with each passing year. The important thing is, I *want* to forgive. God has been so very amazing to me and my motivation to forgive is to make Him happy. He forgave me, so I MUST forgive others! I meditate on **Psalms 51:10** a LOT, *"Create in me a pure heart, O God, and renew a steadfast spirit within me."* Let me repeat, forgiveness is a daily *decision*, not a feeling! We don't have to make that decision in our own strength. God's Word is our powerful tool, and the Holy Spirit is our Helper.

If we are talking to *God* on a regular basis about forgiving a person(s), and not venting to anyone else, He is faithful to change our hearts to match His. Don't fall into the trap of gossiping or complaining by venting to people instead of God. Venting to God is allowed. He already knows our every thought and He is the only one who can change the condition of our heart. He will not leave us to figure it out on our own. A humble and sincere plea for help to forgive will move the heart of God to come to our aid. That's all I know to do until those deep wounds are completely healed.

When we can meditate on the many times God has forgiven us for our mistakes, our deliberate sinful acts that broke His heart, and the ways we have treated others, we too can be instantly healed from bitterness and anger out of the ability to forgive our enemies too.

I challenge you to try some of these principles covered in this chapter. If you are struggling with unforgiveness, try the 30-day prayer challenge that the preacher gave me back then. It may take longer than 30 days, but don't give up! Just keep asking the Holy Spirit to help you.

Again, forgiveness means to *"lovingly*, voluntarily cancel the debt." Voluntarily means YOU decide you are going to forgive that person, **EVEN IF THEIR BEHAVIOR REMAINS THE SAME**. Lovingly means you decide to live with a heart like Jesus, to the best of your ability! If your offender responds in a hurtful way, your LOVING response is God's way. It doesn't get THEM off the hook, it gets YOU off the hook with God. Let God be your avenger. Let HIM deal with them. Stay in good graces with God and be the bigger person. IT WILL TRULY SET YOU FREE!!!!

Finally, another very important principle of the Kingdom is THE POWER OF PRAYER. Prayer enabled me to forgive those who hurt me. I look back now and realize that I didn't know the power of prayer as I was going through those storms. If I had known to pray against darkness over my husband(s) like I know today how to pray against darkness over my loved ones, I might have seen great miracles. If I knew to pray against unbelief and anger in Rob, it might have changed things. If I had known to pray against insecurity and addiction over Calvin, it might have changed the end of our love story. If I had known to pray against depression and addiction over J.J., he could still be alive today. If you are in the midst of a similar situation in your life and you see no happy ending in sight, PRAY! Prayer can change everything! It doesn't always happen instantly, but while you pray, GOD will change YOU! All I knew to do was to pray for my escape. God answered every one of those prayers.

Let me make myself perfectly clear! If you ARE a prayer warrior and you HAVE prayed endlessly in a similar situation, do not lose faith! It is possible God HAS answered your prayer with a "No child. This is not the path I have chosen for you." When we pray first about any situation, especially about getting a divorce and breaking up a family, God is FAITHFUL to guide us down the right path. Spend time with Him. A lot of time! He will give you concrete signs on what His will is for your life! He knew J.J. would only get worse until it was time to take him Home. He knew the atmosphere for my boys would only get worse if I stayed. He knew I was too "young in my faith" to know how to pray strategic prayers of warfare. I still had a lot of growing up to do. If you are perplexed about what is God's will in your situation, war for it on your knees! Just be prepared in case God gives you His answer you may not want to hear. Trust Him and obey! His perfect will is the best place for everyone involved in your surroundings.

By forgiving myself and the other men I was entangled with, I was free to live and to love unconditionally. As I received the forgiveness of God by asking Jesus into my heart and gave Him my life, I was transformed by Love. He taught me how to love like Him – even if it took 4 decades to get me there. As a new creation, my past no longer held me in its grip, and I was free to move forward into a new chapter I could never have known to ask for or even imagined.

CHAPTER FIFTEEN

The Dawn of a New Day

"Now the Lord is the Spirit, and where the Spirit of the Lord is, there is freedom."

~ 2 Corinthians 3:17

I was in a very good place when the day came that I bumped into my destiny. We can wait for decades, but when God decides to move, He can move quickly! I wasn't even looking for it. Notice I didn't say met. I had a chance encounter with a man whom I had known since the 6th grade during an outing with my girlfriends. I knew of his family and their name was well-respected in the community. I had heard through small-town gossip that he had gone through a divorce from his first wife of 20-plus years. There was an instant spark when we saw each other this fateful night.

This could sound like a rerun of the start with Brian when that relationship started while he was separated from his wife of 20+ years. However, Craig (his real name) was *completely* opposite of Brian, and all the other men in my life. He was *already* divorced – not just separated. I don't have to change his name to prevent any offense, like I have done throughout this book with most of my other men. Craig is my happily-ever-after. I don't have to protect his privacy due to toxic stories connected with him. Craig is the exact opposite of toxicity.

Craig pulverized all of Satan's lies; *"A decent man would never have you. You have messed up too many times for any good man to ever want you."*

The night we ran into each other, we began catching up on the last 30 years following high school. Our attraction to one another was instant. It was strong. It was PURE. It was the first time a man didn't try luring me into bed right away. Instead, he only walked me to my car and gave me our first innocent kiss goodnight. I remember going home that night and telling Mom, (my "roomie" after Dad moved to Heaven), "Mom! I think I really like a GOOD guy! I'm pretty sure he likes me too!" When I told her who he was, Mom and I did a praise dance right there in the kitchen. She knew his family since her high school years and concurred when I said he was a good man. He comes from a good family – very well-known and respected. My hopes and dreams were coming to pass!

Craig and I went on our very first lunch date a few days later. We became exclusive immediately and married on the one-year anniversary of that fateful first night we connected. Every day spent with this man is like living in a dream that I thought would never come true. He is kind, gentle, supportive, TRUSTWORTHY, and a faithful Jesus follower. From the moment we started dating, I felt so safe and secure with him. I knew that he was a man of his word. He proves over and over how dependable and honest he is. Not once have I doubted his devotion. We have a complete trust bond between us. I truly have found my best friend to do life with.

My two sons and his three children call each other "brother and sister." Cliff, Chad and Caylie are my "bonus children". Here are some amazing fun facts. Cliff and I share the same birthday; and Caylie and I share the same middle name! It's as if God had this planned from the very beginning of their lives on earth. The word "step" is never used in our perfectly blended family. Now, we all have been blessed with other additions to our family with Chad's wife, Michelle and Cody's wife Kari; and my adorable grandsons from Cody and Kari – Canyon and Kingston. All of our children have instantly bonded and been so loving and supportive of one another. We could be on a reality show for "model" blended

↑ Don't Fall For It ↓

families, though it would get canceled the first season for lack of viewers. No drama means no entertainment. There *have* been millions of laughs and meaningful conversations.

When I *finally* surrendered my future to God's plan and released it out of my own hands, God brought me the desires of my heart in Craig. Craig isn't a stepdad to my boys; he is a "stepped-up" dad. God brought him into our lives in the season when they needed a father figure the most. Craig is the PERFECT surrogate father. He loves them as if they were from his own bloodline. He is always willing to extend a father's hand, but also respects their boundaries when they just need a friend. He never has the heart to replace the boys' dads but only to fill in for them when needed.

Our family TRULY is a God-ordained union that no man can ever separate. Craig and I do have our challenges, but we know that when God is in the center, every obstacle is taken care of in His time.

Unlike any past life I've known, I can only count on one hand the number of arguments Craig and I have had. Yes, we disagree sometimes, but we never FIGHT! Craig is the first man I have ever been with who insists, and practices the art of, amicable conflict resolution. We are in no way perfect, as we have raised our voices with one another, but it has never escalated into name calling or shouting the "D" word – divorce. It always ends with sincere apologies and a good heart-to-heart conversation that only brings us closer.

One of my fondest memories came early in our relationship and depicts the nature of our love story. When we first started dating, I was so paranoid that this new world would clash with my past. I just knew that if my darkness surfaced in the town gossip, I would surely lose Craig. One memorable night, my fear was completely obliterated. We were about to walk into a social gathering. My anxiety intensified with the dread of possibly seeing someone from my past. Our courtship at this time was exclusive going on three months, but new to the general public. Word of our courtship had not gone beyond our closest friends and family. We had already started talking about a forever future together, despite being a new couple. I remember holding his hand as we were about to enter the unknown, saying something to the effect that he may be embarrassed to be seen with me. I made a joke about "people will see I'm with candidate #4," referring to my multiple divorces and long list of previous last names. It was a word of caution to him. I don't remember my exact words, but I will never forget his words. He took my hand and held it tight, saying, "You have nothing to fear. You're with me now and one day you will be a Dunnam, for good." I never felt more relieved and safer. God changed people's names in the Bible when they crossed over into their eternal destiny. Saul became Paul. Simon became Peter. In July of 2009, I was given my new name, representing dignity and respect in our small town. God had changed my name to be forever associated with a man who didn't care where I'd been. He could only see who I *truly* am.

After God delivered me from the den of iniquity, He continued His miraculous work in me. As soon as we returned from our honeymoon and settled into our new life together, God delivered me INSTANTLY from my marijuana addiction! I remember I was sneaking a puff in the early morning hours the day after we came home. Craig was still asleep. He knew nothing about my addiction and that a few puffs had been my regular morning routine. After only one toke, I started feeling the effects. The worst case of paranoia came over me and it was not the usual relief from anxiety. That had never happened before. It was followed by an overwhelming sense of conviction. The Holy Spirit made it clear to me that my new life could not include my double life. I threw my stash over our back fence, and I never looked back. I never had a craving after that day either! The absence of a stressful environment made all the difference. The step of faith to "toss it" was all that God required to complete a work of healing in me.

One morning, very soon after that, I realized I hadn't taken my anti-depressant medication for over a week. I kept forgetting to take it. There were no physical or emotional symptoms, reminding me I had missed several doses. I thought, "Hmm, well, let's see how long I can go without them before I start feeling symptoms." So far, I've gone over 14 years without them! Any doctor who prescribes anti-depressants will tell you to NEVER quit those types of drugs "cold turkey" because it can have an adverse effect. I had even experienced that before, when a certain kind of antidepressant made me too lethargic. After a few days of missed doses, the effects hit me so hard, I thought I was having an emotional breakdown. So, **I am not advising you to go against any doctor's orders.** Yet, THIS WAS A TRUE MIRACLE! I have been completely delivered from those mind-altering chains I "drug" around for years. It was instant and it was so easy! Praise God!

As I finally finish writing this book, we have been married 14 years and have been a couple for 15. Craig has been a strong shoulder to lean on and a source of comfort and support as I've recalled and described here, the tumultuous past I experienced before he came into my life.

Craig had never heard about my past until right before our 10th anniversary. It's because *he never asked*. The only reason he heard about it was because God told me it was time to make my story public. When I was asked to go before the congregation at my church in full transparency with my testimony, Craig was there hearing it for the first time, too. Oh sure, I had divulged bits and pieces of my story to him, giving him some idea of my sordid past. Naturally, he knew my past wasn't as seamless as his, having three divorces under my belt. Yet, he had only heard the tips of the icebergs. He never asked for the gory details, so I never had to relive them, nor explain them. When I was commissioned to air my dirty laundry in public, I was somewhat concerned as to what he would think of me. After the service was over, he approached me with tear-filled eyes, hugged me and said, "I'm so proud of you. You are so brave." My story only strengthened Craig's admiration and respect for me. The lie that Satan had me believing for decades was no longer a threat. A decent man DOES love me, with warts and all. Craig sees me through the lens of Jesus, my Redeemer!

God's will is for us to marry within His family. **2 Corinthians 6:14** says, *"Do not be yoked together with unbelievers. For what do righteousness and wickedness have in common? Or what fellowship can* *light have with darkness?"* My past relationships are a perfect illustration of what happens when we are yoked with men who chose the world instead of Jesus. Thankfully, our sins and mistakes are covered by the blood of Jesus! When you wait on the Lord and His plans for you and your marriage . . . when you are yoked with someone who loves Jesus first, you will be joined with someone who sees you through the lens of Jesus. Righteousness and unconditional love will navigate your life when you both find your joy from Jesus first, then share that joy with one another.

Jesus, Craig and I have had 15 years of happy times so far. Our story began with a beautiful church wedding. Our children stood beside us as attendants. Our photo album is FULL of fun trips. We started with a romantic honeymoon to Hawaii. We have taken many anniversary trips and fun vacations following. Our story isn't over yet! Craig bought our new home right before the wedding. From the day we got back from our honeymoon, it has been our own safe haven. We live in perfect harmony and do everything together. We bought a business together. We work it, day in and day out, TOGETHER. Most importantly, we start every day in the Word and prayer. I literally spend time with my man 24/7 and we never grow tired or weary of one another. He is truly the closest to someone who acts like Jesus I could have on this earth. He is my best friend. He reminds me every day, by his actions, who Jesus is and how much He loves me.

The thing that continues to blow me away is on occasion during our prayers listening to Craig weep before God, saying, "Thank you God for bringing me Lisa. I don't know where I would be today without her." WOW. I always tell him, "I KNOW where *I* might be without *you*! I could easily have slipped back in a dark pit, knowing my tendencies." This gentle, humble man with a squeaky-clean past, is thankful for ME. Jesus is the Giver that just keeps on giving. His promises never fail!!! I'm loved so much better than I deserve by both of them.

Since I've lived under the covering of a godly husband in safety, I have grown EXPONENTIALLY in my walk with Jesus. I was

↑ *Don't Fall For It* ↓

baptized in the Holy Spirit five years into our marriage. That was a life changer. I have grown so much closer to the Holy Spirit and I know His voice and His ways. I've become more confident in Whose I am, and I am bold in my convictions. I feel free to be transparent with my story. It glorifies God, and I know I am protected from the enemy's attacks. I'm sure there will be others who judge and criticize me about my story. The amazing part is, I don't care! I'm not bound by man's opinion. Satan can't touch me with guilt and shame anymore. I realize now that I have ALL AUTHORITY over the enemy because my Savior redeemed me from his chains.

Craig was baptized in the Holy Spirit a few years later. His experience was different than mine. I received my prayer language. He did not. He was slain in the Spirit. I was not. That's ok. Craig lets me be me and I let him be him. We never try to control one another, nor change one another. We have our individual journeys with Jesus, and we support each other in our personal relationships with Him. We don't make each other try to follow our own protocol and we don't make each other "our gods." Jesus is our God. We worship Him together. That's the key to a long, happy marriage. I'm a slow learner, but I finally figured that out.

In case you haven't gotten my point yet, let me reiterate. I'm living proof that God is merciful and powerful! God is patient. God is kind. He never gives up on us when we give our hearts to Jesus, even when it takes decades to understand Jesus! God's heart is that none shall perish! He will wait as long as it takes and do whatever it takes for us to return to Him when we stray. When we turn and repent, He doesn't *even remember* our pasts sins! The beauty of God is, He is our Heavenly Father and no matter what WE decide – to love Him or not to Love Him – it doesn't change His love for us. God doesn't love us according to our decisions and behavior. God IS Love. It's His true nature and He rejoices when one of His lost sheep are found.

"The Lord is near to all who call on Him, to all who call on Him in truth. He fulfills the desires of those who fear Him." ~ **Psalms 145:18-19**

Our Wedding - 2009

LORI'S FAMILY: ALLISON WITH SON RYDER, (HUSBAND) LANCE; DREW, US WITH NIECE/FLOWER GIRL - HANNAH (ALLISON & LANCE'S), MOM, AUNT LYNN, LORI AND (HUSBAND) KERRY

ME, MOM, & THE BOYS

LORI & ME

THE BOYS' NEW SIBLINGS: CLIFF, CHAD, & CAYLIE

HONEYMOON IN HAWAII

BEST FRIENDS!

CHAPTER SIXTEEN
Look What God Did!

"For my part, I am going to boast about nothing but the Cross of our Master, Jesus Christ. Because of that Cross, I have been crucified in relation to the world, set free from the stifling atmosphere of pleasing others and fitting into the little patterns that they dictate . . . It is not what you and I do . . . It is what GOD is doing, and He is creating something totally new, a free life! All who walk by this standard are the true Israel of God – His chosen people. Peace and mercy on them!"

~ Galatians 6:14-16 [The Message translation]

The moral to my story is this . . . even when we mess up God's plan, He still sees us; He still hears our cries, and He always has a divine plan to get us back on track. Jehovah never fails!!! God's plan was never for me to go down the dark roads I traveled, yet He still made beauty from ashes!

JESUS is MORE POWERFUL than our worst mess. He can take our messes and turn them into a powerful message. He IS the "God who sees us"! I can confidently preach this because He has illustrated in my life His grace over my children – even with all *my* mess!

You may be wondering where my boys are today. As I give you my account, please know I am ONLY bragging on God! My sons are perfect examples of God's mercy and grace. **Psalm 136:23** says, *"[God] remembered us in our lowly state, for His mercy endures forever."*

The reason for writing this book started as an encounter I had with the Holy Spirit a few years ago. I was awakened very early one morning, by a notification on my phone. Cody, already a husband and father, was living out his true destiny as a Worship songwriter and recording artist. On that day, he had released his latest single on *You Tube*. It was a live recording of him, singing his new release, at the *Passion Conference 2019*. The song is called, "Nothing Else."

When my phone pinged, I shot out of bed and eagerly ran to sit and watch the video. Cody was seated at his keyboard on a stage that was positioned in the middle of the room. Cody was literally surrounded by hands raised in worship and the sight melted my heart to the point of sobbing with gratitude. Suddenly, I heard the Holy Spirit whisper so plainly, "Your little drops of faith are now a sea of worshipers." That definitely got my attention. So, I inclined my ear to hear more. "All of those countless mornings, I saw you at your kitchen table, tearfully pleading for Me to guide your children down a different path than you took. Asking Me to protect them from the enemy's schemes. Those prayers. I heard every single one, long and short Lisa, and I collected your tears in a jar. They were never spoken in vain and look where Cody is now. Your fervent prayers, I have answered. I am giving Cody songs from Heaven to pour out on My Body – the Church."

At that moment I was undone. My emotional response to my Lord was "Oh God! I wonder how many single moms are at their own kitchen table this morning begging you to protect their children because they're in a mess like I was. Some may even listen to Cody's music and think he was raised in a 'perfect Christian home'. How I wish I could tell them their prayers are heard!" A strong desire arose within me to speak to every single mom who has a similar story, "Hear me! A MOMMA'S PRAYERS ARE POWERFUL!" You do NOT have to be perfect to get our Perfect God's attention!"

As you have read, Cody was conceived by two messed-up people. Calvin was extremely talented but used every ounce of talent to try furthering his career in the Country-Western genre. Singing

↑ *Don't Fall For It* ↓

and playing the drums in nightclubs only lured him into the world of drugs and sex addiction. I was bound by the many lies Satan fed me throughout my life that caused me to worship man, instead of God. Calvin and I had many challenges in our marriage that ultimately led to divorce when Cody was only 3 years old. Despite his broken beginnings, Cody has always had a strong heart for God, even before he came into this world.

When I was pregnant with Cody, I had an overwhelming urge to go worship at a Pentecostal Church across town with a congregation of African American believers. I had never had this desire to worship the Pentecostal way before. I was still a "sit-still-and-be-quiet" Protestant! Still, I couldn't shake the urge, so Calvin eagerly agreed to go, as that was familiar to him and his upbringing. Although we were the only white people in the room, we never felt out of place or unwelcome. They embraced us as if we were family. The gospel music and the on-fire preaching were captivating and contagious! We became regular visitors until Cody was born. After Cody entered the world, I didn't feel the urge to go any longer. To this day, I still believe it was Cody's spirit drawing us to go where worship was authentic, powerful, and Spirit-filled! God knit Cody in my womb for His divine purpose! Cody grew up with a never-wandering heart for Jesus, EVEN THOUGH his surroundings were not exactly Christ-like from his early childhood years.

He was a very obedient child growing up. He was like Lori, my sister. He simply followed the rules and did what he was told with no argument. His innate motive was to please God and so, naturally, he pleased his parents.

In high school, he wore a Christian t-shirt EVERY DAY and was labeled a "Jesus freak" by his peers. He took that as a compliment, not an offense. It was impossible to persecute Cody. He knew who he was and Whose he was!

I always knew Cody had a special calling on his life and I knew he would always be in love with Jesus. I never thought I would see him where he is today though! My limited vision never went that far. God gets ALL the GLORY! *"As the heavens are higher than the earth, so are My ways higher than your ways and My thoughts [higher] than your thoughts."* **(Isaiah 55:9)**

Cody is a dedicated Jesus follower who honors God with his gifts and talents. He is also a loving husband to my daughter-in-love, Kari, and an amazing father to my two grand-boys. It never ceases to astonish me that Cody knows how to parent in a healthy way. He grew up with an unhealthy, single-parent example. He understands what it takes to have a healthy and happy marriage. **That's all God, none of me. My only contribution was my PRAYERS, not my wisdom!** Today, in a lot of ways, I'm thankful for my wilderness journey. At least Cody learned from my example how to cry out to God in repentance. He saw a lot of that!

This is the irony of God. Cody and Kari recently recorded a song on his latest album, *God Is Good*. The song is called "Forever and Amen." The bridge says, "When we pray – in our secret place – You bend to listen; You love to answer." That's the full-circle blessing of God! God is so faithful to help you train your kids in the way they should go, if you constantly ask Him! He bent to listen to my prayers in my secret place. Wow. I still pinch myself sometimes to make sure I'm not dreaming. Never under-estimate what God has planned for YOUR kids.

Cody has not always had a perfect story, though. He grew up facing many struggles with his dad as well as me. Calvin went to rehab and got clean from his drug addiction during our divorce proceedings. He ended up going to college and became a licensed Respiratory Therapist and was a productive member of society throughout Cody's upbringing. So, some normalcy was provided in raising Cody. There was just one problem. Calvin stayed bound in all the attitudes that addiction instills in a person. He remained bitter and became self-righteous, never healing emotionally from our divorce. This spilled over into Cody's surroundings. We were never able to reach an amicable friendship and co-parent Cody in a way that was best for him. There was a lot of animosity and strife between us. His attitude toward me was constant resentment for not forgiving him and staying married. I forgave him – I just refused to live with a man I couldn't trust. He never saw my side. BUT GOD. He sheltered Cody in so many miraculous ways that didn't interfere with his joy of growing up. He still had lots of good times with his dad that he will cherish forever. Cody didn't even realize until after he reached adulthood, through counseling, that his dad wasn't as emotionally healthy as he thought. God's grace kept a divine covering over Cody's emotional well-being. Unfortunately, Calvin's story ended too short.

When Cody left home at age 18, something drastically changed in Calvin. He started using drugs again, was fired from the job he had held for many years, and he left our hometown, trying to escape his regret, anger and unforgiveness. As the years passed in Cody's adulthood, his dad only became more bound in addiction. Cody was forced to make the excruciating decision to protect his family and set boundaries for his dad. He refused to be his enabler and was forced to show him "tough love." Soon, we lost track of Calvin's whereabouts because he refused to answer Cody's phone calls. We eventually learned through mutual resources that he was homeless. Cody never stopped praying for him and grieving over him. We were both concerned about his well-being. Calvin severed all contact with everyone who loved him. Finally, we lost him when God ended his misery and took him Home. Cody was just shy of turning 33 years old.

I surprised myself at how I reacted to the news. All those years of lingering animosity exploded into an outburst of grief the minute Cody told me. We had clung to the hope that Calvin would find a way to get clean again and re-gain his ability to lead a productive life. Cody did an amazing job of organizing a memorial service that honored his dad with so much love and devotion. Before I left home to attend the funeral, the Holy Spirit led me into a task to deal with my grief by writing a list: "The things I loved about Calvin." I knew it was an exercise on forgiveness. My plan was to give it to Cody so he could always remember that he was conceived in love. The Holy Spirit had a different idea. He didn't tell me His idea until I arrived at Cody's house, and he was briefing me on the funeral plans he had made. "Ask to speak too," the Holy Spirit whispered. I asked before

I argued, but with a slight reservation that Cody would be opposed. Instead, he confirmed the Holy Spirit's word with, "I would LOVE for you to speak Mom!" So, I got up and read what the Holy Spirit had helped me write.

That experience was the most liberating few minutes of my life. Any shred of unforgiveness I had held onto toward Calvin was left at that podium. I struggled to hold back tears as I read about our love story. I could sense Calvin with me and embracing me through every word. It was my final apology and truce with him for all the hurt I had caused him, no longer harboring the hurt he had caused me. As I concluded my speech, and started my way back to my seat, Cody ran to me on the stage, with everyone looking on. He had tears streaming down his face as he held out his arms to embrace me. I saw that little boy who used to come running to me, crying when he needed his Mama. We held that tight embrace for several minutes, in front of the spectators, exchanging tearfully "I love you" several times. That was the moment God wrapped His loving arms around all three of us: Calvin, Cody, and me; with His infinite love, forgiveness and reconciliation.

Cody received closure and peace, no longer worrying about where his dad was and if he was ok. I received the gift of total forgiveness and the reminder of why I was in love with him, at one time. As I stated in my comments, *"We will never know what caused Calvin to return to the dark side, but we DO know he is now free, living in the Light of his Savior."* Through it all, Calvin always loved Jesus. He just didn't love himself. I personally watched Calvin battle with his addiction when we were married. I saw him on his knees begging God to forgive him and set him free. The problem was it was in those moments he was high. When he was sober and felt better, he thought he was strong enough to stay in the environment where drugs were easily accessible. Alcoholics Anonymous teaches this is not possible and rightfully so. I knew Calvin's heart was to get clean, but his mind and his flesh won the battle. I believe God heard Cody's cries to save his dad and He answered with His grace to take Calvin home. He will never be homeless again!

Don't Fall For It

I believe Calvin is looking down from Heaven today with so much pride over his only son. I truly believe the Holy Spirit guided my thoughts and my pen when I wrote those words, HE told me to write. It's what gives me peace. Although Calvin forfeited his divine calling on earth, he is now singing praises to our God, with his incredible voice. He is healed, whole and grateful that Cody didn't travel down his dark road, either. Cody took the baton his dad should have carried and is running the race set before him and fighting the good fight.

It's a tragic story that God turned into His victory. It was during those trying times Cody endured with his dad (while he was still with us), that the Holy Spirit gave him the song, "Run to the Father." It stemmed from Cody's prayers to his Heavenly Father about his earthly father. Now, Cody's story can help to set other people free as well. To GOD be the GLORY!

My second son, Will, was also born in a mess. His beginning had similar setbacks in a different setting. God gave Will a funny sense of humor, a zest for learning and a photographic memory. Will ALSO has an innate love for Jesus that began at a very early age. Will was prayerfully spoken over, at age eight, that he would be an evangelist one day. I have no doubt that will come to pass. When he was a preschooler, J.J. and I would giggle with pride watching Will witness to his teammates on the sideline of his soccer games. He was more worried about their salvation than the scoreboard. He was only four years old!

I remember a time when Will was in junior high school. He was invited to a birthday party with a friend who was two years older. They played little league ball together and had become close buddies. This boy lived in a community outside of ours and went to a different school. So, he was the one with the actual party invitation for one of his classmates. Will was the tag-along, since he was spending time with his friend. When I dropped them off, the words that came out of that boy's mouth will forever be etched in my heart. "Now Will, please remember, you *can't* talk about Jesus the whole time. These kids will think you're weird!" I never felt prouder! Will is not of this world.

Will has an overwhelming compassion for the homeless and people with challenges of all kinds. Will is also blessed with the "gift of gab." He never met a stranger; another trait that comes in handy, for an evangelist. To this day, he still cringes when I call him that, mostly out of fear that I'm right. It's difficult for us when God's calling is so uncomfortable, especially for a people pleaser. He gets that from me, unfortunately. As he grows closer to age 30, I can see how he is maturing in the Spirit more and more each day. He is such a lover of the Word of God. He calls himself a "Bible nerd" and there is no better music to a momma's ears. I definitely know Will has a high calling on his life, whether the world sees it or not. God sees what he does in the secret places. I cannot wait to see how his story unfolds. It's so easy to see all the gifts God knit together in Will while in my womb, for His divine purpose.

Will has overcome so much tragic loss in his short lifetime. He has seen a lot of sorrow in his young life, starting at age 11, when J.J. died at the young age of 47. Several more losses followed. For a time, Satan tried to steal Will's love and devotion for Jesus through those tragedies.

By the time Will was 18, he had lost all his relatives on his father's side, except for a few cousins and an uncle. Untimely deaths occurred like falling dominoes, due to years of alcohol and drug abuse. Will suffered a long, dark season of grief and anger, mostly at God, for taking his family. He developed a paranoia that he might lose me and Cody. With his dad's addiction, Will developed a common side effect for loved ones: codependency.

When Will began his freshman year in high school, classmates made fun of him for carrying his Bible to school. He did not see it as affectionate teasing from friends, but instead rejection. The enemy was already working on stealing Will's sense of identity in Christ. He didn't have the same assurance of Whose he is, due to life events that shook his solid ground. So, Will left his "life compass" at home, no longer carrying it wherever he went and tried his best to fit in with the world.

↑ Don't Fall For It ↓

The enemy had Will bound in a way that took him on a journey of wandering away from God. I always say, "Will's college years enhanced my prayer life." Will never lost his belief that Jesus was his Savior. He just couldn't see Jesus as his Best Friend. I was constantly on my knees, praying for God to set him free. "Let his rebellion be short-lived, God! Don't let him take decades like it took me!" That was my daily battle cry!

God answered! In His perfect timing, God already had Will's deliverance written in His playbook, while he was still a young man. Today, Will is a free, sold-out lover of Jesus, making MUCH better decisions than I did at his age. He is on a journey to bring honor back to his family name in breaking the generational curses he was born into.

He and his first cousin, Natalie, are sole heirs to the family fortune and they are making good decisions with God's blessings. Natalie lost her mom, Will's aunt Diana, when she was a freshman in high school. "Nat" has had to travel a treacherous road of abandonment and has overcome every obstacle the enemy used to try to take her out. God won. Both Natalie and Will believe in living the Kingdom way. They refuse to take the dark path that the generations before them chose. People get confused because they refer to one another as brother and sister; not as cousins. It's because their journeys to overcome, have brought them closer than just first cousins. As the only children born to a brother and to a sister, they see each other as brother and sister.

Will is now very successful by living according to Kingdom principles. God has blessed him with a financial fortune that he NEVER takes for granted. Will uses his monetary fortune to show others the love of Jesus. He lives comfortably, modestly and gratefully, with an incredible amount of generosity. God heard my countless prayers to send "earth angels" to guide Will with his inheritance. His dad left this world too soon before he could mentor Will about the responsibilities of being a landowner. When Will was approaching his college years and searching for his major course of study, he was riddled with anxiety. Me being an academic advisor and career counselor, I tried to help Will see he needed to follow his interests, without considering the paycheck. He insisted he needed to major in farming and ranching, even though the subject did not really appeal to him. He would say, "But Mom! I need to learn how to ranch, since it's going to be my responsibility to manage the land!" He felt so alone and helpless. I always responded with Blessed Assurance, "Will – God will bring you people who will help you! You need to major in a subject that sparks your passion!" Thankfully, Will decided on a pre-Vet agricultural major because of his love for animals. He didn't buy into the lie he HAD to major in a subject that didn't interest him. He could've easily dropped out of college. Instead, he earned his bachelor's degree because he loved studying something that he was interested in.

God confirmed my words that I knew were His promises. Today, Will is surrounded by Kingdom-minded financial advisors that mentor him with Biblical principles. He is being mentored by "surrogate dads" who help him make the most profit out of the land he owns. It has nothing to do with ranching. He has other advisors that help him invest the Kingdom way. I feel safe in knowing Will is guaranteed a secure future no matter how much money he has, because he trusts in God, not his money.

Will is storing up his treasures in Heaven. He is always willing and EAGER to bless others with the financial blessings God pours out on him. God continues to flood Will with financial blessings, because Will constantly lives by his motto, "It's not my money. It's God's money."

God gave Will a strong interest in His Word, along with a photographic memory for a reason. I believe he will be a teacher of the Word in some capacity. I'm just waiting for the praise-worthy announcement, while he continues to find his destiny. Whether he is called to be in front of large crowds like his brother or preaching one-one-one in the streets, I know Will is going to make an impact on our broken world in some capacity.

Cody married his dream girl and "perfect-for-him" mate, Kari Jobe-Carnes. They both love Jesus and have the same calling on their life. It is BEYOND my wildest dreams to get to watch them serve Jesus and His people by writing and recording His songs together. Their hearts are purely devoted to leading people into the presence of God when they lead worship. "The Blessing" is their life story, as much as it is God's Aaronic blessing over the world. It is my story too, and I sing it with all the breath in my lungs since the day they wrote it.

Will has a steady girlfriend for the first time in his life. He always dated with a purpose to find his wife, not just date casually for a while. He always felt uncomfortable dating more than one girl at a time. He is definitely a "different breed" of a single white male. He is so much smarter than his parents. For that reason, he rarely made it past the second date in his search. Most often if he didn't feel "a spark" right off, he would end it before he had to make a decision that would hurt her feelings. Other times, he would get his feelings hurt a little when the girl wasn't interested as much as he was. *I* could see that was God's protection although *he* only saw it as "he wasn't enough." Will is still working through some deep emotional scars through Christian counseling, and I know he will come out stronger than ever and free from the enemy's lies. At the time this book is published I am very hopeful he has found his true love. Jenavee is his FIRST "real girlfriend" as they date God's way in a mature and intentional courtship to seek God's will and explore a possible forever together. I am so excited and blessed to watch their courtship grow into a devotion to one another with all the signs that a marriage is in the near future. I name it because I'm claiming it! God picked the perfect mate for Will. She loves Jesus first and she loves William well. She has influenced Will to be the best version of himself.

As I said from the start of this chapter, I'm bragging on God, not necessarily my children. Our Loving Father broke the generational curse of unplanned pregnancy and dysfunctional marriage off of my children. New generations of Jesus worshippers have been birthed in our family. My momma prayers were never ignored, EVEN when *I* needed desperate prayers for myself! God answered those small prayers in ENORMOUS ways! His favor is on my children and their children and their children's children.

I SAY ALL THIS TO SAY . . .

If you are a single mom, who is walking in guilt and shame, feeling like you are failing as a parent, look at me and be encouraged! I was *nowhere near* being a perfect mom. When the boys were little, I was stressed, addicted, and depressed. I constantly felt the pressure of playing both parental roles while also hiding my demons. Stress instigated the bad habit of exploding on the boys when it became too much. Yes, on top of all my other flaws, I was a screamer too. The boys knew not to push me too far, or they would see "psycho mom." I also have many regrets for the times I chose to do all the chores first, instead of letting them pile up and get on the floor to play with them. Although I promised to play a game with them as soon as the chores were done, on most occasions, time ran out and I missed those opportunities. Now, I realize how fast the years went. In the life of a single mom with young children, the *days* are LONG, but the *years* FLY BY! I now wish I had those days back, knowing what I know now. It never occurred to me they would grow up and leave home one day. I could only see as far as 24-hour segments and took for granted they would always be with me. I'm so thankful today that I get a "do-over" with my two precious grandsons. I don't take one moment for granted, fully aware of how fast they are growing up. The chores can wait!

There were a few things I DID get right, besides praying without ceasing. To be honest, some days those prayers were more like complaining. But again, by God's grace, I still had some healthy maternal instinct during my years of living a double life. I give the Holy Spirit ALL the credit! ONLY by His guidance, did I even think to do these things and He gave me the wisdom to know how to.

I constantly talked to the boys about making good decisions in their future. "You MUST go to college!" "You must have a Christ-centered marriage, or it won't work!" You get the picture. My list was long. I was transparent enough to admit my faults to use myself as an example of what NOT to do. My "go-to" statement was "Look at me and learn!"

I also taught *them* to pray. Not like a Sunday school teacher would instruct, but by example. My boys tease me to this day about our bedtime prayers. If I had a bad day, I would start off with a childlike prayer that they understood. Soon it morphed into an all-out cry-for-help petition! They usually fell asleep on me. I guess that's better than a bedtime story! I'm thankful it showed them how we can always enter boldly into the Throne Room and cry out to Abba, because Jesus made a way. We can use our own words too. No fancy religiosity is required.

Every time God performed a miracle of provision, I always told them about it out of sheer excitement and awe of His signs and wonders. The boys loved it when we would praise Him together. My boys grew up KNOWING God was real because they saw Him work in tangible ways. I'm so thankful I didn't keep those miracles to myself!

Most importantly, when I messed up, like "blowing my top", screaming or spanking them in anger, I always went to them and apologized. I was just honest and transparent and let them know they deserved better. Children are SO resilient and love us unconditionally when we first love and respect them. A healthy and honest conversation helps them to see that even as parents, we are still human, and we are going to mess up. It's a good parenting lesson they can use on their own children.

If any part of my story sounds familiar to your story, I pray this book will inspire you to forgive yourself and just run to the arms of your Father. He will take it from there. He will lead you out of your wilderness, no matter how long it takes you to fully repent and be transformed. Never give up, no matter how many times you mess up.

I can testify by experience that God's grace will cover all your flaws if you have given your heart to Jesus! Jesus paid for your sins – past, present, and future – at the Cross. If you have accepted the free gift of salvation, God only sees the righteousness of Jesus when He looks at you! You are covered by the blood of Jesus. He shed His blood for you! God will send angels to shelter your children from the enemy's schemes. Cling to the Holy Spirit and He will lead you to full repentance where you will be set free from the bondage of a repeated sin! All it takes is trust in Him and fervent prayers for yourself and your children. I cannot stress that enough. Not only will it ensure your children's safety, but also give you so much peace. Single moms (actually, all moms) NEED PEACE!

Parenting does not require perfection. It only takes a sincere desire to know Jesus, to talk to Jesus, and teach them about Jesus. When your parenting has those basic principles, the Holy Spirit will guide you through every storm that comes. That's true even when *you* are the cause of your own storms! Put your children in the loving arms of their Heavenly Father. He is the BEST parenting Partner you could ever ask for! He will blow your mind when He reveals what His plans are for them.

"Now to Him – who is able – to do immeasurably more than all we ask or imagine, according to His power that is at work within us, to Him be glory in the church and in Christ Jesus throughout all generations for ever and ever! Amen." **Ephesians 3:20-21 [NIV].**

Lastly, don't quit praying for yourself. If you are trapped in a dark pit of any kind, Your Daddy is waiting to rescue you. He pursues us with His reckless Love, even when we are not aware of it. God sees you and He's not giving up on you, so don't give up on yourself. So, on that note, enough about me . . . let's talk about YOU! I pray my final chapter will leave you with a powerful message of HOPE.

CANYON, CODY, KINGSTON

KINGSTON & KARI

WILL & JENAVEE

WILL'S COUSINS: NATALIE, JACK & SLOANE

KINGSTON & CANYON

FAMILY CHRISTMAS

CODY & KARI'S WEDDING

WILL & ME

MOTHER & SON DANCE

KINGSTON & ME

CANYON & PRESENTS

GIGI & WILL

CRAIG, ME, WILL, CAYLIE

WILL, CRAIG, ME, KARI, CODY

PLAYING BALL!

KINGSTON & CANYON

OUR PERFECTLY BLENDED FAMILY!

CRAIG'S SIBLINGS: JILL WITH HUSBAND JOHNNY (FAR LEFT), CLARK (FAR RIGHT), AND FAMILY

THE BEST INLAWS EVER! JOLENE & CHARLES DUNNAM (AKA, Ma & Pa)

CHAD & MICHELLE WITH THEIR SIBLINGS AT THEIR DESTINATION WEDDING

DUNNAM COUSINS: CHLOE, JENNA & JUSTIN

SLEIGH RIDE WITH THE COUSINS (LORI'S FAMILY)

CODY WITH ALLISON & DREW

ALLISON & WILL

COUSINS AS KIDS

COUSINS AS TEENS

KINGSTON'S 1ST BIRTHDAY!

WILL & KINGSTON

WILL & ME ON MOTHER'S DAY

CODY & KARI

CODY, ME, & WILL

TRIP TO DISNEYLAND

WILL & JENAVEE

WILL & NIECE SLOANE

KARI & KINGSTON

FAMILY VACATION

CHAPTER SEVENTEEN

My Final Plea...

PLEASE Don't Fall For It – You're Worth MORE

"I pray that out of His glorious riches He may strengthen you with power through His Spirit in your inner being, so that Christ may dwell in your hearts through faith. And I pray that you, being rooted and established in love, may have the power, together with all the Lord's holy people, to grasp how wide and long and high and deep is the love of Christ, and to know this love that surpasses knowledge – that you may be filled to the measure of all the fullness of God."

~ Ephesians 3:16-19 (NIV)

Throughout my story, I pray you understand by now there was a core reason I traveled this long, dark, winding road of sorrow from bad decisions for *decades*. Let me reiterate what I stated at the beginning of my story.

I DIDN'T KNOW WHO I WAS IN CHRIST! The enemy stole my identity in my early childhood. Keep in mind, throughout this journey, I still loved Jesus very much and had a hunger for His Word. I got up at 5:00 a.m. every morning for alone time with Jesus and Bible study. The problem was I didn't TRULY believe His words. I couldn't fully *receive* all the revelations I was reading because I didn't TRULY believe He loved ME. I couldn't see myself as a child of the Most-High God.

My Abba (which means "Daddy") wanted me to grow up understanding I was a treasure in His eyes. Had I truly believed that - I may have guarded my heart and my body from broken men who didn't understand, they *too*, were meant to be holy as He is Holy. Sexual sin is one of Satan's most sinister plots to separate us from the love of our Father in Heaven. We simply don't recognize how our Father sees us and how precious we are to Him, so that we VALUE ourselves. My response to any dysfunctional situation should have been "No thank you. I'm worth more than a one-night stand, or to be cheated on, or to be insulted and degraded, and certainly not to be punched, choked, or kicked! I will WAIT for the TRUE love my Father sends me!" Instead of constantly looking up with my eyes fixed on Jesus, I looked horizontally - to the left and to the right, trying to fit into the world.

We were created to live vertically and strive to fit into God's plan for our lives!

At a young age, I learned to compare myself to others. The enemy would constantly tell me I didn't measure up. To this day, I must admit that I still struggle with those lies and tend to compare myself on occasion. I'm getting better. God is not finished with me yet. Very recently, Holy Spirit whispered to me, "You know Lisa, it is an outright insult to God for you to try to be like someone else." That got my attention! He elaborated, "This downplays the Divine Creator. He is greater than creating everyone the same." As I said in the beginning of my story, God is not a cookie-cutter Creator. He uses His Sovereign creativity to knit together every one of His children with excellent *uniqueness*. That includes you. God knit, in you, YOUR UNIQUE PURPOSE while in your mother's womb.

You don't have to believe me. I didn't say it. God did. In **Luke chapter 1,** He tells us the story of Mary the virgin, conceiving Jesus by the Holy Spirit. In the same season, her cousin Elizabeth, who was barren, miraculously conceives a child from her husband Zechariah. God told her it was a boy, and his name was to be John. When Mary finally wrapped her head around the fact that she was

↑ *Don't Fall For It* ↓

to give birth to the Messiah [Jesus] by immaculate conception, she decided to leave town for a while [probably to escape the town gossip] and go be with her pregnant cousin Elizabeth. **Verses 40-41** says, *". . . she entered Zechariah's home and greeted Elizabeth. When Elizabeth heard Mary's greeting, the baby leaped in her womb, and Elizabeth was filled with the Holy Spirit."* John already knew while he was in his mother's womb what his purpose was. He felt the spirit of Christ even when he couldn't see him or wasn't yet born himself. But, his purpose was already established that he would be the one that would go before Jesus and pronounce to the Jewish people, "Prepare the way for the Lord" and "Repent! For the Kingdom of heaven has come near!" This all came to pass right before Jesus' began His 3-year ministry.

You may be saying, "yeah, well I never have felt I'm supposed to do anything as grand as that." I get it. Me neither. Satan loves to tell us lies that unless we are called to do something grand in the public eye that we don't have a purpose. I learned a blatant lesson that is a lie during a very sobering moment in church. Please allow me to tell you one more story to illustrate.

When I went on my Walk to Emmaus retreat, where I met Jesus, the theme of that weekend was "Say Yes to God". I took that literally and didn't hear the part about asking Him first what He is calling me to. I thought I had to volunteer for every ministry I was asked to, in order "to save the lost souls in town." My life became extremely busy by piling up MORE responsibilities on top of the ones I already had. I was burning the candles at both ends, dashing from meetings to events and dragging my small children with me.

On this particular Sunday morning, I was singing in the choir in our small/quaint church and my seat in the choir loft positioned me to be noticed by everyone in the congregation. I had a front and center seat on the stage. When it came time for the children's sermon, as always, my heart melted when I would watch Cody and Will run as fast as they could to get next to the pastor. I had a full view of both of them, where Cody and I could make eye contact. I don't remember the actual question the pastor asked the children. I do remember it was a pre-k level question that my 5- and 9-year-olds would know. Yet all the children sat with no response. As the awkward silence grew, the more anxious I became. I kept thinking, "Answer Cody! You definitely know the answer!" Suddenly Cody looked right at me, and I mouthed to him, "Answer! You KNOW this!" He looked back with a puzzled look as he shrugged his shoulders to say, "no I don't."

A WAVE of conviction fell on me, and I heard The Lord say, "No daughter – he doesn't know the answer. You've been so busy "going out to *save the world*", you've neglected the most important calling I've given you – teach your children My Word. THEY may be the ones I am calling to go out and save the world – not necessarily you. Your job for now is to partner with Me to equip them." I then busted out in the most dramatic, snot-slinging cry of my life! I could not hold it in – so, along with conviction, I got a big dose of embarrassment as well. When I was able to contain my cry and looked up at the congregation, I cratered again at the sight of their tilted heads and "puppy dog question mark look" on their faces. When I was finally able to laugh at this scenario, I imagined they were thinking, "Wow – she really takes Children time serious!"

Kidding aside, I'm thankful God called me out and put me back on the right path again. I learned just because it's "good", doesn't necessarily mean it's God's will for me. I needed to pray about it each time I was asked to volunteer for another ministry. I thought "saying Yes to God" was an automatic response. The enemy LOVES to tweak God's relationship with us "just a notch" to get us off course. The TRUE purpose God had for me was ministering to my own children for a season. I could've done another ministry – He wouldn't be mad about that – just as long as it didn't interfere with my most important priorities: 1) my relationship with Him; and 2) my duty as a mom to teach my children how to have a relationship with Him too.

We judge "purposes" by the size of the calling, according to our own limited vision. God's ways are higher than our ways.

What we may think might be insignificant, God sees it as grand, if it is in line with His will.

In other words, when HE calls, we obey.

If you aren't sure what His will is, seek His will in His Word; keep talking to Him about it until He answers. Don't move forward until that happens.

He makes all our purposes according to His plan and His glory, not our own.

For example, if you are moved to help your elderly neighbor with errands or housework, while a friend is called to go preach to a group of troubled teens, God sees both of your calling equal in His eyes. Just because your calling may not look as "glamorous" or important to the world, it's extremely important to God. Even if your neighbor refuses the help, and the troubled teens break out in a fight – God STILL has a purpose in the situations – we cannot see it, but He can. So, our purpose is not about results and outcomes – **it's just about obedience to His call.**

He instills unique personalities, gifts, and talents in each of us for His divine purpose. No one else can be you! Only you can be you. It is like spitting on God's workmanship by wanting to be someone else. If only I had grasped that truth as a young child. There is no telling what amazing stories I could write today about the adventures God took me on --- holding His hand as He showed me my divine purpose. I didn't start that adventure until well into my 50's. I wasted my youth and half of my adult life. However, He is making up for lost time in my golden years. I know He no longer remembers the mistakes I've made because I've repented. So, He doesn't look at my life and say, "what a waste"; He says "what a woman of faith". His mercies are new EVERY morning! Praise God!

What if *YOU* grasp this truth now? Seek Jesus! You will find Him! You'll find who you were uniquely created to be! Don't live in a dark pit of despair for decades like I did. Walk with Jesus and He will show you how you are infinitely loved and created for a divine purpose. He will take you to places you never thought you could go! In Jesus, you have HOPE and a future that is full of joy, no matter your circumstances!

Thank you for taking this journey down memory lane with me. It's been a rocky road, as I've had to recall and process even deeper about my troubled past. But, I'm so thankful I can use it to warn you, if you (or someone you know) are: 1) headed down this path; 2) are in the middle of this path; 3) or are in a transition season from darkness to light. Don't forget – Jesus is with you EVERY step if you have given your life to Him.

If you haven't made that decision, I pray you will start sensing that the Holy Spirit will chase you down like He did me and show you with tangible proof - HE IS FOR YOU! Stop running and receive His free gift of salvation today. Then, you can write your own story. Your mistakes do not define you. You are who HE says you are.

If you are still in a pit of despair and cannot climb out of it, be comforted by God's Word in **Psalm 107:13-15,**

"LORD, help! They cried in their trouble, and He saved them from their distress. He led them from the darkness and deepest gloom; He snapped their chains. Let them praise the LORD for His great LOVE and for all His wonderful deeds to them." [NLT]

That sums up my story and it can be the summary of your story too. If you've learned nothing else, I pray you at least know this: GOD. LOVES. YOU! Everything He is revolves around this. Even if you cannot feel it, you can still believe it because He declares it in His Word over and over. God is not man, that He can lie! Believe it, receive it and allow your Loving Father to write you a beautiful love story about your life as well.

He created you for an important purpose on this earth – that no one else can fulfill. It's yours and yours alone. Cling to Jesus, find your TRUE identity and watch what He will do with you!

Walk by faith, not by sight.

May God bless you and keep you in a tight grip in His arms!

- Lisa

Psalm 71:18 *"Now that I am old and gray, do not abandon me, O God. Let me proclaim your power to this new generation, your mighty miracles to all who come after me." [NLT]*

Made in the USA
Middletown, DE
13 August 2024